QUEER

GENEALOGIES

IN DOMINICAN

LITERATURE

AND CULTURE

Queer Genealogies
in Dominican Literature
and Culture

MAJA HORN

UNIVERSITY OF FLORIDA PRESS | *Gainesville*

Cover and frontis: Ritual nocturno de amor / Charcoal on canvas / 36 × 60 inches / 2024 / Dominican artist Noa Maria Batlle

This book will be made open access within three years of publication thanks to Path to Open, a program developed in partnership between JSTOR, the American Council of Learned Societies (ACLS), University of Michigan Press, and The University of North Carolina Press to bring about equitable access and impact for the entire scholarly community, including authors, researchers, libraries, and university presses around the world. Learn more at https://about.jstor.org/path-to-open/

Copyright 2025 by Maja Horn

All rights reserved
Published in the United States of America
30 29 28 27 26 25   6 5 4 3 2 1

DOI: https://doi.org/10.5744/9781683405498

LIBRARY OF CONGRESS CATALOGING-IN-PUBLICATION DATA

Names: Horn, Maja, author.

Title: Queer genealogies in Dominican literature and culture / Maja Horn.

Description: Gainesville : University of Florida Press, 2025. | Includes bibliographical references and index.

Identifiers: LCCN 2025020177 (print) | LCCN 2025020178 (ebook) | ISBN 9781683405498 (hardback) | ISBN 9781683405542 (paperback) | ISBN 9781683405597 (pdf) | ISBN 9781683405641 (ebook)

Subjects: LCSH: Queer theory. | Gay culture—Dominican Republic—History. | Gender identity in literature—History. | Dominican literature—History. | Sexual minorities in literature—History. | BISAC: LITERARY CRITICISM / Caribbean & Latin American | SOCIAL SCIENCE / LGBTQ Studies / General

Classification: LCC HQ75.16.D65 H67 2025 (print) | LCC HQ75.16.D65 (ebook) | DDC 306.7601—dc23/eng/20250514

LC record available at https://lccn.loc.gov/2025020177
LC ebook record available at https://lccn.loc.gov/2025020178

University of Florida Press
2046 NE Waldo Road
Suite 2100
Gainesville, FL 32609
http://upress.ufl.edu

GPSR EU Authorized Representative: Mare Nostrum Group B.V., Mauritskade 21D, 1091 GC Amsterdam, The Netherlands, gpsr@mare-nostrum.co.uk

To my son Lukas, who has taught me
>the beauty of unforeseen paths

and all that can be said
>without uttering a word.

#STXBP1

CONTENTS

ACKNOWLEDGMENTS
ix

INTRODUCTION
Queer Dominican Genealogies | Between the Tacit and Streetwalking
1

ONE
Dictatorship and Same-Sex Desire | Engendering the Tacit in the Writing of Pedro René Contín Aybar (1907–1981) and Hilma Contreras (1913–2006)
16

TWO
Queer Nightlife during the Balaguer Years in the Novels of Rita I. Hernández (1977–) and Rey E. Andújar (1977–)
38

THREE
Waddys Jáquez's Theater, Travestis, and HIV/AIDS in the New Democratic Era
56

FOUR
Divagaciones 2006 | New Directions in Dominican LGBTIQ+ Politics and Literature
78

CONCLUSION
Queer Dominican Genealogies
99

NOTES
111

BIBLIOGRAPHY
133

INDEX
143

ACKNOWLEDGMENTS

THIS BOOK HAS BEEN OVER TWO DECADES IN THE MAKING. I FIRST wrote and talked about queer Dominican cultures in 2003 at a graduate student symposium at Cornell University. This is the book I thought I would then write, but first felt the need to grapple with a longer history of gender, and in particular of masculinity, central to Dominican political and popular culture. This critical detour led to my first book, *Masculinity after Trujillo: The Politics of Gender in Dominican Literature* (2014). My commitment to thinking through Dominican gender genealogies reflects this book's insistence on how nonheteronormative desires are shaped by gender as well as crucially by race and class and urban versus rural contexts. Each chapter aims to balance male and female voices, reflecting how gender matters in these representations of queer experience, and at least half of these come from Afro-Dominican perspectives. Apart from the authors from the early twentieth century discussed in the first chapter, I am honored to personally know most of the writers, performers, and artists mentioned in these pages, precisely through the networks of queer relationality that I aim to capture here, and that Rita Indiana Hernández first introduced me to. Among them is also Dominican artist and disability advocate Noa Maria Batlle, whose artwork graces this cover; I hope that in some small way this book honors and celebrates their brilliance and queer irreverence, which has captivated me since the early 2000s.

Since then I have frequently changed my mind about how to best write this book, there have been many starts and stops, but there are without doubt key turning points that moved me forward. First, during my Heyman Center Faculty Fellows program at Columbia University in 2016–2017, the group responded to a draft that they had wished for more local detail and specificity and less lofty theorizing: who were the central voices, the places, the key events? This pushed me to conceive of this book as the telling of a "micro" history that aims to capture a slow change over time in how queer experiences were articulated in Dominican literature and more broadly in Dominican culture and society. This was a change that I myself witnessed unfold from 2002 to 2006 when I spent more than half of my time living in Santo Domingo. The other key impulse has been the scholarship of my colleagues Carlos U. Decena and Ana-Maurine Lara, whose work on the "tacit" and "streetwalking" in the Dominican Republic, along with Rosamond S. King's insistence on the interdependence on sexuality and gender in the Caribbean, are the conceptual framework that underwrites this analysis. In fact, the field of Dominican Studies has beautifully grown over the past two decades, and there are so many scholars whose thinking and intellectual generosity have made it a joy to consider myself first and foremost a Dominican studies scholar—Raj Chetty, Lauren Derby, Anne Eller, Lorgia García-Peña, Ramona Hernández, Jacqueline Jiménez Polanco, Sharina Maillo-Pozo, Elizabeth S. Manley, Sophie Maríñez, April J. Mayes, Miguel D. Mena, Danny Méndez, Mark Padilla, Rachel Afi Quinn, Dixa Ramírez-D'Oleo, Celiany Rivera-Velázquez, Angelina Tallaj, Silvio Torres-Saillant, Elena Valdez, Ramón Arturo Victoriano-Martínez, among many others.

It was during the COVID pandemic that I sat down in earnest to finish this book and found myself, like so many, feeling isolated and missing the scholarly conversations and exchanges that had taken place in person at conferences and at local events; I ameliorated this feeling of isolation by designing two new courses for Barnard College: the seminar "Queer Quisqueya: Same-Sex Desire in Dominican Literature" for my department of Spanish and Latin American Cultures, and the seminar "Queer Caribbean Critique" for the department of Africana Studies. I have taught each several times now and each iteration has been a salve for making this project feel continually alive; I am immensely grateful for the conversations with my students about the texts we read and their own experiences, which have deeply shaped my ongoing thinking and have taught me so much about how to be accountable to the constantly evolving genealogies of queerness. I am deeply grateful to teach for two departments, Spanish and Latin American Cultures and Africana Studies, in the midst of fantastic colleagues, who give me the freedom and support to design courses focused on my interests; I am deeply grateful that I work at an institution where this kind of combination of scholarship and teaching is possible and encouraged;

and I am deeply grateful that there is a generous sabbatical policy as the bulk of this book was made possible by two semester-long leaves. As I was starting to envision that this book of over two decades in the making might be nearing completion, I was fortunate to be in conversation with Stephanye Hunter, Editor-in-Chief at the University Press of Florida. Stephanye's interest and keen engagement with this manuscript has been a driving force in making this the book it is today.

It was not only the COVID pandemic but also the birth of my oldest son in 2018 with a severe neurodevelopmental genetic disorder (*STXBP1*-related) that led to a few years of introspection, self-interrogation, and a degree of stepping back from the world as I was grappling with the implications of his diagnosis and the lifelong care he would need from me and others. Lukas laid bare to me all the assumptions I had unknowingly held dear about independence, about self-expression, about what a good life might be. He has taught me what truly being "in relation" with others means, our fundamental interdependence on others, and all that is lost if we don't recognize the many ways that others sustain and care for us. Here are some of those who have sustained and cared for me in the past years in essential ways: my sister Mirjam and the rest of the Horns; Mike Boland and the rest of the Bolands; my far away but close to the heart friends Anne and Lisa; my colleagues and *compinches* Abosede George, Cristina Pérez Jiménez, Kaiama L. Glover, Kelly B. Josephs, and Orlando Bentancor; my rare genetic "mom" friends, who are always there in the hardest parenting moments; and the women who have helped me care for my children, Lukas, Marcus, and Oscar, which allowed me to finish this book, especially Nyasia L. Collier, Evelin Bottocano, Keelin Pogue, and Lizeth Nava Pastor.

QUEER GENEALOGIES IN DOMINICAN LITERATURE AND CULTURE

INTRODUCTION

Queer Dominican Genealogies

Between the Tacit and Streetwalking

IN JANUARY 2003 I ARRIVED IN THE DOMINICAN REPUBLIC FOR THE first of several prolonged stays ostensibly to advance my research on intersections of Hispanophone Caribbean literature and performance. One of the reasons that my progress would be slow was because I was drawn into the vibrant queer cultural life in Santo Domingo that cut across the realms of literature, theater, performance, and visual arts. The very first play I saw shortly after my arrival at the Dominican National Theatre exemplifies this. *Puentes* (*Bridges*) was co-directed by Henry Mercedes and the late Jorge Pineda, the latter a prominent visual artist.[1] Mercedes himself acted in the play along with Isabel Spencer, Vicente Santos, and two other renowned Dominican actresses. The play is based on short stories by Rita Indiana Hernández and hence was the result of the collaboration of creatives from different fields—literature, visual arts, and theater—and it was suffused with the queer relationalities that crisscrossed the cultural sphere at the turn of the twenty-first century.

Puentes was in no way an explicitly "queer" play, a term that would only become more frequently employed by Dominican LGBTIQ+ activist groups in the second decade of the twenty-first century and, arguably, not until the third decade in the cultural realm; however, many of its contributors would later create works and events more explicitly tied to LGBTIQ+ projects.[2] The writer Hernández would go on to become the renowned "out" lesbian musician with her group "Rita Indiana y Los Misterios" around 2009; Mercedes would also in 2009 help found the first annual "Outfest: Festival Internacional de Cine GLBT," alongside his long-standing work in LGBTIQ+ and HIV/AIDS activism and documentary production; Pineda, a nationally and internationally renowned visual artist, participated in 2016 in the path-breaking "Queer Caribbean Visualities" symposium and in its accompanying exhibit (both organized and curated by David Scott/Small Axe Project); Spencer in turn would direct in 2018 the first explicitly LGBTIQ+ Dominican play, *Varones* (written by Rafael S. Morla), as well as create the first Dominican theater workshop for trans people in 2019. Indeed, I argue that these shifts to a more overt affiliation with markers of LGBTIQ+ identity and politics index a larger epistemic change in Dominican society and culture when it comes to addressing gender and sexual difference, which I argue crystallized around 2006.

This book attempts to trace this gradual change without falling into the pitfalls of a celebratory developmental history where the Dominican Republic, and the Caribbean region more broadly, is slowly "catching up" with the more "developed" Global North regarding LGBTIQ+ discourses, cultures, and politics. Many key voices in queer Caribbean studies, including Omise'eke Natasha Tinsley, Rosamond S. King, Vanessa Agard-Jones, Carlos U. Decena, Alison Donnell, and Rinaldo Walcott, among others, critique the broader geo-political implications of such developmental narratives. They push back against how globalized LGBTIQ+ frameworks tend to map out the Caribbean as a "backward space."

To avoid this developmental narrative and the problematic teleologies that underwrite it, Donnell in her recent study *Creolized Sexualities: Undoing Heteronormativities in the Literary Imagination of the Anglo-Caribbean* (2022) argues for what she calls a "feeling sideways" rather than "backward" approach: "If we accept the Caribbean as beside (another place) rather than as before or behind (as is often implied in the historical model of less 'developed' or progressive areas), then we need to account for the possibility of a creolized queerness that is not erased by the absence of the historically and geographically specific touchstones of pride, assertion, display, outness, naming, and parade that have come to signify queerness under the global rubric."[3] I embrace Donnell's terminology of "creolized queerness" to index Dominican literary and theatrical works whose critiques of heteronormativity unfold outside the language of LGBTIQ+ discourses and identities, including the aforementioned play *Puentes*.

At the time, in 2003, *Puentes* was in every sense of the word a bridge for such creolized queer creative synergies and collaborations that thrived in the Dominican cultural landscape at the turn of the twenty-first century, which, as the staging at the Dominican national theater already suggests, were in no way marginal to national cultural life but often at the very center of it. Yet, if on one hand this book attempts to foreground and archive the vibrancy of this creolized queer cultural production, it also wants to capture a change over time and the consolidation of more globalized LGBTIQ+ vocabularies and repertoires. The wager of this book is that we must do *both*: account for present and past forms of creolized queerness and account for change over time, including an increased anchoring of globalized LGBTIQ+ repertoires and discourses in Caribbean social and individual imaginaries. I hope to do so without falling into a simplistic developmental narrative or assuming that this change is always and inherently evidence of the march of "progress" or is the *only* possible path toward greater sexual justice in the country. In fact, it would be neo-colonial to insist that Caribbean societies must follow a prescribed path of LGBTIQ+ politics and rights to achieve greater sexual justice; yet, it would also be neo-colonial to assume that globalized LGBTIQ+ repertoires taken up by local Caribbean activists and subjects will inherently follow predictable routes and inevitably lead toward what Lisa Duggan has termed homonormativity.[4] At the same time, creolized queerness is deeply shaped by a history of coloniality and the culture of respectability and emphasis on discretion produced by it, while also positing a powerful anti-colonial challenge to these. Decolonizing queer Caribbean genealogies means grappling with these multiplicities, apparent contradictions, and their ambivalent interstices.

In 2003, the vibrancy of creolized queer cultural life but also its centrality to the cultural sphere came as a surprise to me, an outsider in the Dominican Republic, in part due to commonplace portrayals of the Caribbean as a particularly homophobic region and of the Dominican Republic as a predominantly Catholic nation. More significantly, I was influenced by the fact that in my graduate studies in Latin American literature and culture I had not encountered any discussions of queer Dominican literature or culture. At the time, in the late 1990s, the two path-breaking anthologies *¿Entiendes? Queer Readings, Hispanic Writings* (1995), edited by Emilie L. Bergmann and Paul Julian Smith, and *Hispanisms and Homosexualities* (1998), edited by Sylvia Molloy and Robert McKee Irwin, had helped consolidate homosexuality as a legitimate field of study in Hispanophone literary and cultural studies. As Lawrence La Fountain-Stokes, a key voice in the field, recalls, "The 1990s were a very exciting period for the development of Latin American LGBT studies."[5] Notably, in these two key anthologies an impressive one-third of all essays is dedicated to the Hispanophone Caribbean, about half to Puerto Rican and half to Cuban literary representations of same-sex desires—with essays on Julián del Casal, Virgilio Piñera, Reinaldo Arenas, Luis Rafael Sánchez, and Manuel Ramos Otero, among others; yet, not a single essay addresses Dominican literary representations of same-sex desire.

It is true that if one set out as a literary studies scholar at the turn of the twenty-first century to look for "Dominican LGBTIQ+ literature" specifically, one would have been hard-pressed to identify many, if any, works, since texts were not explicitly framed as LGBTIQ+ literature either by their authors or by critics; indeed, the controversial 2004 *Antología de la literatura gay en la República Dominicana,* edited by Miguel de Camps Jiménez and Mélida García, defaulted largely to selecting texts or even just excerpts that featured *any* kind of same-sex desire, including very homophobic ones, as I discuss in detail in the third chapter. Yet this is not to say that there were no Dominican literary works with complex portrayals of same-sex desire and subjects albeit without referring explicitly to LGBTIQ+ identities. Dominican literature was not exceptional in this; Tinsley recounts how in 2005 her intent to write a book about "twenty-first-century Caribbean fiction by queer writers" faltered when she found that the terms she was "using to describe these authors, the descriptors that they used for their own identities—queer, lesbian, transgender—appeared nowhere in their work. *Nowhere.* No characters, no narrators, no one in the novels used these words. Instead they talked about many kinds of desires, caresses, loves, bodies, and more."[6] Over a decade later, Donnell echoes Tinsley, in that she finds that in "most of the literary works that I discuss, non-heteronormative attachments, desires, and orientations remain unnamed."[7] Yet, more so than other forms of creative expression, such as visual or performance art, literature and the written word spell out same-sex desires on the page and make them legible, even if outside a LGBTIQ+ nomenclature. Even if unnamed, same-sex desire is written about, described, and put on the page in literary and dramatic works, creating a queer archive that allows us to reconstruct past forms of creolized queerness, as I set out to do in chapter 1 and chapter 2, set during the Rafael L. Trujillo dictatorship (1930–1961) and the Joaquín Balaguer regimes (1966–1978; 1986–1996) respectively. At the same time, literature also allows us to reconstruct the emergence and sedimentation of more globalized LGBTIQ+

vocabularies alongside and intersecting with creolized queerness, as I show in chapter 3 and chapter 4.

QUEER CHRONOLOGIES

The late E. Antonio de Moya (1949–2014) was arguably the most important scholar of Dominican masculinity and homosexuality who lived and worked in the Dominican Republic. His work foregrounds the specificities of Dominican masculinity and non-heteronormative sexuality, which he conceptualized as a "being and not being," as he frequently described it, including in a meeting with this author. This "ser y no ser" is indicative of "a distinct, complex and contradictory sexuality" in the Dominican Republic according to him.[8] It is not coincidental that this critical formulation by de Moya features prominently in the first two monographs about Dominican male same-sex practices and desires, Mark Padilla's *Caribbean Pleasure Industry: Tourism, Sexuality, and AIDS in the Dominican Republic* (2007) and Carlos U. Decena's *Tacit Subjects: Belonging and Same-Sex Desire among Dominican Immigrant Men* (2011). This "ser y no ser" is discussed by Padilla in the context of "public performance and private subversion" that he observed among male sex workers who had sex with men, and Decena, in a related vein, highlights "the contradictions of living in and through various identities, positionalities, and commitments" among the gay Dominican immigrant men he interviewed.[9] Indeed, Decena and Fátima Portorreal Liriano, who published a moving tribute and critical review of E. Antonio de Moya's life and work after his untimely death in 2014, more broadly assert that "contradictions were central to Tony's life, his intellectual pursuits, and his vision of Dominican identity," and that he felt no need to resolve them.[10]

For de Moya, these contradictions emerged out of a Dominican history shaped by Spanish colonialism, Catholic dogma, and slavery. In a little-known essay titled "La Constante Homoerótica en la Historia de América," de Moya traces possible lines of historical continuity from indigenous and colonial practices to present times. He points to pre-Columbian indigenous artifacts that depicted same-sex practices that he suggests persisted later on, especially between male youth as well as with older men in return for goods/money; in either case "the main reason that this could take place seems to be that there was a sort of vow to secrecy among the participants, a kind of 'law of silence.'"[11]

Silence and discretion were thus central to how same-sex practices between men were negotiated. He also points to the indigenous tradition of *bardaje* surviving to some degree: "The bardaje is a person with 'two spirits' (male and female) or a ritual androgynous person: a man raised as a woman or a woman raised as a man."[12] He then traces a line to the present by suggesting that Dominican *travestis* are one of the ways in which the practice of bardaje persists.

During colonial times such gendered transgressions along with the presumable sexual transgressions of "sodomy" were of great concern to Spanish colonizers and their chroniclers. Federico Garza Carvajal shows in *Butterflies Will Burn: Prosecuting Sodomites in Early Modern Spain and Mexico* that as early as the "first quarter of the sixteenth century," colonial texts already were "a genuine tour de force used to depict sodomitical cultures in the Indias that was subsequently cleverly embellished by theologians and historians as just causes for Spanish empire."[13] This is to say that gender and sexuality and the Indigenous peoples' presumable homosexual practices and gender deviance, particularly in relation to masculinity, were not marginal preoccupations but absolutely central to colonial domination and its justification. For example, as Garza Carvajal details, Bartolomé de la Casas, in his fraught attempt to defend the Indigenous peoples "vehemently denied the practice of sodomy among the Indios," though he eventually "did provide his reader with examples of sodomy in the Indias" and had "witnessed the existence of *bardajes*."[14] It is in this same vein that later "indigenous historiographers resorted to previous perceptions of sodomy in the peninsula as they explained and argued that indigenous cultures in the Indias had also always abhorred sodomy."[15] Such repudiation was essential and necessary within the colonial and Catholic matrix in order to claim their own humanity as Indigenous chroniclers were writing "in defense of their cultures."[16] This shows how Indigenous peoples' claims to humanity or to being "man" and later citizens with rights depended on their gender/sexuality, namely their heterosexuality and non-effeminate masculinity—or heteropatriarchy—that they had to assure to the colonizer.

I want to gesture to the larger critical implications of this colonial dynamic and history in relation to now-globalized understandings of the imperatives of LGBTIQ+ discourses and politics. Michel Foucault in *The History of Sexuality* described the emergence of the "discourse on modern sexual repression" in nineteenth-century Europe, in response to which "the sexual cause—the demand for sexual freedom, but also for the knowledge to be gained from sex and the right to speak about it—becomes legitimately associated with the honor of a political cause."[17] Such demands, knowledges, and the speaking/naming of sexuality are still at the very heart of the globalized LGBTIQ+ politics and its causes. Foucault, of course, famously questioned this "common sense" assertion of sexual repression and that "sex is negated" or the "repressive hypothesis"—and instead highlights the "veritable discursive explosion" and "an institutional incitement to speak about it," "in the form of analysis, stocktaking, classification, and specification, or quantitative or causal studies."[18] Hence, Foucault claims that "[w]hat is peculiar to modern societies, in fact, is not that they consigned sex to a shadow existence, but that they dedicated themselves to speaking of it *ad infinitum*, while exploiting it as *the* secret."[19]

What Foucault's conception of "modern societies" failed to fully account for, as Ann Laura Stoler shows in her pivotal *Race and the Education of Desire: Foucault's History of Sexuality and the Colonial Order of Things*, was how race and the "colonial order" underwrite and shape them. For one, Stoler emphasizes how while Foucault foregrounded the proliferation of discourses surrounding sexuality in nineteenth-century Europe, a "colonial perspective ... could easily offer a different chronology with other prefigurings."[20] Indeed, such "other prefigurings" are clearly evident in Carvajal's study of some of the earliest Spanish colonial texts and their manifold discourses about sexuality and same-sex practices, in particular with the island of Hispaniola being one of the first places where these descriptions and discourses proliferated.

There is of course a significant difference between sixteenth-century colonial discourses and later nineteenth-century discourses about sexuality, as much in content as by who produced them. Stoler describes in her later work *Duress: Imperial Durabilities in Our Times* (2015), how during colonial times "issues of sexual morality and its normative regulation vacillated between visible legal forms of control and others that were as imposing but went without saying—inscribed in the racial grammar of colonial common sense."[21] These colonial "prefigurings" of discourses on sexuality, as well as the particular ways in which sexuality was regulated and always already shaped by "racial grammar," including through forms of control that went "without saying," are key deep historical contexts for the creolized queer Caribbean. What are the implications of the discourse of sexuality proliferating from colonial governance as early as the sixteenth century versus through scientific, criminal, and medical discourses in nineteenth-century Europe? How would this historical context shape the demand to speak one's desires as a form of liberation—as critiqued by Foucault—differently? Such a "Caribbean" History of Sexuality still remains to be fully written and theorized.

Importantly, not only did colonialism produce discourses on sexuality but these also were "heavily gendered"; as Stoler describes, "if there is any discourse that joins the triumph of rational bourgeois man in colony and metropole, it was that which collapsed non-Europeans and women into an undifferentiated field, one in which passion and not reason reigned."[22] This indexes how deeply the affirmation of one's masculinity, specifically one's heteromasculinity, mattered within the racial politics of empire as a precondition for claiming one's status as subject with rights and later as citizen. This colonial imbrication may also offer a deeper historical context for the repeatedly noted interdependence of sex-gender in Caribbean queer studies today; Rosamond S. King in her impressively comprehensive study *Island Bodies: Transgressive Sexualities in the Caribbean Imagination* (2014) foregrounds the centrality of gender and the difference it makes. She describes "sexualities that are intimately connected to gender codes and expectations," and that ultimately "the enforcement of gender codes is much more common" so that the "public gender transgression is more problematic than private homosex."[23] This connection is also foregrounded by Decena in *Tacit Subjects*, where he describes the "deep investment in the privileges of masculine identification" in many of the gay Dominican immigrant men he interviewed.[24] Those who could "perform normative masculinity," could "access a respect" and claim a right to "privacy" about their sexual preferences that others "whose self-presentation was considered effeminate and whose gender non-conformity got conflated into their sexuality" may not have access to.[25] In this way, "gender conformity and male privilege" facilitated these men's ability to make their sexuality a "tacit subject," defined by Decena as "something present yet not remarked upon, something understood, yet not stated, something intuited yet uncertain" particularly in the context of "family and close interpersonal relationships."[26] They inhabited a space "both 'in' and 'out' of the closet," emphasizing that "what is tacit is neither secret nor silent."[27] Importantly, Decena's finding among Dominican immigrant men in New York is echoed by Padilla's study based in the Dominican Republic, where he found that "the vast majority of gay-identified men ... had not explicitly 'come out' as such to their families, and often gave responses to my inquiries ... : everybody knows, but we haven't talked about it."[28]

Other Caribbean and Latin American studies scholars have discussed similar negotiations of same-sex desires and subjectivities in other parts of the Americas and the Caribbean in particular. King usefully summarizes their discussions of the "open secret" or "secreto abierto" when someone's sexuality is "common knowledge" but is not "commonly discussed," referring to the work of Lawrence La Fountain-Stokes on Puerto Rico, Gloria Wekker's work on Suriname, David A.B. Murray's work on Martinique, Dolores Pourette's work on Guadeloupe, Jafari Allen's, Susana Peña's, and José Quiroga's work on Cuba, and Roger Lancaster's work on Nicaragua, among others.[29] King also foregrounds how the secreto abierto differs from the notion of coming out of the closet, where "one insists on the right and necessity to tell," while the secreto abierto "insists on the necessity and right 'not to tell.'"[30] King ultimately concludes that "this emphasis on respect and discretion over disclosure exists throughout the Caribbean."[31]

King, along with others, including Decena, push back against the tendency to devalue this emphasis on discretion as an inherently "lesser" or more "backward" choice for Caribbean LGBTIQ+ subjects than "coming out" and openly claiming a LGBTIQ+ identity. As King points out, such evaluations are based on terms that are "set by the global North" where "'coming out' and public, explicit, audible visibility will be prioritized, and Caribbean subjects who engage el secreto abierto—who in fact make up the majority of Caribbean same-sex desiring subjects—will always be considered backward failures."[32] In fact, much can be possible within the realm of the open secret that may seem surprising; as José A. Quiroga points out in *Tropics of Desire: Interventions from Queer Latino America* (2000), there were enormously famous non-heteronormative public figures, like the Puerto Rican astrologer Walter Mercado, "who dresses in long robes and satin shirts and is surrounded on the set by Orientalist kitsch," or the Mexican singer Chabela Vargas, at a time when Quiroga, as far as he knows, is not aware of any "comparable figure" in the U.S.[33] I echo this in my first chapter in which I describe the lives of two Dominican men in the 1950s and 1960s, the *letrado* Pedro René Contín Aybar and the comedian Paco Escribano, who were very public figures and well-known homosexuals, even very visibly so, without ever disclosing themselves as such.

While King and others caution against mapping the prerogatives of LGBTIQ+ politics, discourses, and identities onto the Global South and critique the developmental narrative this creates, this does not mean that these prerogatives are not relevant in the Dominican Republic and other Caribbean places. This is reflected in Decena's study where he finds that the gay Dominican men he interviewed "drew from a collective repertoire of understandings that were, themselves, embedded in Dominican culture as well as globalizing 'gay' discourse."[34] We must thus attend to both collective globalized *and* local repertoires in any study of queer Caribbean culture today. King also emphasizes the importance of doing *both*, as she finds that "what is too often missing in discussions about same-sex desire in the Caribbean are the *variety* of ways in which sexual minorities live and love and work for change, including taking seriously different traditions such as el secreto abierto."[35] This *variety* of ways includes the growing sexual rights activism in the Caribbean, where by the twenty-first century LGBTIQ+ organizations have consolidated and many places, including the Dominican Republic, have multiple activist organizations.

In fact, there is a growing body of scholarship that foregrounds the histories of local Caribbean LGBTIQ+ activist organizations, including recent work by Lyndon K. Gill (Trinidad/Tobago), Erin L. Durban (Haiti), Matthew Chin (Jamaica), Ana-Maurine Lara (Dominican Republic), and of course the long-standing work of Angelique V. Nixon and Rosamond S. King with the Caribbean International Research Network (Caribbean IRN). What this scholarship attests to is how local LGBTIQ+ organizations often draw from vocabularies of globalized LGBTIQ+ activism and identity discourses while savvily negotiating these in the context of local possibilities and constraints and engaging in a *variety* of strategies. Indeed, Lara's *Streetwalking: LGBTQ Lives and Protest in the Dominican Republic* (2021) offers a crucial analysis of Dominican local strategies that LGBTIQ+ activists employ to counter the repression they encounter in the Dominican public sphere—locally shaped strategies that she terms "Confrontación," "Flipping the Script," and "Cuentos." Such localized strategies coexist with a tactical use of the globalized language of LGBTIQ+ politics and rights that Lara terms "strategic universalism" (in counterpoint to "strategic essentialism").[36]

These localized as well as the more globalized strategies are part and parcel of what Lara terms "streetwalking," where "*la calle* serves as a space of *Resistencia*—a space where people streetwalk in order to occupy public space by hanging out."[37] This being "out" (quite literally) and about in the Dominican public sphere is contrasted by Lara with Decena's notion of the tacit.

While I could relate to Carlos's theories and knew those subjects and had experienced these understandings of the world and states of being myself, I was also seeing and experiencing something else while in community with others in the D.R. Since 2000 ... some Dominicans had been choosing to publicly articulate a visible and known LGBTQ presence.... small groups of people began to walk the street while mobilizing LGBTQ political identities.[38]

This practice of "something else," encompassed under the term "streetwalking" by Lara, "ruptures and exposes Christian colonial public/private spatial dichotomies because those of us streetwalking bring into the public that which is supposed to be private, tucked away, masked, and unknown/unknowable."[39]

I also witnessed in the early 2000s during my time in Santo Domingo the change that Lara describes, including an increase in public LGBTIQ+ events and LGBTIQ+ participants as much in more formal conferences and activist gatherings as in more informal social gatherings in public spaces. As I describe in the fourth chapter, this time period saw the first academic conference dedicated to (homo)sexualities at FLACSO (Facultad Latinoamericana de Ciencias Sociales), organized by Jacqueline Jiménez Polanco in 2005, and the emergence of an annual government co-sponsored "sexual rights" forum—both of which I participated in as well—along with an increase in official pride celebration events and public protests. Jiménez Polanco also founded a lesbian writers group "Divagaciones Bajo la Luna" with the aim of putting together an anthology of lesbian writing—I attended a few of these meetings and later helped write the grant for its publication in 2006. Yet, alongside these remarkable "new" initiatives I also encountered the long-standing work of creatives in the cultural sphere, especially in the realm of the visual arts, who had powerfully pushed against existing gender and sexual norms in their works since at least the 1980s outside the language of LGBTIQ+ identity and politics, as I describe in chapter 3.[40]

At times these artists were conscripted to support LGBTIQ+ activist causes; for example, the aforementioned Rita Indiana Hernández and Isabel Spencer both participated in July 2005 in a bookstore event organized by the lesbian writing group "Divagaciones" celebrating the revised version of Juanita Ramos's *Compañeras: Latina Lesbians/Lesbianas Latinoamericanas*. As Frances Negrón-

Muntaner has described, this interview-based anthology and other similar oral histories emerged out of a feminist and queer ethos of "documenting 'hidden' voices" and were part of "a practice of community and movement-building" that was at the heart of the "Divagaciones" project as well.[41] However, many queer Dominican artists at the time found an explicit framing as LGBTIQ+ reductive for their work and expressed their refusal at having it named as such. This identity framework felt too narrow for the multifaceted critiques that their works articulated about Dominican society and its deep-seated racial, gender, and sexual prejudices and social and economic inequalities, perpetuated by corrupt governmental politics in conjunction with neoliberal policies and economics. While this may be read as not wanting to be "outed," that seems an unfair interpretation, given that most of these artists were anything but "closeted" and lived their same-sex desires openly with friends, family, and their communities.

In a similar vein, Dominican literature did not generally explicitly feature positive portrayals of LGBTIQ+ characters or terminologies, and authors did not identify themselves as LGBTIQ+ until later in the twenty-first century, but this is not to say that there is not a history of representing same-sex desire since at least the mid-1950s. My study of twentieth- and twenty-first-century Dominican literary and dramatic texts traces a changing queer Dominican geography over time, from the Trujillo dictatorship to the early twenty-first century. In chapter 1 I show how during the repressive and starkly heteronormative Rafael L. Trujillo dictatorship (1930–1961) such spaces of same-sex desire and queer possibility were necessarily away from society and the public eye—either in the relative privacy of the home, as in the work of Hilma Contreras (1913–2006), or in a secluded public space, specifically at the beach, as in the work of Pedro René Contín Aybar (1907–1981). Contreras's short story "La espera" and Contín Aybar's prose poem "Biel, el marino," thought to be the first open representations of same-sex desire in Dominican literature, index how gender limits the access to public space to mostly men and the possibilities and limitations of private space for women's same-sex desire. Yet, despite these differences, I argue that the visibly male and female non-heteronormative characters are both tacitly supported by their environment—even in the midst of the tyrannical Trujillato—in part as a result of their secure middle/upper-class status and non-Black racial identities but also because of what Lyndon K. Gill and Alison Donnell usefully describe as Caribbean forms of queer embeddedness.[42]

In chapter 2 I discuss how, surprisingly, already in the mid-1970s, during the semi-authoritarian Joaquín Balaguer years (1966–1978 and 1986–1996), new urban nightlife spots in Santo Domingo became key spaces for queer life and encounters. Focusing on the debut novels of Rita Indiana Hernández (1977–), *La estrategia de Chochueca* (2000), and Rey E. Andújar (1977–), *El hombre triángulo* (2003), set during the second Balaguer regime in the 1990s, I foreground the centrality of queer nightlife and the proliferation of local queer typologies, of *la loca, travestis,* as well as same-sex prostitution of so-called *bugarrones*, as part of it. I trace how both novels portray urban nightlife as a space of new queer possibility but also as one suffused with steep class and racial inequalities that result in tensions and even violent conflict. Ultimately, both texts insist that the strongest challenge to existing Dominican social and cultural norms is not posed by what happens in the semi-privacy of queer nightlife spaces, but rather when the protagonists challenge existing gender norms of femininity and masculinity in the public sphere.

Then, in the late 90s with the so-called full return to democracy in 1996, there was an increase of new mainstream representations of LGBTIQ+ subjects in the Dominican media, television, film, theater, and literature, but these tended to wield reductive stereotypes often for the purpose of comedic relief. Yet, as I show in chapter 3, at the same time various cultural institutions and arts collectives offered new spaces for creative and public challenges to such reductive portrayals of gender and sexuality. These cultural spaces were suffused with queer synergies at the turn of the twenty-first century as Dominican writers, visual and performance artists, and theater playwrights and actors, who were hardly siloed from each other, formed thick networks of relations both professionally and personally, as the aforementioned play *Puentes* exemplifies. At this time we also see creative works emerging that explicitly name LGBTIQ+ subjects as LGBTIQ+, in particular in the award-winning plays of Waddys Jáquez (1966). In my analysis of the representation of trans subjects in the play "P.A.R.G.O." (2001) and of HIV/AIDS in Latinx America in the play "CERO" (2005), I show how these plays proffer a challenge to respectability politics and insist on naming their LGBTIQ+ subjects while not suggesting that LGBTIQ+ frameworks are sufficient or adequate for representing their queer Caribbean/Latinx lives.

In the fourth and final chapter I foreground 2006 as a moment of change, as noted by other scholars as well, when the Dominican LGBTIQ+ movement significantly expanded with new activist organizations and increased public presence; this key moment is reflected in literature as well, with the publication of three new works in 2006. These books were written from beyond the urban cultural circles and networks traced in the previous chapters. Instead, they foreground other spaces, including rural spaces, beyond the capital Santo Domingo; notably, these texts were also written in part in languages other than Spanish, including in English and French: the anthology *Divagaciones bajo la luna: voces e imágenes de lesbianas dominicanas/Musing under the Moon: Voices and Images of Dominican Lesbians* (2006), edited by the political scientist and activist Jacqueline Jiménez Polanco, with personal and fictional texts by Dominican women who desire women, more than half from the Dominican diaspora, is written in Spanish and English; *Erzulie's Skirt* (2006) by Dominican diaspora writer and scholar Ana-Maurine Lara (1975–) is written in English and is the first Dominican novel focused on the long-term relationship of two poor rural women, one of Dominican and one of Haitian ancestry, whose lives and love are deeply intertwined with their practice of vodun; and lastly, the novel *Dólares de arena* (2006) by the French writer Jean-Noël Pancrazi (1949–), is written in French, later translated into Spanish by a small alternative Dominican press in 2010, and lastly turned into an internationally successful movie by the Dominican-Mexican director duo Laura Amelia Guzmán and Israel Cárdenas in 2014. This novel focuses on the deeply unequal (and paid) relation of a French tourist with a young Afro-Dominican *bugarrón* in a north coast tourist town; while deeply dissimilar from *Erzulie's Skirt* and its message of love beyond all economic and social challenges, and even death, both novels address how same-sex desires are lived in rural settings outside urban Santo Domingo, away from spaces of queer nightlife and artistic and cultural spaces. Both texts also suggest how gender continues to shape access to private and public spaces for male and female same-sex desire, but also how for both men and women the tacit acceptance of their surrounding community helps sustain these same-sex relations.

This circularity, whereby we re-encounter some of the key themes and findings of the first chapter set during the 1950s, much later again in 2006, more than half a century later, pushes back against this chronological study being simply a story of LGBTIQ+ "progress." While like others I note a palpable change in the LGBTIQ+ landscape by 2006 that has continued since, and despite this book's chronological structure, my argument is not simply a developmental one. I do not argue that earlier representations and experiences of same-sex desire were necessarily "overtaken" by more overt and globalized LGBTIQ+

politics, identities, and languages. Instead, I argue that early queer Dominican literature moved in the interstices of what Decena terms the "tacit" and what Lara terms "streetwalking" as they make same-sex desire explicit in writing but without references to their subjects being a "lesbiana," "bisexual," "hombre gay" or "trans" person. However, we also see how over time, from the Trujillato, through the Balaguerato, up until the new democratic era, epistemic frameworks are changing, reflected in the new spaces for queer desires and subjects that emerge in these writings and in the Dominican public sphere. Yet, it would be reductive to describe this shift simply as a progressive teleology erasing the actual multiplicity of ways in which same-sex desire and gender differences are negotiated. In the chapters that follow I aim to capture this multiplicity and a multifarious and shifting queer Dominican cultural genealogy.

ONE

Dictatorship and Same-Sex Desire

Engendering the Tacit in the Writing of Pedro René Contín Aybar (1907–1981) and Hilma Contreras (1913–2006)

BEGINNING AN ACCOUNT OF SAME-SEX DESIRE IN DOMINICAN literature during the country's most repressive and virulently heteronormative time period, the Rafael L. Trujillo dictatorship (1930–1961), may seem counterintuitive.[1] Yet it was during the Trujillo dictatorship that the first open representations of same-sex desire were written by two key Dominican writers: Pedro René Contín Aybar (1907–1981) and Hilma Contreras (1913–2006).[2] The repudiation of homosexuality was integral to Trujillo's embodiment of political power: his all-powerful persona hinged on a performance of grandiose masculinity and virulent heterosexuality.[3] A much-told anecdote, captured by Dominican sociologist Lipe Collado, encapsulates this: he recounts how Trujillo, informed by an intelligence officer (SIM) of a *New York Times* article critiquing his regime, exclaimed, "Come to me when you find in the U.S. press an article that says that Rafael Leonidas Trujillo Molina is a faggot!"[4] Trujillo thereby declared that only a questioning of his masculinity through an imputed homosexuality would be of concern to him and not any form of political critiques, even if emanating from the most powerful nation in the region and his country's recent military occupier (1916–1924). This anecdote speaks to the centrality of heteronormative masculinity, not only to the dictator's personal identity but also to his regime's political identity in its national and international projection; homosexuality becomes that which must be avoided at all costs, a sign of powerlessness and the obverse of personal and political strength and sovereignty.

Not surprisingly then, in Dominican society being named as a homosexual was a fundamental threat to a man's social and political standing, and within the phallocratic politics of the Trujillato such "outing" would have meant certain social death or worse. As E. Antonio de Moya and Rafael García describe, "in the twentieth century, during Rafael Trujillo's dictatorship (1930–1961), homophobic authoritarianism seemed to reach its peak. A homosexual or bisexual orientation or identity was regarded as a family disgrace and shame . . . Homosexual and bisexual males were frequently subject to blackmail and aggression, ostracized, or even driven to commit suicide. Many were also forced by social pressure to marry women and to father children, as a means of disavowing the imputation of homosexuality."[5] The media, in particular the Dominican national newspaper *El Caribe* and its public commentary section, "El Foro Público" ("Public Forum"), played a key role in making such imputations. The historian Lauren Derby and others, including Collado, describe how the "Foro Público" functioned as a form of repressive control where anonymous denunciations could discredit even the most elite members of society.[6] One discrediting strategy was to denounce someone as homosexual; "when one wanted to associate someone with homosexuality, the correspondence that came to the newspaper was signed with the name 'Pajarito Pichón'"—"pájaro" being a colloquial term for homosexual.[7]

There were more physical forms of persecution allegedly as well, as de Moya and García describe, "in the early 1950s, Trujillo went so far as to create two concentration camps for middle- and upper-class-intellectual and/or political male dissidents suspected of being, or known to be, homosexual or bisexual."[8] This history is notably absent in the dossier on "Homofobia, represión y resistencia durante la dictadura de Rafael Trujillo en República Dominicana y sus efectos en la sociedad actual" (2020) published by the Museo Memorial de la Resistencia Dominicana (Memorial Museum of Dominican Resistance). Perhaps little is known about these camps, because as de Moya and García add, "this control measure was short-lived because of strong societal resistance."[9] This brief reference to "strong societal resistance," however, opens up a set of intriguing questions: if homosexuality was a family disgrace and necessarily led to ostracization, how does one explain this "strong societal resistance"? Does this not suggest that there were other ways of relating to homosexuality beyond ostracization, and that homosexual men were an integral part of their families and communities, who then strongly resisted their arrest and seclusion? This reference to "strong societal resistance" at a time when any resistance was supremely dangerous complicates any picture of Dominican society as simply coinciding with the Trujillato's explicit and virulent homophobia and points to relationalities that cut across the putatively stark divide between heteronormative society and homosexuality. It evokes precisely the kind of "queer embeddedness" in Caribbean societies that both Lyndon K. Gill and Alison Donnell foreground that is often missed in accounts "overemphasizing exclusions" and "systemic homophobia."[10]

The explicit references to homosexuality one can find during the Trujillato are mainly about men who desire men; women who desire women are rarely mentioned in the existing literature. For one, this can be explained by how existing gender norms at the time rarely considered women a political threat or persons of public concern, even as the dictatorship did bring women into the public sphere and politics in new ways, as Elizabeth S. Manley has crucially shown in *The Paradox of Paternalism: Women and the Politics of Authoritarianism in the Dominican Republic* (2017). Yet key gender divides remained in how men and women were perceived and how they operated in the public sphere. In fact, Manley argues that when this divide was overstepped by the regime when it assassinated the Mirabal sisters in 1960 for political reasons, this led to a backlash and strengthening of resistance to the dictatorship and ultimately its "demise" because of how it grossly violated widely shared notions of "traditional familial and feminine 'protections'" that the state failed to uphold.[11] For better or for worse, as Lauren Derby describes, "[w]omen were not perceived as full and equal participants in the Trujillista project," and as a result "[t]hey were not subjected to the same constraints and pressures that men faced in the definition of their public identity."[12]

At the same time, in the private sphere, women were often part of female-led households and lived with multiple other women; "many families . . . were made up by various generations of women, grandmothers, sisters, aunts, granddaughters who lived in the same residence."[13] This, as the Museo de la Memoria's dossier notes, makes "the search for lesbian women who lived during the Trujillo dictatorship . . . a very difficult task," since women's same-sex relationships would have been hard to distinguish from the common practice of women living with other women in female-led households.[14] On the other hand, these close familial settings also created dense networks of surveillance for women, and "despite this certain invisibility, there were gossip and rumors about certain women who were considered 'butch' and of questionable femininity."[15] Alongside such familial and popular practices of gossip and rumor as forms of social control, there were also more formalized practices of denunciation directed at women just as with men: "in the Public Forum some epithets were used that questioned the reputation of intellectual women or those who were opposed to the regime to 'discredit' them and their professional and personal integrity because society condemned and demonized any type of manifestations of lesbianism between women."[16] The historian April J. Mayes gives a telling example of this in the life of the first woman to become a doctor in the Dominican Republic, Evangelina Rodríguez, who dedicated herself to "the healthcare needs of poor women of colour."[17] Being a Black and unmarried woman led to accusations of Rodríguez being a lesbian, and her life ultimately ended in ostracization and tragedy.[18] This shows how women's gender performance and sexuality were surveilled and questioned in ways not necessarily dissimilar from men's, even if many fewer women at the time had access to the kind of public intellectual and professional roles that made them susceptible to public denunciations.

The homophobic discourse of the Trujillato was not only reproduced by the media under his control but also reinforced by two institutions that were greatly strengthened by the dictatorship: the military and the Catholic Church; both institutions vastly expanded during the dictatorship and remain very powerful actors in Dominican society up until today. The church and the armed forces propagated a particularly virulent homophobic discourse with long-lasting consequences for LGBTIQ+ people. As the dossier by the Museo Memorial de la Resistencia Dominicana recounts, in the case of the Dominican military, this included legislations during the Trujillato "that contained explicit prohibitions and sanctions for persons who sustained sexual relations with the same sex."[19] These legislations, the Public Forum, and the Trujillato's political rhetoric at the time show how there was an officialist concern with homosexuality; the propagation of explicitly homophobic discourses during the dictatorship was mostly, but not entirely, male-focused, where homosexuality stood for femininity and hence weakness and the obverse of proper masculinity that the heteropatriarchal regime propagated.

Yet, even during the Trujillato there were some paradoxical-seeming spaces of tolerance and public expression of non-heteronormativity for men that reflected precisely their embeddedness in Dominican society, which enabled some not only to survive but also at times to thrive. One telling example is the comedian and radio and television personality "Paco Escribano" (1917–1960). Born Rafael Tavárez Labrador in Santiago de los Caballeros, Paco Escribano, also known as "Paquita," named himself after the Spanish female singer Paquita Escribano. He performed as "Paquita" while cross-dressing in the 1940s and 1950s, a relatively common comedic and theatrical practice at the time. Lipe Collado remembers warmly how "one of the renown public figures on the radio, who beat audience records in the Dominican Republic in the forties and fifties, was don Paco Escribano, the Laugh Out Loud Big Shot, the King of Nonsense, and the King of Happiness, presenter, humorist, theater actor and peculiar homosexual who cross-dressed as a variety show dancer and who liked to proclaim his condition [as a homosexual]."[20] Indeed, as another source describes, Paco Escribano was an exceptional figure in the Dominican media at a time when "homosexuality was a mistake and no one was allowed to parade themselves around freely," yet he was the "one exception"—"a dissimulated gay man of renown trujillista solvency and with almost obligatory public acceptance in and outside of the allowed groups during the era of El Jefe."[21] These two accounts offer an interesting counterpoint; while the first states that Paco Escribano liked to "proclaim" his homosexuality, the second describes him as being a "dissimulated gay man," pointing to some of the ambivalences and nuances of what "telling about" one's sexuality might mean in the Dominican context that are not captured by being "in" or "out of the closet."

How knowledge about his sexual preference was managed by Paco Escribano and those who knew him is described by a longtime acquaintance in a Dominican short documentary about the comedian: "one *knew* that he was homosexual, he did not speak of it, . . . but his gestures, his mannerisms, his friendships denoted it."[22] Paco Escribano's negotiation of his sexuality, which Collado claims he hardly made secret ("le gustaba pregonar su condición"), as his longtime acquaintance notes, was not spoken of directly but was "denoted" by him. This is indicative of what Decena conceptualizes as the "tacit," a more nuanced way of understanding how Dominican men who do not explicitly identify as homosexual are not necessarily "secret" or "silent" about their sexual identity in their relations with others who are aware of their sexual preference without discussing it.[23] Instead, Decena's notion of the tacit offers a space in-between speaking and silence, shifting attention to the "ambiguity and shared understandings [that] are crucial to the sustenance of individuals and collectivities."[24]

Paco Escribano was able to sustain the complicities needed not only to survive but also to thrive during the Trujillato by how he presented himself in public and by what he kept private. As Decena explains, when it comes to the tacit, the ambiguities and complicities it relies on are made possible by "the understanding that one's sexuality was a private matter best kept away from scrutiny outside one's immediate family."[25] Pablo Escribano did just that, as the documentary describes: "he was a very dignified man, he was not a man who went around exhibiting unpleasant things, far from it, but it was evident that he was a homosexual."[26] This statement suggests how refraining from making his homosexuality explicit facilitated Paco Escribano's ability to claim respect from others: "he managed everything with respect and dignity and that is why many people visited Paco Escribano's house no matter the prejudices that existed in that era against homosexuality."[27] The claim to respectability was crucial in sustaining social complicities that could override presumably deep divides of hetero- and homosexuality, as long as sexuality was managed as a "private" matter and not made explicit public knowledge.

The stakes of keeping such knowledge in the realm of the tacit—understood but not made explicit—and of the social complicities that underwrite it were probably at no time more heightened than during the Trujillo period. Thus, although Decena's discussion of the tacit is anchored in his study of late twentieth- and early twenty-first-century Dominican immigrant men, one may speculate how the Trujillato, when sustaining social and familial complicities were matters of life or death, was a crucial moment for making tacit negotiations of homosexuality a particularly entrenched practice in the Dominican Republic.

Successful tacit negotiations of one's sexuality depend to a good degree then and now, as Decena points out, on the access one has to "privacy" mitigated by one's class, racial, and gender identity. This is evident in Paco Escribano's home ownership that granted him privacy, as well as the ability he had to demand "respect" from others as a white upper-class man. Pablo Escribano's surprisingly successful tacit negotiation of his homosexuality during the virulently heteronormative Trujillato was also facilitated by the respect he earned for his ability to make light of Dominican idiosyncrasies and to capture Dominican vernacular culture; he earned this respect *despite* his generally obvious sexual preference—as long as he did not publicly name it as such. What this suggests is, again, that there were forms of social capital—in this case Paco Escribano's humoristic talent alongside his social status—and social relations that overrode straightforward rejections of homosexuality even during the most repressive time period in Dominican political history.

The strong social support that Paco Escribano was able to elicit even at the highest levels became evident when one of his *chistes* ("jokes") with *riesgo político* ("political risk") got him in trouble with the Trujillo regime. He was arrested, but shortly after, reportedly at the behest of the dictator's own mother, Doña Julia Molina, who listened to his program every day, he was freed and reinstated. Paco Escribano's preeminence during the Trujillo regimes makes him, like others, an ambivalent figure, but he also boldly claimed a public space for his non-heteronormative persona and has been reclaimed at least by some as "the father of Dominican transvestism."[28]

In contrast, lack of economic independence, access to one's own private space, and ability to manage one's public reputation due to one's class, race, and gender made the "tacit" in various ways less accessible to many others, including women, especially in the early and mid-twentieth century. Decena addresses this gender limitation as well; the men he interviewed "enjoyed less scrutiny of their lives precisely because their private lives were severed from the spheres most relevant to the sustenance of their families. What mattered was not which bodies populated their fantasies and their beds, but that they helped sustain their family units." In turn, while "women might also enjoy certain respect when they become providers in their families, the socialization of Dominican and Latina women and the regulation of their bodies in the domestic sphere suggest that ... they might negotiate these dynamics differently."[29] Decena here suggests how the right to privacy that men with same-sex desires could claim was much less accessible to women whose sexuality and whereabouts were more closely surveilled in the private sphere and by family members and neighbors.

This gender difference is discussed at length by King in the chapter "El Secreto Abierto: Visibility, Confirmation, and Caribbean Men Who Desire Men," where she foregrounds the notion of the "open secret," closely akin to Decena's notion of the "tacit"; King suggests that "it is especially appropriate to study el secreto in relationship to Caribbean men because it relates to the trope of visibility of Caribbean men as opposed to the dominant trope of *invisibility* in relationship to Caribbean women who desire women."[30] It is important to pause and consider with King the gendered dimension of the "tacit" or the "open secret," because these have been foregrounded to conceptually capture the particularity of Latin American and Caribbean homosexualities; yet, such a discussion would remain wholly incomplete if women remain largely excluded from it. King precisely pushes against this gendered division in relation to the "open secret" in her following chapter "'This is You': Invisibility, Community and Women Who Desire Women," in which she deconstructs "the myth of the invisible Caribbean lesbian found throughout the region and its diaspora."[31] Instead, King notes that "assertions of invisibility often either imply or are accompanied by *tacit* acknowledgment of these women's existence" and, moreover, "women who desire women . . . are not always invisible to each other."[32] King thus points to how the foregrounding of the invisibility of female same-sex desire, in part because of how it is obscured by the prevalence of female-led households, has detracted from how the tacit/open secret is in fact relevant for women as well. Hence, like King, I want to move beyond tropes of lesbian invisibility by teasing out the role of the tacit in negotiations of women's same-sex desires, while remaining attuned to the gendered differences of their experience through a comparison of Hilma Contreras's and Pedro René Contín Aybar's writings about women's and men's same-sex desire.

HILMA CONTRERAS AND PEDRO RENÉ CONTÍN AYBAR WERE BOTH part of elite Dominican intellectual circles and like many, though not all members of these circles, they were considered white in Dominican society and came from "respectable" middle-/upper-class families. Contreras was born into "una familia notable" ("a notable family"), especially on her mother's side from Santiago.[33] Her father was the distinguished doctor Darío Contreras who studied medicine at the Sorbonne in France and later famously operated on Trujillo, saving his life. Contreras lived her early years in France during her father's medical studies and then returned to the Dominican Republic for a few years, where she attended a prestigious school directed by Ercilia Pepín.[34] Ercilia Pepín is a pivotal figure in Dominican women's history and her influence on Contreras's life is palpable; as Mayes describes, Pepín followed the *normalista* tradition that emerged in the late nineteenth century from the collaboration of "[Eugenia María de] Hostos and Dominican Salomé Ureña Henríquez, the Dominican poet laureate, who founded Santo Domingo's Institute for Young

Women in 1881," which "helped make public secular education available to young women in the nation's major towns."[35] The *normalistas,* the women who graduated from these schools, came to symbolize "the virtuous, educated Dominican woman committed to social reform"; as such they "challenged the public/private binary" since teaching gave them access to the public sphere and transformed "educated women's physical movement into and through public spaces otherwise dominated by the working poor as forces of civilization rather than threats to the social order."[36] Indeed, Contreras would become one of these educated women as a writer who participated in the intellectual and artistic sphere and through her work at the French Embassy giving her access to the public sphere in ways that were not the norm in the mid-twentieth century for Dominican women.

Ercilia Pepín seemed to have played a key role in preparing Contreras for this trajectory; not only did Hilma Contreras attend Pepín's school, but also, in 1925 when the then twelve-year-old returned to France alone, her father, "doctor Contreras sends the educator Ercilia Pepín to accompany Hilma."[37] Pepín, who that same year gave a speech in Santiago that emphasized that women could acquire the same level of "culture" or education as men, thus indubitably had a direct impact and influence on Hilma Contreras.[38] Back in France, Contreras put this into practice as she continued her education at an exclusive school and then at the university; however, her parents' divorce forced her to return to the Dominican Republic in 1933 and led to her estrangement from her father while she remained very close with her mother throughout her life. Back in the Dominican Republic, Contreras began to write and publish in local newspapers, and by 1937 the renowned Dominican writer and politician Juan Bosch (1909–2001) commended her for a short story she had sent to him under a pen name. By 1942 she had moved to the capital and become part of Santo Domingo's literary and intellectual circles while working for the French Embassy for several decades.[39] With Contreras's education and her administrative role at the French Embassy, she followed in the footsteps of other *normalistas,* such as Pepín, who had their own incomes and did not necessarily rely on marriage and family for their livelihoods; in fact, Contreras would never marry, and she staked out a public role for herself as a writer, even if only a modest one at the time.

Contreras was close with a group of writers, including Aída Cartagena Portalatín, who was part of the group La Poesía Sorprendida (The Surprised Poetry), thought to be critical of the Trujillo dictatorship. Several members from this group, including Portalatín, Franklin Mieses Burgos, Freddy Gatón Arce, and Manuel Rueda, created the publishing series "La Isla Necesaria," and their third publication was a collection of four stories by Hilma Contreras, *4 Cuentos*, her first monograph, published in 1953. As I discussed elsewhere, the first story, "Viernes Santo Sangriento," is a barely obscured scathing indictment of the heteropatriarchal Trujillo dictatorship.[40] Sheila Barrios Rosario, who has written the only book-length study about Contreras, assures that "definitively Hilma Contreras did not support the dictatorial regime of Rafael Leónidas Trujillo."[41] Yet it appears she made it through the dictatorship relatively unscathed, perhaps because as a woman she did not play a key public role, or perhaps because her father's relation with the dictator, whose life he had saved, protected her in certain ways, even if she was estranged from him after her parents' divorce.

In contrast, Pedro René Contín Aybar was a much more visible public intellectual figure during the Trujillato and thereafter, but less is known about his personal biography. Arguably this reflects his ability, as a man, to keep his personal life "private" and separate from his prolific public life. Like Contreras, Contín Aybar was also part of the elite, an *aristocrático* ("aristocrat") with an established family genealogy and a taste for *cultura francesa* ("French culture").[42] Yet, in comparison to Contreras, he had a much more public role in Dominican intellectual life and was considered the "main critic of his time," according to Miguel D. Mena.[43] In fact, Contín Aybar was most known as a critic rather than a writer: he was the editor of the *Antología poética dominicana* (1943) and an associate editor of the *Antología de la literatura dominicana* (1944), part of the "Colección Trujillo," which are considered foundational for the creation of the Dominican literary canon.[44] Contín Aybar also held important positions as director of the National Library, and he was subdirector of the prominent radio program La Voz Dominicana, where he undoubtedly crossed paths with Paco Escribano.

As one of the premier literary critics during the Trujillo regime, Contín Aybar had to do its dirty work as well. According to the Dominican poet and critic Ylonka Nacidit-Perdomo, his scathing critique of the writer Melba Marrero de Munné "buried" her work, and she became a "victim of Pedro René Contín Aybar's misogyny"; Contín Aybar had "assimilated as a 'first rate intellectual' at the service of the Trujillo dictatorship, [and] he lent himself to critique Melba, with the greatest perversity possible for a 'critic': on order of María Martínez de Trujillo"—the dictator's own wife.[45] Interestingly, it was again the relation with one of the Trujillo women which helped sustain the career of this very publicly non-heteronormative man; at the same time, this attests to the powerful role that men played as arbitrators in the public sphere in ways that women did not generally have access to—including the Trujillo women!

The unfortunate Melba Marrero de Munné in turn had close links with the Contreras family: her brother, Héctor Marrero Oller, was married to Rosa Julia Contreras, the sister of Hilma Contreras. This personal history gestures to how Hilma Contreras and Pedro René Contín Aybar appeared to be personally and politically on opposite sides during the Trujillato. Contín Aybar was one of the main editors of the *Cuadernos de cultura* (1943–1952), an important journal that was funded with government resources and thought to follow officialist lines, in contrast to the group La Poesía Sorprendida, which also published a journal (1943–1947), and which Hilma Contreras was aligned with.[46] As Eugenio García Cuevas's study of La Poesía Sorprendida describes (citing Max Henríquez Ureña), the group was formed in part as a reaction to "another group of poets and intellectuals who led by Pedro René Contín Aybar founded with officialist support by the Trujillo regime the Cuadernos Dominicanos de Cultura."[47] Yet this presumable dichotomy between one literary group being complicit and the other resistant to the dictatorship does not necessarily hold up. The literary critic Soledad Alvarez argues that while unquestionably the *Cuadernos* were tied to the Trujillo regime via funding, once "repression tightened its claws and *La Poesía Sorprendida* had disappeared, [*Cuadernos*] opened its pages to writers who in the first few years [of the journal] had been excommunicated, as had been the surprised poets," and "in diverse occasions as much Contín Aybar as Incháustegui Cabral and Manuel Arturo Peña Batlle served as a shield for writers who for some reason were frowned upon or watched by the regime."[48] Such cross-cutting social allegiances and relations could override presumable political divides. In fact, Hilma Contreras would publish one of her most well-known stories, "La Ventana," in the journal *Cuadernos de cultura* as well.

Though Contín Aybar and Contreras affiliated with different intellectual groupings, their personal lives at least superficially resembled each other in that they led relatively non-heteronormative lives—both lived without spouses and had no biological children—though Contín Aybar had been briefly married and later adopted two sons. Contín Aybar's sexual preference has been addressed, albeit obliquely, by the writer and critic Manuel Rueda (1921–1999), who calls him "an exceptional figure"; Rueda describes how "his opinion was always heard with reverence, and the notoriety he reached was so . . . that his *eccentricities* were accepted as something natural to the degree that he became a myth, one of those figures who dictate the worth of others, *without having to situate himself*" (my emphasis).⁴⁹ Here again references to Contín Aybar's "eccentricities" as well as his "elegant posture that was underlined by the fluttering of a perfumed fan," while not having to "situate" himself, speak to how during the Trujillato he publicly and tacitly managed his sexual difference with great success, reflecting his deep embeddedness in Dominican society at the time.⁵⁰

Hilma Contreras's sexuality is more ambivalent and tellingly has remained much more privately guarded. A much-circulated picture of her in France wearing pants—scandalous for women at the time—and looking androgynous next to a similarly dressed woman, gestures to the possibility of her same-sex desires; yet, Nacidit-Perdomo, who manages Contreras's literary estate, has uncovered more details of Contreras's romantic life. She posthumously published Contreras's letters from a decade-long romantic attachment to a married Spanish intellectual in exile, Segundo Serrano Poncela (1912–1976), from 1941 to 1951, whom she met in Santo Domingo and continued to write to once he (and his wife) moved on to Puerto Rico and then Venezuela, where she visited him many years later, in the 1970s. The published portion of these letters attests to Contreras's chaste-seeming romantic and intellectual infatuation that complicates prevalent readings (including my own) of Hilma Contreras's possible same-sex desires that her famous pants-wearing and androgynous-looking picture as well as her writing may suggest.⁵¹ Indeed, Nacidit-Perdomo, who was also Contreras's confidante in the final decades of her life, pushes back against such interpretations without, however, dispelling some of the ambiguities surrounding her sexuality. In her preface to the anthology *Cuentos completos: Hilma Contreras* (2021), Nacidit-Perdomo insists that Contreras "dressed as a man in Paris" only to go to a party ("para ir de fiestas"), while also alluding to her "misterios y secretos" ("mysteries and secrets"), which she did not live "because of prejudice, because of stereotypes and fear of her mother's judgement."⁵² Here the close surveillance of women's behavior, and sexuality in particular, by family and community members, is clearly connected to Hilma Contreras leading such a visibly "chaste" public life.

Whatever these authors' sexual preferences may have been, both writers stand out for their open literary renderings of same-sex desire during one of the most repressive times in the Dominican Republic. As their biographies suggest, their "respectable" position in society, due to their race and class, and the allegiances, complicities, and relations in which they were embedded in the Dominican intellectual and social milieu facilitated a writerly space for their bold challenge to the officialist heteronormative Trujillato.

PEDRO RENÉ CONTÍN AYBAR'S HOMOEROTIC LITERARY TEXT "BIEL, EL marino,"

published in 1943 in a very small edition of twenty-five copies for a set of friends, tellingly opens Decena's *Tacit Subjects*.[53] For Decena, "what may be most scandalous is the way this short piece of writing, which was accessible only to a select group of people, worked its way into literary circles of writers and critics who gossiped about it, wondered who the characters were, claimed they knew one of them."[54] In this way, for Decena, Contín Aybar's book "describes and performs connections that cannot be said. It is about what words say, but also about the way words produce circuitries of sociality," and it "foregrounds the importance of unspoken bases of connectivity for the making and sustenance of socialities."[55] The circulation and knowledge of this short work thus exemplifies for Decena a key insight of *Tacit Subjects*: "what binds people to one another and what makes networks, solidarities, and resource sharing possible and sustainable are forms of connection that cannot be fully articulated but can be shared, intuited, and known."[56] These kinds of queer networks, solidarities, and connections are what I will attempt to trace in the two literary texts by Contín Aybar and Contreras discussed in this chapter. While Decena opens his study with "Biel, el marino," he also notes that the text's actual literary analysis is beyond the scope of *Tacit Subjects* and that "[t]he specifics of the story and the lyrical prose the author uses to tell it deserve literary critical treatment"—it is this literary critical treatment that I would like to offer here.[57]

Dominican literary critic and writer Andrés L. Mateo declared that with the publication of "Biel, el marino," "Contín Aybar cast a historic provocation to Dominican society at the time, which was not prepared to assimilate the naked crude frankness of homosexual love."[58] Mateo's hyperbolic description of this "naked" "crude" and "frank" description of homosexuality indicates how this text breaks with more metaphorical and allusive ways of invoking homoeroticism. The narrator in "Biel, el marino" is closely identified with the author himself, an older intellectual who expresses his admiration and love for a younger (white) lower-class man, "Biel." In fact, as Miguel D. Mena recalls, "years after the death of the critic and poet, Antonio Fernández Spencer, at one of those mythic tables at the Cafetera El Conde, would speak of Biel as a lover of the poet, who lived in the Borojol neighborhood, and whom the poet did not want to let go."[59]

Biel is idolized in terms of his youth, strength, and beauty but is also significantly differentiated from the narrator in social stature. When the narrator meets him near the ocean, he finds him "strong and morbid, the color of peach and of magnificent proportions"; moreover, he "smelled like freedom," and "he was vibrant and ample song. Like the ocean."[60] The narrator declares, "that creature, half-wild, attracted me for his candor and strength. Flesh to bite and field where to sow."[61] With this description he both idealizes and marks his social difference from Biel—Biel being "half-wild" and "free" in contrast to the narrator's "civilized" status—and demarcates the erotic dimensions of their relationship ("flesh to bite and field where to sow"); indeed, he speaks various times of his "amado" ("beloved") in the prose poem.[62] This social distance and contrast between the two is also evident in how the narrator recalls Biel always using the formal "Usted" with him when they speak, and how Biel is "respectful of our distance, enlarged, who knows, by a form of admiration for this other world where I traveled, far from his reach."[63] The narrator describes himself as hailing from another world and sphere of Dominican society, due to his class and education, and he, unlike Biel's poor relative, is "able to give Biel what was not in his power to give him," alluding perhaps to financial support or a form of worldliness and erudition inaccessible to him otherwise.[64]

The text follows the narrator's various visits to the ocean to see Biel, where he feels freed from society and the world he belongs to. There he finds not only Biel but also the friendly company of "young boys like him and like him bold, light and vibrant," as well as the solidarity of a loyal male family member of Biel's who passes notes between the two.[65] Their relation is thus embedded in and supported tacitly by a network of homosocial relations where the narrator is embraced despite or perhaps precisely because of his class difference. For the narrator the homosocial space of the beach and Biel are a key form of escape from society, away from "deaf and sterile concerns, free of stupid conventionalisms."[66] When he is there he "enjoyed forgetting the worry about the War, the stupidity,—inevitably!—the day-to-day of my work to earn a crust of bread, a bouquet of roses, and to gain a position where when they see me lying in the sun, they say of me:—he has strange ideas [ideas raras]."[67] This reference to his "ideas raras," "raro" being a common Latin American term to allude to non-heteronormative subjectivities and desires, gestures powerfully to the narrator's sexual difference and how this distances him from others; but his being "raro" does not prevent him from being deeply embedded in Dominican society with a successful professional life that is evidence of his efficacious tacit negotiation of his sexual difference in the public sphere.

This tacit negotiation of his sexuality relies on a stark divide between the narrator's public and private life, his professional role and his personal pursuits at the beach. Only once does the text describe a tentative challenge to this division when the narrator and Biel go to the cinema, where the narrator laments the social constraints placed on their interaction in public, "Why could I not lean my head on his shoulder there, in the midst of everyone, without anyone being scandalized, and caress on his face the dreams that those scenes produce in his soul?"[68] The threat of scandal constrains the possibility of any open show of same-sex desire and affection, a constraint that the narrator laments and that contrasts with the freedom he feels when they are on the beach away from the public.

This homoerotic beach idyll ends one day when "Biel" sends a note saying that he will go search out adventures and says "good-bye forever" to the narrator. The narrator remains in silence knowing that it would be impossible for him to forget Biel. The narrator returns once more to the ocean where his surroundings and his memory of Biel converge ("Each wave is a thought. Each thought is a desire. All my desires converge in one point. And without thinking even, I am full of you, Love").[69] Yet in the end he concludes that even though he thought he had been in love with Biel, it is the eternal ocean whom he loves, and it is love itself whom he loves.[70] With this ending the narrator declares that there is no end to his same-sex desires, even when Biel is no longer there; he lays claim to a futurity for his desires albeit away from society's conventions in proximity to the beach and the ocean, despite the loss of his lover and his alienating social surrounding. As the narrator laments again, "I am surrounded by people who are so unlike me!"[71] Yet, even as the narrator proclaims his "unlikeness" caused by his (sexual) difference, this does not affect his social and professional status, and at the same time he knows that at the beach there is a space for his same-sex desires, even with Biel gone, alluding to other possible future sexual encounters.

Contín Aybar is hardly alone in finding the beach and the ocean to be propitious for homoerotic encounters in the Caribbean. Cuban writer Reinaldo Arenas goes with great gusto and detail into his sexual adventures with other men at Cuban beaches and in the ocean in his memoir *Antes que anochezca* (1992); in Martinique, as Vanessa Agard-Jones describes in her essay "What the Sand Remembers," "a secluded cove" on a beach is "one of the island's few meeting spaces for same-sex desiring men," though women attend parties there as well, making this a space "critical for the 'queer' culture of island," including as a "space of both cross-class and interracial connection."[72] Interestingly, Omise'eke Natasha Tinsley in *Thiefing Sugar* also foregrounds the beach as a space of same-sex erotic possibility for women in the works of Caribbean writers such as Dionne Brand (Trinidad), Lydia Cabrera (Cuba), and Michelle Cliff (Jamaica), but even as these "beachscapes" are imagined as spaces of sexual possibility, they "end by not being able to carry this possibility through—by leaving this space as myth, rather than reality."[73] This mythic potential of the beachscape as a homoerotic site for women contrasts with the very real sexual encounters that Arenas describes with other men and which Contín Aybar describes as well; indeed, his encounter with Biel may just have taken place at one of the beaches closest to the capital, Santo Domingo—in Boca Chica—which by the late twentieth century had become a key site for international male sex tourism, as shown in Mark Padilla's *Caribbean Pleasure Industry*.

These gender differences suggest how women often did not have access to the same spaces for homoerotic encounters outside the home that were available to men, however limited; indeed, Hilma Contreras's writing portrays how such encounters were limited to the private sphere, and even there the ever-watchful eyes of family members and neighbors strongly constrained them. Contreras's most renowned short story collection *Entre dos silencios* (1987) played a key role in her becoming the first woman to receive the Dominican national literary award in 2002. Yet the stories in the collection are thought to have been written largely decades earlier during the Trujillo regime and the repressive "doce años" of Joaquín Balaguer from 1966 to 1978; among these stories is "La espera" ("The Wait"), which Miguel D. Mena dates to 1953, and which is most known for Contreras's representation of same-sex desire between women.[74]

In "La espera," the female protagonist is falling asleep in her small private room, which is suffused with the many noises of close-by neighbors, attesting to how she lives in a household and place with little privacy. Then suddenly another woman sneaks into her room and tries to seduce her. In fact, rumor has it that the story is about Aída Cartagena Portalatín's attempted seduction of fellow writer Contreras. Incidentally, Cartagena Portalatín is mentioned right after Contreras in Mena's incisive essay "Letras saliendo del closet," though he describes Cartagena Portalatín's writing as exhibiting a more "subtle eroticism" ("erotismo sutil") in comparison with Contreras's more explicit story.[75] Perhaps Cartagena Portalatín, who has been recently claimed by Dominican writer Johan Mijail "as a *cuir* mother for the nation" but whose "dissident lesbian writing" has yet to be fully taken into account, had to negotiate her sexuality in more tacit ways at the time in her life and writing.[76] In Contreras's short story, Aída Cartagena Portalatín's putative seduction attempt—if one gives credence to rumors—ends when she notes that a neighbor seems to have taken notice: "Old María has heard us."[77] The fear of others and the claustrophobic ambience in this small private room contrasts greatly with the "free" experience at the ocean in Contín Aybar's homoerotic text. As Decena in his own suggestive reading of Contreras's short story notes, "Old María's attentiveness and insomnia point to the function of gossip and women's discipline of the behavior of other women as mechanisms of gender restriction during and after the Trujillo era."[78]

This gender restriction is clearly evident when comparing "Biel, el marino" and "La espera," and it starkly divides male and female homoerotic experiences. Women are constrained by the domestic/private space and closely surveilled by those surrounding them. The only freedom the protagonist finds is when she is alone in silence, when she is "without any kind of interference."[79] Not only the neighbors but also the discovery by the protagonist's *hermanos* poses a grave threat and represents the prevalence of patriarchal surveillance of women—"imagine your brothers' faces if they saw you stark naked," says the woman who enters her room.[80] While in "Biel, el marino," the male narrator can rely on a stark division of his public work life and private love life on the beach, for these women the private/public divide is much more porose and bleeds into their private lives through a close circuit of familial and social surveillance. There is no beachy escape possible for their same-sex desires.

What both Contín Aybar's and Contreras's texts share is the fear of public scandal and the imperative of same-sex desire to remain tacit. In Contreras's story the attempt at seduction ends when the woman who entered, Lucía, notes, "I don't want a scandal either."[81] Indeed, both texts fear scandal and describe silence as something positive: it is "refreshing," "like a limitless cool bath" in Contreras's story;[82] and silence is a space of openness and possibility in Contín Aybar's text, "a silence full of suggestions, of sun and sea breezes."[83] Here we see that both texts do more than simply mark "the myth of silence and isolation as the essential characteristics of gay life"; rather, as Agnes I. Lugo-Ortiz has argued in another context, there is another kind of silence, "a deep silence" that "may be read as a radical deconstructive proposition against any pretense to political absolutes," including "the specificity of sexual politics."[84] This might be particularly true for these texts written about sexual difference under the political absolutes of the Trujillato.

Yet, each protagonist and text is situated differently in this network of power struggles, in large part due to their gender differences. In Contín Aybar's text the narrator and Biel share this silence in a moment of homosociality, while the narrator, Josefina, in Contreras's text only experiences the positive valences of silence when she is alone. In Josefina's world the sudden intrusion of same-sex desire is ambivalently portrayed as an undesired interruption that makes her feel "rage" and a desire to "slap that face."[85] In Decena's interpretation this scene of same-sex desire is "an elaboration of women's erotic ambivalence" and not a straightforward celebration of women's homoeroticism.[86] The woman who enters is not the light, beautiful creature described in "Biel, el marino," but instead "she had mannish looks, rather fleshy" and with "tobacco breath."[87] Female masculinity is described in not very flattering terms here, and the story centers on the rejection of her advances.

However, it would be too simple to merely focus on this rejection and not on what makes this encounter possible in the first place: the tacit knowledge and acceptance that underwrites it. For one, the woman, Lucía, who enters Josefina's room is not a stranger; she has been welcomed to spend the night at the family home where Josefina and her brothers live closely surrounded by their neighbors. Her female masculinity makes her visibly diverge from heteronormative gender norms, but this does not preclude Lucía from clearly being part of the protagonist's social fabric and circle of friends; unlike in "Biel" the two characters are social equals here, reflected also in the use of the familiar "tú," rather than the formal "usted" that we see in "Biel." Moreover, Lucía's same-sex desires are clearly not a complete surprise to Josefina, even if she rejects the advances, as she exclaims, "Te has quedado a dormir para eso?" ("Did you stay overnight for this?"). "Eso" names and yet stops short from naming Lucía's same-sex desire and is Josefina's tacit acknowledgment that she knows of Lucía's same-sex desires already, that they are not a complete surprise for her.

While in many ways this story does attest to the invisibility of women's same-sex desires, hidden away in a private bedroom, this encounter is also embedded in the tacit knowledge of Lucía's same-sex desires; while her same-sex desires may be rejected by Josefina in the moment, this does not forestall Lucía's acceptance into the family household as a social equal.

In the end the story takes an unexpected turn when Josefina is alone again and seems to address the woman who just left, promising that she will save herself, "Love, although we may only meet in a better world."[88] However, alternatively, this sentence could also be directed at the man whom Lucía suspects is "in this somewhere."[89] Depending on the interpretation, these endings give the story quite different valences when it comes to same-sex desire: either Josefina is yearning for a not-yet possible same-sex love, given the public scrutiny, or she is chastely saving herself for a male lover (possibly echoing Contreras's own biography); yet, what is more important is that the story offers a representation of female masculinity and same-sex desire not as radically othered or ostracized, but as tacitly accepted and integrated into the protagonist's social circle. It seems that the prevalence of Dominican women living with other women in matrifocal households may indeed offer some room—quite literally—for sexual relations, even if closely constrained by gossip, rumor, and other forms of surveillance by family members and neighbors. At the same time, despite these networks of surveillance, there is room for Lucía's gender nonconformity in the social relations and familial circles surrounding the protagonist.

I NOW TURN TO A MUCH LESS-KNOWN STORY BY CONTRERAS IN THE same collection *Entre dos silencios* which tells of the threat of the tacit becoming explicit and disrupting the familial and social webs that sustain it. Contreras's short story "Canícula" ("Dog Days") already alludes through its title to a sense of discomfort, in this case the threat and disordering of same-sex desires made public. The story takes place within the well-off home of Don León, who employs a butler ("mayordomo"), and Laura, the female character from whose perspective the story is largely told; it is unclear if Laura is Don León's wife, a female relative, or a secretary living in the same home. The story begins with "la joven" Laura not wanting to get up in her room where there is "sure contrariness" and a threatening heat outside: "up above, a white torment stagnated, inflaming everything with its damp tongue of heat."[90] In the midst of this oppressive atmosphere, Laura hears the butler laughing in the hall, and he asks her "Supo usté" ("did you know"). The laughter and question if she "knows" reveals that something that was not meant to be known has been found out and is subject to ridicule. Laura answers that she did not know anything and asks *when* it happened, revealing her tacit understanding of what may have happened. The butler says "last night," as someone suddenly enters the house.[91] The butler greets the man, whom he calls "Su Excelencia" ("Your Excellency"), indicating the visitor's high social status and class, while his whiteness is alluded to in the description of his rosy flesh and "the smiling blue of his eyes."[92] Laura, in response to the arrival of this unexpected visitor, "turned around, tingling in every nerve," her emotional reaction indicating the stakes and tension in this situation.[93]

Su Excelencia asks if the butler has seen his belt—a hardly veiled phallic symbol—that he lost last night. "Last night?" asks the butler. "Yes, last night.... *You know very well*," answers "Su Excelencia."[94] With "You know very well," Su Excelencia again affirms the tacit knowledge that the butler has of what conspired the previous night and calls him out for trying to disavow this shared knowledge. Don León himself then emerges and asks, "What does my steward [butler] know?"[95] Laura answers that "His Excellency has lost his belt," and Don León replies, "It's not difficult.... Look for it where you were fooling around last night."[96] Laura, when she hears Don León's answer, thinks, "*Too smooth... he knows where to find it or he would be shouting.*"[97] As it becomes openly clear that something happened the night before that led Su Excelencia to take his belt off, emotions become increasingly tense: "The steward [butler] laughed without moving a muscle of his face, but his body trembled" indicating his amusement and mockery, while Don León's "face tightened," and Laura's "tingling nerves hurt, sending a feeling of malaise throughout her body."[98] As that which is supposed to remain tacit threatens to become explicit in broad daylight and with the knowledge of others, the discomfort becomes all-encompassing.

Then the story shifts to the past night in question, referring to it as "an old story of besieged nights and days."[99] It is three in the morning and Don León and Su Excelencia are drinking. Don León wants to go to bed, but Su Excelencia looks for the butler to get more ice for drinks but does not find him. When he returns, he finds Don León in bed, and despite Don León's protests, Su Excelencia responds, "Do you think it's shameful to see me naked?" and then "he took off his clothes with saintly calmness."[100] Returning to the present moment, Su

Excelencia reappears after having looked for the belt and not finding it, saying "I'm sorry... but it was a gift from my wife. And I couldn't have left it anywhere else. I'm certain..."[101] Don León quickly asks his butler to show Su Excelencia out as he and Laura have a lot of work to do. It is then that Laura tries to "intervene," and "from her tone, don León understood" and immediately cuts her off; "His Excellency, who also had understood" says his good-byes to Laura as well and leaves.[102] Both men "understand" that in this moment Laura is about to articulate what was tacit and ever-present knowledge between all those in the house, but it must remain unnamed, and the two men forestall her utterance. In the end even the brazen Su Excelencia wants to dissimulate what they all know, creating an atmosphere of unbearable and suffocating tension, so that for Laura, the story ends with her thinking, "But why should she get up, if the heat and the mute, serene and fascinating presence of death were exhausting the will to live?"[103] The mute presence of death speaks to a different kind of silence, not a refreshing one as described before, but an oppressive and dangerous one. Su Excelencia's return in broad daylight and evocation in front of the entire household of what was supposed to remain under the cover of the night creates a deeply troubled atmosphere. The story is full of allusions to what is known but cannot be named, and the tense feelings that arise when the tacit is made explicit in the presence of others. When the possibility of same-sex desire is no longer just part of a *noche asediada* ("besieged night") between two men with too much to drink while everyone else is asleep, but rather becomes a shared knowledge in broad daylight, the social and familial balance of the household is threatened.

Contreras's story as well as Contín Aybar's and Paco Escribano's personal lives during the Trujillato speak to the power of the tacit as articulated by Decena—of that which is known but not made explicit—that allows these elite men to sustain respect and assume positions of power even within the homophobic outlines of the Trujillato. Yet their same-sex desires must remain out of the public eye, as "Canícula" shows so clearly, and be relegated to other spaces: nighttime encounters and spaces removed from the public realm, like the beach in "Biel, el marino." However, these "other" spaces, such as the beach or the *noches asediadas* of drinking late at night are not accessible to women in the same way; rather, as seen in "La espera," women remain in the domestic space and their privacy is closely surveilled, including by women themselves, making the private/public divide more porose for them and leaving them less room to maneuver their sexuality than the male protagonists. Yet, as Contreras's short story "La Espera" suggests, within and despite these constraints, there is also opportunity for intimate encounters between women that are disguised or made "invisible" by the social reality of female-headed households where women living and sleeping in close proximity is the norm.

The male same-sex encounters in Contreras's story "Canícula" and in Contín Aybar's "Biel, el marino," as well as the encounter between the two women in "La espera," is facilitated and underwritten by the tacit knowledge and embeddedness of non-heteronormative desires and subjectivities. Both the male protagonist in "Biel, el Marino," despite being *raro,* and Lucía in "Entre dos silencios," despite her female masculinity, are deeply woven into the Dominican social and familial fabric. While Contreras's and Contín Aybar's stories attest that a history of Dominican same-sex desire must take into account gender differences that were given even sharper relief during the Trujillato, they also highlight the tacit knowledge and acceptance of non-heteronormative desires and identities of these men and women even during a time as repressive as the Trujillo dictatorship. In all cases, their experiences are mitigated by their access to private space, even if only a private room, and the ability to lay claim to the respect of others, marking their middle/upper-class status and white identities; hence, these stories can only tell one part of Dominican experiences of same-sex desires, and it will be several decades before the experiences and same-sex desires of lower-class and Afro-Dominicans are represented in the literary works of a new generation of writers, including in the work of Rey E. Andújar, discussed in the following chapter.

TWO

Queer Nightlife during the Balaguer Years in the Novels of Rita I. Hernández (1977–) and Rey E. Andújar (1977–)

THE ASSASSINATION OF RAFAEL L. TRUJILLO IN 1961 BROUGHT A period of political uncertainty, instability, and hope for a new democratic beginning and political change in the Dominican Republic. For many this hope was encapsulated in Juan Bosch's presidency in 1963, which endeavored to make decisive political and economic changes and as a result was prematurely ended by a coup that same year. A popular uprising demanded Bosch's return in 1965, known as "La Revolución de Abril," but was crushed by a second U.S. intervention (1965–1966). As a result, Joaquín Balaguer (1906–2002), one of the Trujillato's key intellectual and political figureheads, became the president from 1966 to 1978 with the support of the U.S.[1] This period, known as the infamous "doce años," cost the lives of thousands of political dissidents, and students and many others left the country, initiating the mass migration of Dominicans to the U.S. that continues to this day.[2] Despite the rampant repression during the Balaguerato, he did not wield the kind of total power Trujillo had. Political scientist Jonathan Hartlyn describes how Balaguer instead appealed to Dominicans with a "rhetoric focused on the values of order and stability, and he continued to link Dominican nationalism to what he viewed as its Hispanic, Catholic essence and to anti-Haitian themes."[3] Balaguer's policy of co-optation was facilitated by the transfer of Trujillo's properties to the state, which allowed for the vast expansion of the state apparatus and a clientelist politics that created new economic and social opportunities and relations in Dominican society.[4] At the same time, Dominican society and economy opened themselves to the outside through mass migration, the impact of international media, and the inroads that global business interests made in the country, including the steadily growing tourism industry that would become predominant by the end of the twentieth century.[5] This growing industry also encompassed a significant gay tourism presence, so much so that the *Spartacus International Gay Guide* describes the country from the 1970s until the early 1980s as "something of a paradise for gay tourists," adding, "particularly paedophiles."[6] These tourists encountered a growing nightlife scene that was part of a rapidly expanding entertainment sector.

Despite the ongoing political repression and the dominant rhetoric of order, family, and Catholicism, it was during this time that queer nightlife spaces began proliferating. As the Dominican-American writer and poet Jimmy Lam (1958–) recalls in an autobiographical essay in his book *Sexile=Sexilio*, in the 1970s paradoxically there "was a bonanza in meet-up places for gays," even while "in those times, homosexuality continued being a taboo given that Dominican society didn't even remotely accept gay life and, to a certain point, being publicly gay, was like suffering a social death."[7] He points to the favorable economic conditions and "the emerging Dominican middle class" along with the renewed political impetus of his generation that enabled the paradoxical emergence of queer nightlife during this repressive political period.[8] Lam highlights 1974 as the moment when "there was a certain explosion of gay life when it comes to clubs."[9] As he describes,

> There was a disco on Winston Churchill Avenue (presided by a fabulous queen, the famous Perfumista) and appropriately called, the Infinite. There was another around 17th street that ended up being called Pent-House but which initially was called El Bochinche . . . Already by the mid-70s gay clubs had been "desarrabilizados" since there were two more discos, one in Lope de Vega Street (Cinema) and another one in Abraham Lincoln Avenue (Zardoz) and well since forever there had been Marte in Gazcue, which was not officially "gay" but all of us gay men went there.[10]

Lam suggests how establishments catering to an LGBTIQ+ clientele had moved from more marginal *barrios* to the very center of the city. Lam's personal memories are echoed by the now defunct Dominican periodical *Clave*, which in 2006 published a dossier on "Las noches reprimidas" ("The Repressed Nights") about gay and lesbian nightlife in Santo Domingo. The dossier includes a table of gay and lesbian nightlife establishments for each decade, 1970, 1980, 1990, and 2000–2005, and remarkably lists six establishments for the 1970s, including the above-mentioned "Infinito"; indeed, there are more establishments listed for the '70s in Santo Domingo than for the '80s and '90s and just one more for 2000–2005. Though the establishments, with one exception (O-Hara's), change for each decade, hinting at the difficulties of running and maintaining a LGBTIQ+ entertainment space over time, they speak to a relatively stable existence of queer nightlife in the capital during different political regimes in the post-dictatorship period.

The centrality of nightlife for Dominican gays, lesbians, and *travestis/tranformistas* during the Balaguerato is underlined by Lam when he speaks of their "strictly nocturnal life" at a time when "there were no community centers, no organizations, no support groups at all, much less allies. The discos were the only establishments where one could show one's gayness."[11] In this context, queer nightlife spaces played a crucial role in expanding normally private negotiations of same-sex desires and subjectivities into newly available public entertainment spaces. Public roles for men who were perceived to be more openly homosexual remained very limited at the time, as Lam describes, "the only public gay men [pájaros] were those who I called gay men by profession.... that is to say, that in the Dominican Republic of the unhappy years of the 70s, gay were only the dancers, the choreographers, the fashion and interior designers and the hairdressers... The rest of us gays and lesbians were in the closet."[12] Lam's quote reflects how, albeit limited, there were certain public and professional spaces of tolerance and queer embeddedness for men who more obviously presented as homosexuals. However, no comparable public and professional roles are mentioned for more same-sex desiring women, pointing to the lasting significance of gender differences.

By 1978 the widespread political discontent and the new social and economic actors in Dominican civil society successfully led to political change and the coming into power of the opposition party, the Partido Revolucionario Dominicano, for two terms from 1978 to 1986.[13] This period of political opening also resulted in a new Dominican social and cultural effervescence when, as Miguel D. Mena describes, "the nightlife revolution" sees its full realization and becomes both "a space for consumption and for the constitution of new subjectivities."[14] As we will see, queer nightlife spaces also facilitated new local queer subjectivities and terminologies to consolidate. This included the 1980s group "Creadores de Imágenes" dedicated to "el arte del transformismo," for which the group members cross-dressed and skillfully performed as famous Latin American divas while lip-synching; they first performed in a nightlife spot called "Le Club" and then were hired to perform in other entertainment spaces as well.[15] This group lasted until 1989 when various group members migrated, though they eventually returned and took on precisely some of the few available professions for gay men mentioned above, including "make-up artists, pastry chef, visual artist and painter" ("maquillistas, repostero, artista plástico y pintor").[16] The significance of this early group of LGBTIQ+ performers has only recently been recovered, including with a documentary about them called "El Último Show," directed by Juan Carlos Albelo, and screened at the 2018 Santo Domingo OutFest/Festival de Cine GLBT; a revival performance in 2020 with some of the original members called "Creadores de Imágenes Visión 2020"; and a tribute party in 2023 at Califé Bar in Santo Domingo.

Alongside the blossoming of new social and cultural forces, the country also saw new political formations, including the country's first small Lesbian and Gay groups. As the political scientist Jacqueline Jiménez Polanco describes,

> The L & G movement emerged in the early 1980's during the emergence of the formal democratization process that followed Joaquín Balaguer's twelve-year long authoritarian regime. The movement reached its highest peak in the mid-1980's concurrently with the society's growing expectations toward the improvement of the socioeconomic conditions and the recognition and respect of human rights. It vanished in the early 1990's when the socioeconomic effects of the "lost decade" fueled a large migratory process of Dominican citizens who traveled to the United States, Europe, and other Caribbean and Latin American nations in search of a better life. The lack of leadership and the socioeconomic crisis atomized the movement until after its reemergence in 2000.

These initial small Lesbian and Gay organizations were short-lived, with the exception of ASA (Amigos Siempre Amigos), an organization founded in 1989 in response to the HIV/AIDS crisis and supported by international funds, that continues to exist up until today.[17]

The interim time period of the PRD (1978–1986) was a key moment for social transformation and hope for political change, which ultimately gave way to political disappointment when Balaguer returned to power for another ten years from 1986 to 1996 following an economic crisis. During this time, for most Dominican LGBTIQ+ people, urban nightlife remained their primary place of public encounter and self-expression outside of the private sphere. Indeed, some of the most successful queer nightlife places were founded in the 1980s and early 1990s, including the club Penthouse. The legendary Penthouse is the subject of the planned documentary "Noches de Penthouse," directed by Juanjo Cid, which documents the network of extravagant *travesti* performers and gay men in whose lives the "cathedral of gay discotheques" played a key role. Later on, "Disco Free" played a similarly crucial role in the 1990s as recalled by the writer Rita Indiana Hernández. She described in a speech at the Centro Cultural de León in Santiago in 2018 the essential role of "Disco Free" as a space for gender and sexual difference:

> I began to attend the gay disco "Disco Free" . . . In "Disco Free" . . . the body . . . was the protagonist. Under the protection of disco music a population of creatures of the night survived dedicated to exploding into a thousand pieces any presumption of heteronormativity. There difference, the spectacular and the uninhibited were celebrated. Transvestism outside of the security of the disco would have been an act of suicide.[18]

These "seres de la noche," described by Hernández, attest to how urban nightlife was a crucial site for the expression of non-heteronormative and gender non-conforming subjectivities beyond the confines of the private sphere. Elena Valdez in fact argues in *Las ciudades del deseo* (2023) that this phenomenon was not limited to the Dominican Republic, but similarly emerged in the Cuban and Puerto Rican context, attesting to the emergence of "una imagen nueva de la ciudad" ("a new image of the city") across the Hispanophone Caribbean, infiltrated by "queer subjectivities that can be read as a symptom of the failure of heteronormative national political projects."[19]

The centrality of queer nightlife as a cultural alternative and challenge to the Dominican social and political status quo during the stagnancy of the second Balaguer regime (1986–1996) is explored by Rita Indiana Hernández (1977–), in her first novel *La estrategia de Chochueca* (2000), and by Rey Emmanuel Andújar (1977–), in his first novel *El hombre triángulo* (2003). Though these novels starkly diverge in their theme and style, they both make urban queer nightlife spaces central to their plot and reflect the multiplicity of local queer subjectivities—of *locas, maricones,* and *bugarrones,* the male sex workers who by the late twentieth century were an established facet of Dominican society. Both novels attest to the proliferation of these local queer subjectivities and terminologies and the richness of creolized queerness; neither refer to LGBTIQ+ identities even as both novels' protagonists may be described as "bisexually" behaving, with both opposite and same-sex encounters and desires, and do not name or identify their sexual difference explicitly.

AFTER THE EARLIER HOMOEROTIC WRITINGS OF HILMA CONTRERAS and Pedro René Contín Aybar there was a long silence about same-sex desire in Dominican literature. As Mena suggests, there were two writers who each *could* have been "a good poet of homoeroticism" ("un buen poeta del homoerotismo"), Luis Alfredo Torres (1935–1992) and Manuel Rueda (1921–1999), but these poets ultimately did not "put their cards on the table," attesting to how they preferred to tacitly negotiate their sexual differences, including in their writings.[20] Then, according to Mena, "in the 80s and in almost all of the 90s there was absence of this theme" until the publication of *La estrategia de Chochueca* (2000) by Rita Indiana Hernández.[21] Hernández's first novel, published not long after her short story collection *Rumiantes* (1998), established her as key new voice in Dominican literature; in Mena's words, she became "the great surprise of the latest literary promotions," her writing breaking with "the established canons of the insular common sense."[22] The novel, told from the perspective of the seventeen-year-old protagonist Silvia, recounts her forays around Santo Domingo as she tries to return a pair of stolen loudspeakers, as a favor to a friend, while evading police. As she makes her way to different places and acquaintances to resolve the case, she recalls previous outings and get-togethers with her irreverent group of friends, who escape the disenchantment of daily life during the Balaguer years through alcohol, drugs, sex, and nightlife. Hernández's novel differs starkly from Rey E. Andújar's *El hombre triángulo*, which centers obversely on a young police sergeant and his experience as a member of the rigid and hierarchical Dominican police force; yet "Pérez" also seeks to escape from a reality he dreads through alcohol, sex, and nighttime escapades and, like Silvia, this leads him to his own same-sex desires.[23] In this chapter I ask what are, according to Hernández's and Andújar's novels, the possibilities *and* limitations of queer nightlife at a time when nightlife establishments were the main sites of encounter for non-heteronormative Dominicans outside the private sphere during the politically stagnant years of Balaguer's second regime (1986–1996)?

Hernández and Andújar hail from the same generation, both born in 1977, and they each self-published their first novel; *La estrategia de Chochueca* and *El Hombre Triángulo* both appeared first in a small edition by the authors, in 2000 and 2003 respectively, and when their novels garnered significant critical attention, they were republished by the Isla Negra Editores in Puerto Rico, in 2003 and 2005. Eventually both authors left Santo Domingo, each making Puerto Rico and the U.S. their home for prolonged periods of time. Yet they continue to write in Spanish and are considered part of the contemporary Dominican literary sphere on the island. In fact, Mena includes both authors among the generation of "post-insular" writers born after 1965, who have emerged since the 1990s, including Juan Dicent (1969–), Homero Pumarol (1971–), and Frank Báez (1978–), among others, and who are less concerned with the Dominican past than previous literary generations. Hernández's and Andújar's novels both favor contemporaneity over a dwelling on the past even as the Trujillato's and Balaguer's authoritarian legacies are omnipresent and each protagonist is driven by a need to escape the strictures of a society shaped by them; yet, looking back is not their principal concern. This is reflected as well in the marginal role that older generations, the protagonists' families and parents, play in each novel. Instead, both narratives unfold in a condensed present during which the protagonists move across the urban space of the city Santo Domingo while experiencing memories of their own personal life.

Chochueca is a decidedly urban novel taking place during the 1990s in Santo Domingo when Balaguer was once more in power. Dominican society is experienced as politically and socially stagnant and suffocating by the youth in the novel; Silvia and her friends reject "the loathsome trotting of the people, lonely people who go nowhere at all, who at the same time shake their heads to a great symphony of disillusionment and scandal."[24] Steeped in stagnancy and disillusionment as the political opposition has long been co-opted and social and economic inequities run deep, Dominican society continues to be given to surveillance of those who do not follow "respectable" social norms and traditional Catholic and heteronormative values that shape the so-called *moralidad pública*. This becomes evident when Silvia and her roving group of friends actively challenge these social constraints and norms of decency and "moral" behavior in the public sphere, including those related to gender and sexuality. As Silvia describes, they went "up and down, making noise, drinking, smoking one cigarette among ten of us," and "they always threw us out from everywhere . . . it was something about our way of smiling, as if with us and our going to the bathroom in threes, our kissing each other on the mouth men and women, our laughing with a full mouth, splashed those who watched us with an unbearable substance."[25] Rejected in public spaces for their "disrespectful" behavior, including open shows of affection and intimacy, these youth seek out Dominican nightlife in both private and public spaces as an escape and space of self-expression.

The novel extensively describes their parties in private homes and commercial nightlife spaces; for example, "Lorena lived in a huge apartment in Naco . . . there we celebrated some awesome parties that always ended in disaster, an intoxicated rich girl vomiting through her nose on a fifteen-year-old rapist who is pawing his [male] friend who is asleep from the Lorazepan [sic] and the Brugal [rum]."[26] A private home in Naco, an upper-class neighborhood, becomes a staging ground for parties that overstep the norms that structure Dominican public and private life, and allow for a seeming breakdown of class, racial, and sexual boundaries. Indeed, a key figure in this youth's nightlife is Franco, a homosexual man—referred to, albeit lovingly, not insultingly, as "maricón" in the text—who frequently seeks out the Dominican *bugarrones,* young, lower-class and often dark-skinned men who have sex with men for pay. Franco makes no secret of his gender nonconformity and same-sex desires in front of his friends:

> At a party in Franco's house . . . he received us with his eyes made-up and a little green chiffon skirt. . . . In the early morning it was more pleasant seeing him with his make-up messed up, his clothes undone, and the laugh of Marlene Dietrich, this was when he did not cry and hug and love you and wanted you to take various grams of cocaine with him and told you how his last love inserted pieces of a hose or a lantern up his ass . . .[27]

With his group of friends Franco is nonchalant about his non-heteronormative gender identity and same-sex desires, and he openly introduces them to some of the male sex workers he has sex with for pay. Silvia recalls meeting one of the *bugarrones:* "He introduced himself and smiled in a learned faggoty way. He must have already fucked him, because Franco was tenacious and there were two sticky stains on the bedspread. Leo . . . was sixteen and in Ciudad Nueva he had a little girlfriend... Franco petted his head like a little stuffed doggy."[28] Though Franco always kicks Silvia and her friends out if a "bugarroncito" offered his "servicios," his apartment is a crucial private space for their parties and get-togethers.

Hernández's novel attests to how male sex workers—bugarrones—were a mainstay of Dominican nightlife by the 1990s. Mark Padilla in *Caribbean Pleasure Industry: Tourism, Sexuality, and AIDS in the Dominican Republic* (2007), based on ethnographic fieldwork from 1999 to 2001, foregrounds the experience and prevalence of Dominican male sex workers, which at the time were "an undeniable and conspicuous feature of gay life in Santo Domingo."[29] Padilla describes how, just like "Leo" in the novel, "*bugarrones* attempt to assimilate to normative constructions of masculinity, are often married, typically request payment for sex, and almost universally claim to participate exclusively in *activo* (active, or insertive) anal sex with their male partners."[30] Often bugarrones would "frequent many of the spaces where gay-identified men congregate," and they were hence a key part of queer nightlife.[31] Gay sex tourism, which had its "heyday" in the 1980s, according to Padilla, further drove a demand for bugarrones and their hyper-masculinity, making their presence even more ubiquitous.[32] Hernández's off-handed engagement with Franco's search for and encounter with bugarrones in the novel reflects how male sex work had become an established facet of queer nightlife and Dominican society more broadly in the late twentieth century.

However, Franco is not the only character with same-sex desires in the novel. Silvia, who in the novel has a secretive sexual relation with a male friend, Eduard, also desires her female friend, Amanda, a Norwegian exchange student, who is part of her group of friends. Unlike the economic, class, and most likely racial differences that underwrite Franco's relationship with the bugarrones, Silvia and Amanda form part of the same social circles. While Silvia at first desires Amanda from a distance as she watches her friend Salim dance with her and touch her, at another party in a nightclub rented out by Franco Silvia and Amanda get intimate:

> The music was brutal, ... the DJ and his zug zigui zug. ... Come, let's go move a bit, Amanda says to me ... and when I touch her it was a like a warm shower rising in me ... Amanda Amanda loveliest, I said and kissed her lips with patience.[33]

This nightlife setting allows the protagonist to readily explore her same-sex desires with little fear of the censure or backlash that they would encounter in the public sphere. This shows how unlike in the previous chapter, the private sphere (Contreras) or spaces away from the public sphere (Contín Aybar) are no longer the only available spaces for same-sex desire, and it also demonstrates the solidification of queer nightlife as a new space of encounter and self-expression.

As Rita M. Palacios in her essay on "the queerification of space in *La estrategia de Chochueca*," notes as well, "the *queer* interpersonal dimension in the novel is articulated outside of the Dominican private sphere, forging a countercurrent intimacy that alters the normative reach of Dominican social organization."[34] In a related vein, Elena Valdez argues that Hernández's characters create "a type of queer relation that supersedes the regulatory power" and that functions as "a counternarrative to official memory and archives."[35] However, importantly, these "countercurrent" intimacies and narratives, I note, are underwritten by the economic and class privileges of the majority of the youth in this group (though not all), which facilitate their free-roaming lifestyle with seemingly no work, study, or familial obligations.

The deep social inequities of Dominican society are always latently present in the experiences and queer nightlife described in the novel and ultimately lead to its violent ending. While Silvia successfully returns the loudspeakers without being caught by the police, she receives a call telling her that Franco had been violently assaulted likely by one of the male sex workers and is in the hospital; she thinks it might have been someone she just saw him with, "a dark skinned guy with a Mets cap who tries to imitate a Puerto Rican accent when he talks, he has all the appearance of one of the prostitutes who go to the Pent House."[36] Penthouse, of course, is the aforementioned legendary disco that played a crucial role in Dominican queer nightlife at the time. This eruption of violence must be placed in the context of deep class, racial, and economic inequities that structure the relation between Franco and the bugarrones he hires for sex and that reveal some of the limits of queer nightlife in Santo Domingo in the 1990s. Hernández's novel thereby closely reflects the tensions that Padilla's study indexes as well: while bugarrones "often develop close friendship and long-term relationships with gays," there were "palpable divisions between gays and *bugarrones,* making social relations between these groups occasionally ambivalent and contentious."[37] This contentiousness was due to class differences, tied closely to racial differences, between "middle-class and elite gays" and lower-class bugarrones, along with their gender differences: the bugarrones' "self-presentation as *hombres normales*" contrasts sharply with the "self-expression of Dominican gay-identified men."[38] Though queer nightlife offered a space for encounters that cut across class, race, and gender variance, it could not always escape the social tensions produced by these deep-seated inequalities.

In comparison, in the novel the nocturnal same-sex encounter between the two women, Silvia and Amanda, is largely a relation between equals, with no economic stakes for either of them, and tellingly there is no pushback or violent backlash in the novel to their intimacy in this nightlife setting. Rather their same-sex desires fit rather neatly with the youths' desire for irreverence, including sexual irreverence, in a social context they experience as suffocating in its conventionalism. In fact, it is not this brief moment of same-sex intimacy between Silvia and Amanda in a queer nightlife space that is the novel's most provocative stance; rather, it is Silvia's insistence on traversing and "owning" the urban space in ways that are traditionally tied to masculinity, through which she most provocatively pushes against established gender and social norms in everyday life; as Padilla highlights, "the logic of Dominican gender ideology . . . fosters a social permissiveness towards men's street activities . . . not available to women."[39] Through Silvia's movement through the streets of Santo Domingo, often by herself, she takes on traditionally male prerogatives and expresses her gender nonconformity. As Valdez notes as well, while "other male characters are presented as more cowardly and more feminized, . . . Silvia appropriates their space and masculine role of dominating the streets."[40] Her overstepping of the norms of femininity is indexed by how outside her circle of friends other women eye her suspiciously; one of her male friend's girlfriends asks, "What are you doing with that chick?" and screams "that I was a whore [puta], that I was a drug addict, that I was a . . . a . . . a, she did not know what to say anymore."[41] The evocation of the "puta" here is telling, as Padilla explains, "the figure of the '*puta*' (prostitute, or more semantically accurate, 'slut') functions to establish normative boundaries that constrain women's activities to the home," and the "'*puta*' in the Dominican Republic functions as a threat to all women who would deviate from certain notions of appropriate female sexuality, loading the term with negative affect and stigma."[42] The insult of being a "puta" hurled at Silvia precisely indexes the ways that her behavior transcends accepted norms of femininity in the public sphere and how such norms of respectable femininity were closely tied to perceptions of women's sexuality.

Silvia herself speaks of the desire to inhabit the prerogatives of masculinity. In her quest to return the speakers, she says "I had disguised myself [as Octaviano], . . . but it is not easy being the Octano, it's necessary to have balls, one needs an absurd and consistent amnesia, one needs to have one's way to be on his side in his world, one would have to be Chochueca."[43] Chochueca, the title figure, is an urban legend, a beggar who would stop by the houses of the dying to request their clothes; his disregard for social propriety inspires Silvia, just like Octaviano does, her delinquent friend for whom she returns the loudspeakers. She ultimately desires to be just like these street-smart masculinities, or *tígueres,* that are able to side-step social norms in public in a way that women generally cannot. As Padilla describes, *tígueres* are "central to the construction of Dominican masculinity," and "in Santo Domingo, the term *tíguere* is often used to describe a man who regularly engages in a range of street behaviors, including drinking in all-male groups, carousing, womanizing, infidelity, aggression, and various kinds of delinquency" alongside "a kind of self-serving opportunism, deception, or avarice that is simultaneously disparaged and valorized."[44] In *La estrategia de Chochueca* and other novels, including in *Papi* (2005) and *De nombres y animales* (2013), Hernández's female protagonists often claim for themselves the prerogatives of male *tigueraje* and thereby challenge the constraints of female gender roles; this arguably culminates in Hernández's sci-fi novel *La mucama de Omicunlé* (2015), in which the main character seamlessly transforms from androgynous female to fully male through a new medical technology. While sexual difference, same-sex desire, is deeply imbricated with these protagonists' gender nonconformity, reflecting the close link between sexuality and gender noted by critics, it is not the expression of their same-sex desires that is the main stake but rather the demand to take up public space in direct challenge to conventional women's roles and to usurp some of the privileges of Dominican masculinity—including the access to other women.

THE PREPONDERANT ROLE OF MASCULINITY AND ITS PRIVILEGES IN Dominican society but also its constraints, especially in the public sphere, including in relation to same-sex desire, are key themes in Rey E. Andújar's *El hombre triángulo*. The narrative begins when "el hombre triángulo" is arrested in a public park in Santo Domingo for being nude, indexing the ways that "public morality" continues to be closely policed. The arrest and overnight detention of "el hombre triángulo" brings him to Pérez, the police sergeant who is the novel's protagonist. In more ways than one this novel is told from the opposite perspective of Silvia and her friends' lives. While she and her friends try to evade the police throughout the novel, this narrative is written from the perspective of a police sergeant who is deeply immersed in the institution and its masculinist ideologies. Yet, as in Hernández's novel, nightlife, and queer nightlife specifically, play a central role in the narrative and are crucially tied to the protagonist's negotiation of his gender role and non-heteronormative sexual desires.

Pérez's life is unhappily conscripted to the police, which for him, a young Afro-Dominican lower-class man, is one of the only paths for upward mobility and economic and social stability. Indeed, race plays a key role in his enlistment, as he recalls, "you enlist because you are tired of the police bothering you in the streets. . . . Because if you are dark-skinned and clothes don't help and it pisses you off that they don't let you in . . . or they tell you 'We are sorry, private party.'"[45] Some of the places that Silvia and her roving group of friends so easily entered would have been inaccessible to this lower-class Afro-Dominican protagonist; enlisting also appeals to him, as he recognizes, because of the public respect shown to cadets, which bolsters his own sense of masculinity; as he self-critically admits, "already the little worm of masculinity and the damn Dominican hetero-machismo is inflating you."[46] In fact, the novel very self-consciously portrays and critiques the performance of heteromasculinity the police demand. This is reflected, for example, in the peppering of the police officers' speech with homosexual insults; when Pérez receives a report with a flowery description of arrests made overnight, the sergeant mocks the author saying, "It's that the little faggot thinks he is a poet," and in response Pérez states, "well then I will teach him how to write a report like a man."[47] Homosexuality and effeminacy are tightly linked here, and to claim respect for himself Pérez emphatically performs a hyper-masculinity that includes frequent gay slurs and denigrations of femininity; yet it is clear that he is deeply at odds and unhappy with the institution and the role it demands of him—he is described as "a civilian in military clothes, a tormented man," who repeatedly thinks of committing suicide.[48]

The Dominican police force is a notoriously masculinist institution with a long history of homophobia. Both Padilla and Lara in *Streetwalking* chronicle the frequent raids on queer nightlife establishments and gathering spaces in Santo Domingo and the arbitrary arrests carried out there. Padilla describes how during the time in which the novel is set the police vocally and actively pursued anti-gay policies and created a homosexual panic, including through "a high-profile campaign by the chief of the national police, Pedro de Jesús Candelier, to purge all homosexuals from his ranks" in 2001.[49] Distancing oneself from any suspicion of homosexuality and from the effeminacy associated with it was thus a matter of self-preservation for any police officer at the time. Deeply entrenched in the police force and its dogmas, Pérez attempts to escape his everyday life and work at night, drinking in bars and regularly going to a brothel to his preferred sex worker named Rotunda. This reflects how unlike the more itinerant male sex work of the bugarrones, as discussed above, female sex work, as Padilla notes, generally takes place "within various sex-work establishments," including hotels and brothels, with access to private rooms.[50] Indeed, the protagonist's multiple sexual encounters with Rotunda all take place within the confines of a small private room in a bar and sex work establishment.

Importantly for the narrative, Pérez likes Rotunda because of some of her more male-seeming attributes: "what drives me crazy Rotunda are your man-like hairs, never shave your legs Rotunda never shave your natural little mustache and your hoarse voice, so hoarse."[51] The narrative thereby already alludes to the possibility that Pérez's sexual desires push against the constraints of heteronormativity. Furthermore, he also spends many nights at Parada 77, an actual existing bar in the historic city center, La Zona Colonial, described by Pérez as a place that "was always full of faggots [maricones], though the music was good and the drinks were cheap . . . those were good excuses to sit from time to time in Parada 77, the bar where even the devil took off his clothes after three am in the morning."[52] Music and drinks are the "excuses" that Pérez proffers to himself for seeking out a nightlife place where heterosexual norms are regularly put into question. Parada 77 in fact figures as a key site for homoerotic encounters in Andújar's later short story collection *Saturnario* (2011) as well.[53]

The so-called La Zona or La Zona Colonial where the bar Parada is located, is a key space of overlap between Andújar's and Hernández's novels and their sexual geographies: their very different main characters, who live in very different neighborhoods, nonetheless both crisscross La Zona and attest to the vitality of queer nightlife there, as amply documented by both Padilla and Lara as well. Not surprisingly, it is in this bar and neighborhood where Pérez fatefully re-encounters "el hombre triángulo" after their first meeting at the police station. After his initial arrest Pérez interrogates him and is surprised by the man's quick veering into deeply emotional territory: he tells Pérez that he feels like he knows him and his agony, and says "I think I can love you," and "you entered in me without saying anything like I enter into you now."[54] The emotionality and physical sensuality of "el hombre triángulo," who reveals his name to be "Baraka," egregiously oversteps the norms of male discourse, especially in the hyper-masculine context of the police station. Thereafter, Pérez cannot forget him, "drink for drink he thinks of his eyes, his agony, this man, this man so naked, so well-formed, so clean for being a vagabond."[55] Pérez's lingering on the man's naked "well-formed" body again points to his desires that break the heteronormative mold; in fact, when he thinks of masturbating his thoughts jump from Baraka, to Rotunda, and back to Baraka, and in his next encounter with Rotunda he tells her about him and his skin that seemed so soft.[56]

Pérez unexpectedly meets Baraka again during one of his nighttime outings at Parada 77, and they sit down to have drinks and talk. In this queer-friendly nightlife space they are surrounded by "false eyelashes and true feelings of men desiring men, flesh, sweat, sweet water," alluding to the presence of Dominican *travestis*.[57] At some point Baraka looks into Pérez's eyes and takes one of his hands and asks him what pains him so much.[58] Pérez tells him of his feelings of guilt about his young lover Matilde from the countryside, who is in an insane asylum after their young son, whom Pérez did not want to have, was killed in a vehicular accident. This emotional confession gives way to Pérez lashing out and asking how Baraka ended up "in this shit, with so many faggots around, darn drug addict, piece of shit crackhead. So many pretty words and so much crap damn fucking faggot."[59] Yet this homophobic outburst gives way to further emotional confessions and intimacy between them, and Baraka longingly looks at him and imagines touching him: "these brown eyes and get caught in the curliness of this black hair, be lifted until eternity by these brown arms, be blessed by these big and strong hands, and stay with him, in him."[60] Moved by Baraka's own pain, Pérez embraces him: "They embraced. Pérez had been right about how soft his skin was, but now everything was different, now he felt his skin vibrating under his hands. A strong embrace, crossing of faces, a very light touching, almost imperceptible, thereafter: the kiss."[61]

With the kiss between the two men the narrative abruptly shifts to the protagonist's past to tell the reader that this was not Pérez's first kiss by a man; he was sexually abused by a married military man who would stop by the house where Pérez lived alone with his mother. Here a key difference between Andújar's and Hernández's novel emerges: in Hernández's novel neither Franco's nor Silvia's same-sex desires are presented as tied to trauma or internal conflict; in contrast, in Andújar's novel the protagonist's same-sex desires are deeply troubling to him, both because of his childhood sexual abuse by the military man and because they threaten his livelihood as a police officer, given that any suspected same-sex behavior would lead to his dismissal. Driven by personal trauma and fear of public exposure of his same-sex desires, Pérez attacks Baraka after he kisses him: "Blood: what was flowing out of Baraka's mouth after the punches thrown by Pérez because of this lack of respect. Fuck, what is that, a man kissing a policeman."[62] Pérez leaves the bar running while "one of the 'locas' pushes him and yells at him from the door: Accept it, admit it fuck that you are also a faggot [maricón]. Piece of shit abuser, fuck."[63] The danger of his same-sex desires becoming explicit in public, the loss of "respect" for his masculinity that this would bring, as well as the social and economic consequences for him as a policeman produce his outburst of violence, a desperate attempt to forestall any reading of him as a "maricón."

Pérez is represented in the novel as a character torn and anguished by clashing forces. Unlike the countercultural youth in Hernández's novel, he does not have the class or racial privilege to turn his back to society and its gender and sexual norms, as he is deeply embedded in one of its most notoriously masculinist and heterosexist institutions, the police force. Yet his demeanor and desires conflict with the kind of masculinity and heterosexuality his position demands and which he himself performs and violently reinforces. As in *La estrategia de Chochueca,* queer nightlife becomes a site of other possibilities, but again its limits in overcoming deep-seated racial, class, and economic inequities become evident with Pérez's violent homophobic outburst.[64]

The novel ends with Baraka leaving for the U.S., a failed suicide attempt by Pérez, a tentative plan to get Matilde out of the insane asylum, and a final encounter with Rotunda, who is about to leave for Europe to work as a prostitute there. This last get-together brings a reckoning with the anal pleasures he desires, leaving him to wonder "what would become of him in a world that is so straight."[65] Pérez's racial and class identity keep him tied to a deeply homophobic institution, and he is unable to shift between heterosexual and same-sex desires as smoothly as Silvia, nor can he claim as confidently as Franco his same-sex desires; he cannot turn his back on Dominican society as resolutely as Silvia and her friends, enabled by their privileges.[66]

Notably, though Andújar's novel shows a keen awareness and critique of the entrapments of Dominican heteromasculinity, this complexity is problematically not extended to any of the female characters; in *El hombre triángulo*, Rotunda and Matilde remain caught in the flat roles of the prostitute and the virginal mother who deliver Pérez on his path toward self-recognition. It is these restrictive gender roles, where women are much more limited by society and men's options are much broader and their lives much more peripatetic that are precisely rejected by Silvia in Hernández's novel as she wants to walk in the shoes of Chochueca; however, in Hernández's novel this rejection is also made possible by the protagonist's middle-class and white racial identity that frees her of the strictures that Pérez remains constrained by. My counterpoint reading of these two novels reveals how same-sex desires intersect with and are profoundly shaped by gender, racial, and class differences in late twentieth-century Santo Domingo. While at times these desires and subjectivities converge in the thriving queer nightlife scene in the Dominican capital to enable new same-sex encounters and cross-class and racial connections, at other times these differences result in violent confrontations that foreground how queer nightlife is not a harmonious utopian space severed from social and economic realities. The two novels thereby echo the findings of the recent *Queer Nightlife* (2021) anthology, which asserts that queer nightlife is not "inherently or necessarily utopian," and even as "queer nightlife spaces can provide refuge and play, they can also be sites of alienation that are circumscribed by normative modes of exclusion."[67] Yet nonetheless, both public and private spaces of nightlife are a vital site of possibility for creolized queerness in these novels even during the repressive and socially conservative Balaguer years, and they attest to a changing queer Dominican geography.

At the same time, we see in these novels how expressions of gender in the public sphere continue to be shaped by different pressures and demands. For men, claiming respect in the public sphere, and especially in institutions such as the police force, hinges on relatively strict norms of masculinity, of how to talk and act like a "proper" man, avoiding any taint of femininity/effeminacy, including by emphasizing (hetero-)sexual prowess. In turn, for women the focal point remains their sexuality, which quickly comes under suspicion if they move too freely in the public sphere, as Hernández's protagonist does. However, we also see how such norms are being challenged by a younger generation, even openly so, but this is mainly possible for those who, because of their class and race, do not rely as much on society's "respect" for their survival as the lower-class Afro-Dominican protagonist in Andújar's novel. As we will see in the next chapter, this begins to change in the context of the HIV/AIDS crisis, which demands a more open grappling with sexuality, and as trans subjects enter the public sphere while asserting their gender difference.

THREE

Waddys Jáquez's Theater, Travestis, and HIV/AIDS in the New Democratic Era

THE END OF THE SECOND JOAQUÍN BALAGUER GOVERNMENT IN 1996, in response to rising pressure from inside and outside the country, is thought to have ushered in the "full" return to democracy in the Dominican Republic.[1] The election of Leonel Fernández (PLD), who had been part of the Dominican diaspora in the U.S. and embraced a rhetoric of modernization and progress, seemed to signal a significant change to the political system. Yet his government ultimately was also mired in clientelism and corruption, and the political realm remained stagnant. At the same time Dominican society continued to rapidly change under the influence of neoliberal economic policies, rapid urbanization, mass tourism, migration, and the expanding reach of global media, first through cable television and increasingly through the internet by the late 1990s. In the late 1990s and in the early 2000s, the reach of international media and globalization more broadly made itself felt in relation to LGBTIQ+ representations in the Dominican Republic as in many other places. In his study of "The Expansion Process of The Homosexual Community in Dominican Society in the Past 30 Years," Francisco Castillo describes a series of international events related to LGBTIQ+ lives in the 1990s—the legitimization of same-sex unions in Hawaii, the first openly gay politicians in the U.S., and the launching of the gay doll "Billy"—which were reported in the Dominican media with a notable change of tone; as Castillo describes, "by the midst of the year 1997, Dominican newspapers dared to present statistic and analytical reports, without any prudishness about the intimate sexual preferences of homosexuals."[2] The fact that the mere sharing of information, such as statistical and analytical reports, was considered "daring" shows the long-standing constraints when it comes to speaking publicly about homosexuality.

In the Dominican media, particularly in television, homosexuality became increasingly visible as well; according to ethnomusicologist Angelina Tallaj, while until recently, "homosexuality was invisible in the mainstream, today homosexual males are more visible, yet primarily as drag queens on TV shows and in the entertainment business."[3] Yet there were significant limitations to this new visibility, as Tallaj describes: "homosexuality has gained acceptance as performance but not as a domestic activity, and this performance, even though it has created some tolerance towards public displays of homosexuality, has, at the same time helped perpetuate the same old stereotypes."[4] While there was a superficial embrace of a new LGBTIQ+ media presence, old patterns and perceptions of homosexuality persisted. These new local mainstream media representations of LGBTIQ+ identities and lives thus were often riddled with stereotypes and deeply ambivalent portrayals. This is borne out in a study by Aimée Encarnación on the "Tratamiento del personaje homosexual en el cine dominicano, año 1988-2008" ("Treatment of homosexual characters in Dominican cinema, years 1988-2008"). As Encarnación describes, based on an analysis of all Dominican movies that in that time period show a homosexual theme or character (nine), "the presence of the theme of homosexuality and of the characters of this sexual orientation is scarce and the minimal representation offered in these movies of these two elements presents them as laughable, reprehensible, annoying, and socially unacceptable."[5] Her analysis indexes as well how, while representations of LGBTIQ+ characters increased toward the end of the twentieth century, these media representations were generally reductive if not outrightly homophobic.

The first Dominican literary anthology ostensibly dedicated to LGBTIQ+ representations reflects these very same contradictions and tensions. The *Antología de la literatura gay en la República Dominicana* (*Anthology of Gay Literature in the Dominican Republic*), published in 2004 in Santo Domingo, was the initiative of two Dominican writers, Miguel de Camps Jiménez and the late Mélida García. It was the first Dominican literary collection explicitly aiming to represent same-sex desires by uniting forty-three texts by Dominican writers who, as de Camps Jiménez describes, "have touched on the theme."[6] The anthology hence consists of texts with *any* allusion to same-sex desire, often simply extracted from longer literary texts—positive and often very negative ones. As Tallaj notes, most of the texts "present stigmatized homosexual behaviour" and "deal with the shame of having been involved in a homosexual relationship, the fear of being discovered, and the resentment towards the homosexual 'other.'"[7] Jimmy Lam, in his essay "¿Existe una literatura gay en República Dominicana?" ("Is there a Gay Literature in the Dominican Republic") thus concludes that though the anthology is "a magnificent compilation" of *some* Dominican homoerotic texts—including Hilma Contreras's "La espera," Pedro René Contín Aybar's "Biel, el marino," and an excerpt of Rita I. Hernández's *La estrategia de Chochueca*—it generally lacks "a necessary and minimum coherence . . . with regards to the content of the works presented."[8] Lam rightfully proposes in the end that "without modesty" the anthology should be called more appropriately "Anthology of Gay and Homophobic Literature in the Dominican Republic"![9]

How did this contradictory Dominican "gay" literary anthology come about? The editor, Miguel de Camps Jiménez, explained in an interview that the project was conceived after noting that such anthologies abounded in U.S. and European bookstores and that the Dominican Republic lacked such an apparently quite sellable product.[10] The result of this quite forceful mapping of globalized conceptions of "gay" onto the history of Dominican literary production is the awkward cramming of any Dominican literary representation of same-sex desire, including very homophobic ones, between the book's pink and rainbow adorned covers.[11] Among the included texts is, for example, a short story by José Alcántara Almánzar (1946–), "Lulú or the Metamorphosis," which thereafter has stood in as a representation of "gay" Dominican literature in other key anthologies.[12] Alcántara Almánzar's story describes a Dominican *travesti*, "Lulú," readying herself for a carnival dance and imagining the admiration she will garner as the queen of rumba; yet, as the story narrates her pleasant daydream, it intersperses narrative fragments that tell how, rather than stunning her audience, as she had imagined and fantasized about, she ends up fighting with a group of men and is arrested by the police. In the story's presentation of the *travesti*'s apparent total delusion about how her audience will perceive her, and in the tone of ridicule with which her beauty routine and belief that she is beautiful is described there are some notable homophobic overtones. She is described as "falsely majestic" ("falsamente majestuosa") and with an "undisguisable awkwardness" ("inocultable torpeza") that emerges from "the scandalous contradictions of her body" ("la escandalosa contradicción de su cuerpo").¹³ Indeed, Danny Méndez, in his essay "De Travestismos sospechosos y seducciones peligrosas: la identidad sexual en dos cuentos de José Alcántara Almánzar" ("Of Suspicious Transvestisms and Dangerous Seductions: Sexual Identity in Two Stories by José Alcántara Almánzar"), argues that in this story "transvestism is used . . . as an element alluding to a sexuality that is always understood as 'abnormal' or perturbing."¹⁴ Moreover, as the above-cited descriptions suggest, "the transvestite characters of these stories are a grotesque element," and, as Méndez finds, despite Alcántara Almánzar's text being anthologized as such, his stories "do not propose a direct commitment to the elaboration of a positive gay identity."¹⁵ This and other texts in the *Antología de la literatura gay en la República Dominicana,* along with many other Dominican mainstream film and television portrayals of LGBTIQ+ subjects, reveal both an increasing fascination of local Dominican writers, dramatists, filmmakers, and musicians with "sexual others" at the same time as, and likely in part due to, the increasing circulation of international LGBTIQ+ images in the late 1990s and early 2000s; yet these new Dominican mainstream portrayals were often steeped in stereotypes and ambivalence.

THESE CONTRADICTIONS AND AMBIVALENCES IN MAINSTREAM MEDIA representations echo the contradictory presence of new and old patterns in the Dominican public sphere. On one hand, LGBTIQ+ activist groups saw a resurgence in the new aughts: after the early but ephemeral emergence of lesbian and gay groups in the 1980s and the "lost decade" of the 1990s—with the exception of the lasting presence of ASA (Amigo Siempre Amigos), an HIV/AIDS prevention organization for gay men—the movement saw its reemergence in 2000. As Jiménez Polanco outlines, in 2001 several key events took place: that year saw the formation of a new national organization (Gaylesdom: Colectivo de Gays y Lesbianas Dominicanas), the first formal lesbian and gay pride event took place, and significant media attention was paid to LGBTIQ+ issues when a LGBTIQ+ stand at the international book fair (Feria del Libro) was forcibly closed down. In fact, this last event points to the ongoing push and pull between the increasing presence of LGBTIQ+ themes in the public sphere and the control and repression through state institutions, the police and military, as well as the very public role of the Catholic Church in denouncing homosexuality at the time.

After decades of authoritarianism the Dominican police and military continued to have a preeminent role in the country; even after the return to democracy in 1996, these institutions continued to have little public accountability and had much leeway in policing public spaces and arresting those deemed as interfering with public order and morality. In fact, it was reported that the level of police harassment had not changed much since the 1980s and remained the same.[16] The church also continued to maintain a key role as a public voice and arbiter of morality—especially former Cardinal and Archbishop of Santo Domingo, Nicolás de Jesús López Rodríguez, who for decades, until his retirement in 2016, played a particularly vocal and virulent role in denouncing homosexuality. As Lara details in *Streetwalking*, López Rodríguez "carried out a public battle against those who are (or are associated with) LGBTQ people" with a particular focus on "gay clubs and El Parque," a key public gathering spot in the 2000s in the historic part of the city.[17] Alongside such public gathering spots, including El Parque Duarte in La Zona Colonial and El Boulevard in the middle strip of Avenue 27th of February and the now-closed bar Fritos Verdes (discussed in the next chapter), there were a handful of LGBTIQ+ organizations and nightlife establishments alongside the increased media representations of homosexuality and same-sex desire; yet, speaking as a self-identified homosexual in public remained perilous. State-sponsored events and spaces remained largely foreclosed to public expression of same-sex desires and gay, lesbian, and trans perspectives.

However, at the same time the arts and performing art spaces—including some state-run institutions, but particularly non-state-run spaces—offered new venues for cultural expressions of non-gender conforming and non-heteronormative perspectives. While artists and performers at the time generally did not explicitly produce works from the position of identifying as lesbian, gay, trans, or bisexual, and many managed their sexuality in tacit ways, as articulated by Decena, there was a significant cohort of visual artists and theater performers in the late 1990s and early 2000s producing innovative works that questioned existing Dominican norms surrounding gender and sexuality, often with great popularity. These interrogations generally were embedded in their art works' broader critical perspectives on the Dominican national status quo, including its corrupt politics, the government's neoliberal economic policies, sustained social and economic inequalities alongside an often racist and virulently anti-Haitian nationalism, restrictive gender norms, violence against women, as well as sexual exploitation in the globalized tourism economy. Hence, these artists and their works share a wider critical stance, of which gender and sexuality were but one part, which they articulated without drawing from the globalized language of LGBTIQ+ identity and political discourses. This is echoed by Rachel Afi Quinn, who similarly has found that "Dominican visual artists, musicians, dancers, writers, and theatre directors" are producing "new works that engage with the reality of Dominican queerness," that is outside of "hegemonic LGBT politics of identity from abroad."[18]

These artists found support in smaller local cultural institutions and spaces such as Casa de Teatro and the Centro Cultural de España; Casa de Teatro, founded in 1974 in a beautiful historic building in the Zona Colonial, which, under the long-standing direction of Freddy Ginebra, has long played a crucial role in bringing vanguard plays, music, as well as literature and visual arts to Dominican audiences. Since 1987 the Centro Cultural de España, also located in a historic building in the Zona Colonial, has played an important role in fostering contemporary Dominican culture, especially the visual arts, becoming a particularly vital cultural site during the directorship of Ricardo Ramón Jarné (1998–2004). In fact, during Jarné's directorship the first openly homoerotic art exhibit "El doble: El alma en busca de un cuerpo" ("The Double: The Soul in Search of a Body") by Dominican artist and writer Nelson Ricart-Guerrero (1953–) and his French partner Christian Vauzelle took place in 2002, as I discuss at length elsewhere.[19]

The Centro Cultural de España alongside other small local cultural institutions and museums and occasional exhibition spaces, some now disappeared, including Casa de Francia, Casa de Bastidas, Museo de Casa de Tostado, as well as small alternative spaces such as the Bar-Gallery Patín Bígotes (2001–?), Bar-Gallery Tamaño (2002–2003), Galería Modafoca (2004–), and Encuentro Artesanal (2005–2012), opened up new spaces of expression, including for questioning gender and sexual norms that avoided the reductive LGBTIQ+ stereotypes that tended to populate mainstream Dominican film and television at the time.[20] Other key cultural spaces were well-established visual and performing arts spaces such as the Lyle O'Reitzel Gallery, founded in 1995, alongside some national institutions—the Museo de Arte Moderno, particularly innovative during the directorship of Sara Hermann (2000–2004); the National Theatre, with a notable history of women directors; as well as the Centro León in Santiago, which has a long history of organizing national art competitions and which opened a large new space in 2003, where Sara Hermann would again play an important role. At the same time the Dominican Republic saw the emergence of several international art events that played a crucial role in developing vanguard artistic expressions, such as the IV Bienal del Caribe (2001) of visual arts; the (biennial) Festival Internacional de Teatro, founded in 1997; and later the International Performance Encounter ChocoPOP (2003, 2004, 2005) in Puerto Plata.

ONE OF THE MOST CRUCIAL COUNTERPOINTS TO REDUCTIVE LGBTIQ+ stereotypes in the mainstream media and in particular to two still deeply controversial topics at the time—trans subjects and HIV/AIDS—is found in the theatrical oeuvre of Waddys Jáquez. Jáquez has been called the "prodigal son of Dominican theater" by theater critic Mónica Volonteri, and other critics echo this appraisal of his plays as a significant innovation in the Dominican theater scene.[21] Jáquez is a multifaceted Afro-Dominican dramatist who writes, directs, and performs many of his own plays, as well as composes, choreographs, sings, and dances. Jáquez has lived on and off in New York, where his Spanish-language plays have been staged at the Repertorio Español, but his main audience is in the Dominican Republic. His plays have been staged with great success at the National Theatre in Santo Domingo and other important theater venues, including the aforementioned Casa de Teatro, which in 2005 hosted a theatrical cycle of three of his plays titled "Resurección."[22] Nowadays he is a nationally renowned celebrity as one of the judges on the show "Dominicana's Got Talent" that has been streaming since 2019.

The Dominican cultural establishment has recognized the significance of Jáquez's contribution to Dominican theater by awarding him the most important Dominican cultural prize, the Premio Casandra (later renamed Premio Soberano); for example, the two plays I foreground in this chapter, "P.A.R.G.O." (2001), which received the award for "Best Play" and "Best Actor" (2001), and "CERO" (2005), which won the award for "Best Play," "Best Director," "Best Actor," and "Best Actress" (2007). Notably, this enthusiastic appraisal of critics and the Dominican cultural establishment is matched by the enthusiasm of Dominican audiences. When "P.A.R.G.O." was staged first in 2001 its one-month-long run was extended because of its resounding popularity. The enduring appeal of Jáquez's work was again clearly evident when the re-staging of three of his plays at Casa de Teatro in Santo Domingo in 2005 filled the theater to full capacity almost every night, when I was in attendance as well.

The first play that Waddys Jáquez wrote, directed, and performed in was the tragicomic "Yerba Mala." The play, written by Jáquez in 1998 and presented in Santo Domingo in 1999, had two actors, Jáquez himself and the Dominican actress Mariluz Acosta.[23] He later revised this play into a new solo actor version "Requiem por la Damián," performed in 2005 at Casa de Teatro. The main character of the play is identified as a homosexual man, José Alfonso Damián, also known as "La Damián," who speaks as a spirit at his own wake, where he remembers the discrimination he suffered while alive: "Nobody can imagine what it is like to be a gay man in a small town. Ay, Loma alto, insignificant small town, ... if I could I would spit fire over you."[24] Yerba Mala and La Damián offer in no uncertain terms a stark critique of Dominican heteronormative society and its homophobia. La Damián is the first of many LGBTIQ+ characters who populate Jáquez's plays, alongside other marginalized characters, including sex workers, hustlers, nightlife performers, and drug users.

Indeed, the remarkable popularity of his next play, "P.A.R.G.O.," which launched Jáquez's career, has surprised critics, given that it revolves around a cast of four utterly marginal characters—a homeless drug user, a hustler and formerly incarcerated person, a sex worker and former beauty queen, and lastly a trans woman. These marginal characters offer no easy identification for the Dominican middle- and upper-class audiences who primarily frequent the theater. Mónica Volonteri, for example, comments on her surprise that "The audience responded, *put up with the stories,* enjoyed themselves ..." (my emphasis).[25] Volonteri's and others' surprise at the popularity of the play is largely due to how "P.A.R.G.O." makes public and centers characters who fall outside of the parameters of respectability as sex workers, hustlers, drug users, and trans subjects. More importantly, "P.A.R.G.O." offers a humorous but not parodic interpretation that would reduce them to mere stereotypes, as we have seen in other Dominican mainstream media; instead, the particular achievement of Jáquez's play is that he makes "respectable" theater audience not only "put up" with these marginal and often non-heteronormative subjects come alive on stage and, more importantly, relate to their stories.

The play was first performed in 2001 in Santo Domingo and restaged in December 2002 in New York City at the Repertorio Español, where I attended the play as well. "P.A.R.G.O." is described by Cuban theater scholar Vivian

Martínez Tabares as a "hybrid" play "that feeds from the traditions of solo performance, stand-up comedy, and the anthropological questions raised by Latin American theatre."[26] "P.A.R.G.O." revolves around four main characters from the Caribbean diaspora, all played by Jáquez himself, who cross-dresses for three of these four characters, including the last character, Pasión Contreras, a Puerto Rican transsexual and recovering substance abuser whose "husband" is also her procurer. What brings these disparate characters together is the annual celebration at P.A.R.G.O., which the MC, who bridges the gap for Jáquez's costume and character change backstage, explains are the initials of a drug and alcohol abuse recovery program. "P.A.R.G.O." in fact replays the principal structure of popular substance abuse recovery programs, in which one person rises and "testifies" about their past and their experiences to a group of other recovering substance abusers. These programs—Alcoholics Anonymous and Narcotics Anonymous—are not only widespread in the U.S. but are also the only widely accessible (and affordable) programs for Dominicans recovering from substance abuse in the Dominican Republic, and the format of "P.A.R.G.O." imitates and alludes to these meetings. By default the recovery group that the characters testify to is formed by the theater audience, who is implicated not only as part of the recuperation effort but is interpellated as troubled members themselves. As the theater scholar Camilla Stevens describes it, "spectators are incorporated into the fiction of Jáquez's play and stand in for attendees of the support group session."[27] The play's audience is asked to relate to the characters' ongoing effort to "make do" with experiences of shame, injustice, and misfortune integral to their lives in the Caribbean and as immigrants in the U.S. and Europe. There is thus a shift in emphasis away from *who* these characters are and their specific identities toward their difficult experiences and how these relate them to each other and to the audience members, despite their seemingly stark differences in gender, race, class, legal status, and looks. "P.A.R.G.O." thereby achieves an unlikely alliance between these "disreputable" characters and the "respectable" audience by emphasizing the process of working through and making do with less-than-ideal tools in contexts of great economic, social, and racial inequalities through which they become relatable to the audience in ways that some critics have found unlikely.

In these experiences of "making do" with challenging conditions, humor plays a central role. The characters' costumes, gestures, and visual hyperbole might at first suggest that this play offers principally a parodic take that could easily stereotype these figures. Yet, as the play progresses it assures us that these characters cannot be simply grasped as parody. While humoristic elements draw the audience toward the characters, these characters are never passive embodiments of stereotypes. Their nonchalant telling of their misfortunes gives the audience much occasion to laugh, but they just as easily shift the tone toward pain and anger that makes the audience fall silent. The play also forestalls a simply parodic interpretation by slowly stripping the characters of their props and excessive gestures, culminating with Pasión, a trans woman, who takes the stage without any theatrical props. The excess of dress and gestures of the previous two acts, of the hustler and former incarcerated person Papi Chío and the beaty queen and sex worker ZaZa, through which they produce their respective masculinity and femininity, makes Pasión appear much more "real" in the end. The artifice that goes into the production of Papi Chío's and ZaZa's supposedly "natural" gender roles highlights their performativity and makes these previous characters appear strange and funny, while Pasión, in contrast, appears as almost anti-theatrical, a sense that is reinforced by the lack of theatrical props during her time on stage. This shift skillfully forestalls the reception of her trans subjectivity as inherently different, strange, or even grotesque; in fact, she visually appears at first like the one whom a middle-class theater audience most likely might encounter as a neighbor. At the same time, her gender and sexual difference is never underplayed or presented as a problem, but rather simply shared by her as a "detail" when she introduces herself:

> Good evening fellow members of P.A.R.G.O.; for those who do not know me, my name is Pasión, Pasión Contreras is my name. I have been a year and a half in this organization. Ex-addict, nymphomaniac, and alcoholic all due to loneliness, according to my psychiatrist. Latina by descent but born and raised in New York, so I belong to those who are said to belong nowhere. A curious detail, believe it or not my mom gave birth to a boy. I was baptized by the name of Ramón; Ramón, what a pretty name. But when I was 19 I made my crossover to the female sex, I had surgery. Transsexual is the medical term for my present condition. I got my cheekbones and breasts done with injections and years later when implants became available, I enlarged my breasts two more sizes, to keep up with the vanguard of technology.[28]

Pasión addresses herself to an audience of *compañeros,* "comrades," whom she claims thereby as sharing a struggle without positing that they are "like" each other or that they need to identify with her gender and sexual difference. Her suggestion that her ongoing surgical gender transformation was motivated to "keep up with the vanguard of technology," always elicits a laugh from the audience, who recognizes this desire, need, and hard work to "keep up" with a fast moving "modern" world, where they are often at a disadvantage whether as immigrants in the U.S. or as Dominicans in a small Caribbean country in the backwaters of the "modern" world. Pasión Contreras thereby most fully embodies the play's strategy of putting the apparently marginal at center stage since as a trans subject, she is least likely to receive "respect" in the public sphere and most likely to face public derision; while she perhaps does not fully become a "respectable" character, she becomes a relatable one for the audience, achieving thereby, as Volonteri notes, "the humanization of the *travesti.*"[29]

Here the critical difference between José Alcántara Almánzar's aforementioned *travesti* character "Lulú" and Jáquez's "Pasión Contreras" is evident. While in Alcántara Almánzar's story, the *travesti* can only be imagined as grotesque and ultimately abnormal, in Jáquez's play she is the most "real" and "normal" character. It is this realism that is such a bold move by Jáquez's play at a time when representations of *travestis* were limited to variety TV and drag shows—making Pasión Contreras a "controversial" character, as one critic notes.[30] Jáquez does not present his "controversial" LGBTIQ+ characters as inherently different and removed from the reality of Dominican audiences, nor do his plays insist that audiences need to identify with who she is. Rather, the play creates continuities between the audience and its characters by relating them through how they negotiate shared struggles of poverty, social and economic inequality, and marginalization at home and abroad. The play thereby produces a queer embeddedness of its trans character that challenges conventional divisions of the "respectable" and the "disreputable" in Dominican society in relation to gender and sexual norms.

THIS RELATIONAL APPROACH, I ARGUE, SPEAKS TO LARGER DOMINICAN cultural currents at the turn of the twenty-first century. Like Jáquez, Dominican writers, visual and performance artists at the time often foregrounded and related the experience and realities of marginalized Dominican subjects, as much in terms of gender and sexuality, as in terms of race, class, and migration in a rapidly changing and deeply unequal Dominican society; often this led to new formal experimentation in literature as well as in theater and the visual arts, while pushing back against a mainstream Dominican public sphere and media culture that, as discussed above, tended to deal in superficial stereotypes when it came to representations of race, gender, and sexuality, including LGBTIQ+ representations. This media critique in fact is the central impetus in Jáquez's multimedia play "Letal, televisión en vivo" (2004), which he wrote and acted in, and which was directed by Bethania Rivera. As Jáquez describes it, "Letal" offers a critique through "various stories interconnected by sensationalism," and thereby takes aim at how live television thrives on dehumanizing tales that in fact can be "lethal."[31]

One of the invited actors for Jáquez's play "Letal: televisión en vivo" was Henry Mercedes, a theater and television actor and director as well as HIV/AIDS and LGBTIQ+ activist; Mercedes in turn had founded in the early 2000s the theater group Teatro Simarrón together with the late Jorge Pineda, one of the most renowned Dominican visual artists. In the early 2000s there were several innovative small Dominican theater groups, including the long-standing Teatro Gayumba (Manuel Chapuseaux/Nives Santana), Guloya (Claudio Rivera/Viena González), Jaqueca (Dir. Carlos Castro), and Katarsis (Dir. Arturo López)—the group that writer Rey E. Andújar participated in as well;[32] yet Teatro Simarrón arguably foregrounded gender in their productions more so than other groups, reflected in their first three plays being based on texts by Dominican women authors: Chiqui Vicioso (*Salomé U* and *Whisky Sour*) and Rita I. Hernández (*Puentes*), who both collaborated with Mercedes and Pineda for their texts' conversion into dramatic scripts. *Puentes*, as discussed in the introduction, was first staged in January 2003 at the national theater, where I also attended a showing, and the play was later restaged in 2004 as part of the IV Festival Internacional de Teatro de Santo Domingo.[33]

Puentes symbolically brings to the point the relationality of marginal Dominican subjects, those who fall outside of the bounds of respectability that Jáquez's plays index. The title reveals the main location of the play: a bridge, underneath which "the characters intersect, connect, touch each other, tell their stories, live, die and revive."[34] The hyperbolic stylization of the characters resonates with Jáquez's characters, and the play has a similarly episodic nature. Moreover, similar to Jáquez's plays, this is a thoroughly urban drama that looks at contemporary Dominican society from the perspective of the marginalized, and represents, as theater critic Mario Rojas describes, "a complex national reality affected by consumerism, sexual tourism, drugs, poverty, the invasion of international products and the control of national and international hegemonic powers."[35] The plot unfolds in a moment of looming crisis, "under the imminent arrival of a hurricane," during which "a mother [María Castillo] goes out looking for her stray-dog children [Elvira Taveras, Henry Mercedes, Isabel Spencer, Vicente Santos] to protect them, but at the end they rebel and devour her."[36] This matricide is indicative of a new generation no longer willing to remain on the leash of tradition and conventionalism. Instead, as Volonteri notes, they don't submerge themselves in the "melancholy of the past" nor in the "tragedy of the present"; rather, they are always on the move and underneath the bridge—*el puente* is where their paths cross.[37] The building of bridges and high-passes in the capital Santo Domingo was a key project of the new "modern" democratic government, a much-touted but superficial symbol of progress often at the cost of investments in other areas such as education and health and social services and embroiled in corruption scandals.[38] In this context, the characters' location *under* the bridge throughout the play is a key critical move to index those who are bypassed by this development and remain in the shadows of progress. Being underneath *el puente* is the material symbol for the characters' loosely interconnected lives and encounters that converge on shared experiences of marginalization outside the bounds of respectability.

Moreover, as I suggested in the introduction, the play *Puentes*, both symbolically and in real life, presents a crossroads of relations where interrogations of heteronormative gender and sexuality formations are a crucial undercurrent. The *Puentes* actress Isabel Spencer, a self-defined Afro-feminist LGBTIQ+ creator and activist, also acted in some of the HIV/AIDS prevention campaign videos ("La mujer que resuelve," 2012) directed by *Puentes* actor and director Henry Mercedes, who played an important role in Dominican LGBTIQ+ activism as part of the Presidential Council for HIV/AIDS, and who went on to create the annual Festival Internacional de Cine GLBT (2009). Spencer would later go on to found the women's theater collective Colectivo de Teatro Maleducadas and hold the first theater workshop for Dominican trans people in 2019. The Maleducadas staged in 2012 the play *Varones*, arguably the first Dominican play from an explicitly LGBTIQ+ perspective; *Varones* was written by Rafael Stalin Morla and explicitly attempts to "break with the prejudices that exist in society surrounding gender, sexuality, love and human relations" and was conceived as a "freedom song lead by members of the LGBT community."³⁹ Notably, Rafael Stalin Morla is not only the author of *Varones,* but also an actor in Jáquez's play "La Cabeza del Rey" (2009). He also makes an appearance by name in Rita I. Hernández's novel *La mucama de Omicunlé* (2015), and recently published the boldly sexually explicit story collection *Saunatopía: Mariconería y domesticidad en un rincón caribeño* (2019), set in a gay sauna in Santo Domingo—exemplifying the strength of queer relational undercurrents in the Dominican cultural sphere.

These relationalities, which interweave queer, marginal, and countercultural affinities, were formalized repeatedly in the form of different artistic collectives that burgeoned in the late twentieth and early twenty-first century. A key group of Dominican visual artists, including Tony Capellán (1955–2017), Belkis Ramírez (1957–2019), Jorge Pineda (1961–2023), Pascal Meccariello (1968–), and Raquel Paiewonsky (1969–), developed a consistent critique of Dominican gender norms and gender and sexual violence in their works, which often take the form of installations. The first four participated in the paradigmatic collective exhibit "Otras visiones" in 1994 at Casa de Francia/Santo Domingo, later shown in Miami, Caracas, Chicago, and Brussels as well.⁴⁰ In this exhibit they offered their "other visions" or counter-hegemonic challenges that included strong denunciations of gender violence, sexual labor, and the complicity of the Catholic Church in maintaining a violent status quo. Later, in 2008, they formed, together with Raquel Paiewonsky, the successful collective Quintapata and showed their first exhibit "Mover la roca" at the Centro Cultural de España in Santo Domingo in 2009 and whose success took them all the way to the Venice Biennial in 2013.

The collective Quintapata is arguably the most successful Dominican visual art collective of the early twenty-first century, as Carlos Garrido Castellano et al. suggest: "although important precedents for collaborative creativity had already existed in the Dominican panorama, they had never attained the national and international recognition achieved by Quintapata."⁴¹ Yet, the collective Quintapata was only one of a series of creative collectives that formed in the Dominican Republic, so much so that Garrido Castellano et al. suggest that "participative and collaborative strategies have dominated the contemporary art landscape in the Dominican Republic for at least two decades."⁴² Indeed, collectives such as a La Vaina, Modafoca, La Sedería, Patín Bigote, and Colectivo

Shampoo shared the critical and anti-hegemonic impetus that "Otras visiones" in 1994 had first so clearly articulated, but these early twenty-first-century collectives now employed new digital tools and their expertise in the advertising industry to articulate their countercultural critiques, including critical perspectives on Dominican heteronormativity. For example, an exhibit curated by Engel Leonardo called "Arte para llevar" (2007) that brought together individual artists and creative collectives to design affordable posters as a form of critique of the commercialization of art, included a gender-bending artwork by Máximo del Castillo of a rooster who is laying an egg.[43] The collective La Sedería created an ambitious printed "passport" project that critiqued reified notions of national identity and foregrounded the many effects of migration, bringing the works of almost two dozen artists together. This included the work of Noa Maria Batlle, whose drawings would later come to illustrate the first collection of Dominican lesbian writing, *Divagaciones bajo la luna* (2006), and whose recent artwork is on the cover of this book. This wave of new collectives and individual artists articulating their critical perspectives through the medium of graphic design was captured in the crucial exhibit "Gráfica Independiente Dominicana 2000/2010" at the Centro Cultural de España and in its accompanying catalogue.

New groups and collectives with critical impetus were also formed in the realm of performance art by the early twenty-first century. The Encuentros Internacionales de Performance—ChocoPOP in Puerto Plata, organized by Eliú Almonte and Oscar Hungría, initially in 2003, 2004, and 2005, was decisive in cultivating a new performance art scene, alongside other initiatives in the capital, where Sayuri Guzmán and Clara Caminero and their organization Arte-Estudio played a key role. Dominican performance art brought together artists with various educational and artistic backgrounds, especially theater (Francis Taylor, Nancy Vizcaíno), visual arts (Eliú Almonte, Lina Aybar, Caryana Castillo, Fermín Ceballos, Elvin Díaz, Derissé De León, Arlyn Jiménez [known as Buloya], Pery Jiménez, Pascal Meccariello, Checo Merette, David Pérez [known as Karmadavis], Grimaldy Polanco, Raúl Recio), but also dance (Jochi Muñoz, Francis Taylor) as well as writers (Rey E. Andújar, Rita I. Hernández, Patricia Minalla).

For example, Rey E. Andújar, discussed in the previous chapter, created an autobiographically inspired performance titled "Ciudadano Cero" ("Citizen Cero"), first performed in 2005 at the Instituto Cultural Dominicano Americano in Santo Domingo, which I attended in person as well. Thereafter, as

Camille Stevens recounts in *Aquí and Allá: Transnational Dominican Theatre and Performance* (2019), the piece was performed at the Teatro Nacional in 2006 "as part of the V Santo Domingo International Theatre Festival and again at Casa de Teatro," and then in 2007 it was shown in Puerto Rico.[44] Rita Indiana Hernández would also stage several performance pieces and events in the early aughts. She performed as the androgynous super-hero "Azúcal" in the Centro Cultural de España, in 2003; then at Casa de Tostado in 2004, she created a multimedia exhibit titled "Nadie va al Padre si no através de mi" and a performative presentation in conjunction with the publication of her second novel *Papi* (self-published 2004; 2005). She also participated in the ChocoPOP performance encounter in 2005 where she and I presented a joint performance piece titled "Impotencia," and where she also performed with the short-lived experimental music group Casifull (along with siblings Elena and Ricardo Fernández)—an important prelude to her later musical fame. Among the ChocoPop Performance Festival participants in both 2004 and 2005 was also Carlos Ortiz/Soriano, who had previously produced video art with Rita I. Hernández, and who later wrote songs and performed as "Carnegato," including at a "Coming out" party at the gay night club CHA; he and Rita I. Hernández along with Raina Mast collaborated on a puppet performance piece titled "Ready y los Niños Envueltos" (2006). Later on, Carlos Ortiz/Soriano would be one of the two front dancers for Hernández's successful music group Rita Indiana y Los Misterios (2009) along with *Puentes* actor and renowned movie actor, Vicente Santos.[45] Such countercultural collaborations and collectives generated relationalities that crisscrossed the Dominican cultural sphere, producing enormous creative energy that was often deeply suffused with queer synergies.

SUCH RELATIONALITIES, HOWEVER, ARE NOT EXEMPT FROM THE social, economic, racial, and gendered inequalities that structure Dominican society. Relations and interdependencies can also result in deeply wounding relationships fraught with inequalities, dependency, and pain. The wounding that relations can cause are, for example, often at the forefront of Francis Taylor's work. The prematurely deceased Francis Taylor (1971-2016) was an actor, dancer, and activist who, like Jáquez, had initially trained with Manuel Chapuseaux, and later turned to performance art in the early twenty-first century. Like Isabel Spencer and Taylor's close friend Henry Mercedes, Taylor also was an important LGBTIQ+ activist, as well as drug policy activist alongside being an actor, director (*Errores Imperdonables,* 2009), modern dancer, and participant in the burgeoning Dominican performance art scene. His play *Errores Imperdonables* explored questions of intimacy and pain in relationships, as did his performance piece "Punto de Cruz," for the 2009 Dominican art biennial at the Museum of Modern Art, which I attended in person. In his performance, Taylor, dressed in all black, drew a heart on his naked chest and then inserted rounded needles into his skin along the heart's outline; at the end of the performance, he re-buttoned his shirt over the painfully reddened pierced heart that viscerally and symbolically fleshed out the pain of romantic relationships and attachments.[46]

The pain and wounding caused by relations both emotionally and in the very real physical sense of illness and death, is brought to the fore in Jáquez's play "CERO" (2005), which addresses the realities of HIV and AIDS in the Latinx American world. This play challenges mainstream media discourses and taboos surrounding HIV/AIDS as mainly afflicting homosexuals, and ultimately critiques how silences and secrecies regarding sexuality in personal relations can have pernicious and wounding effects; in fact, it gestures to how the private/public divide that has long structured negotiations of sexualities in the Dominican Republic, where sexuality is a "private" matter and homosexuality negotiated tacitly, needs to be challenged in the context of the spread of HIV and the AIDS pandemic.

The HIV/AIDS pandemic demanded a more public engagement with sexuality more broadly and with homosexuality specifically. As Daniel Castellanos describes, "the HIV/AIDS epidemic forced a public discussion on homosexuality that challenged public officials and leaders to take public health, political and legal actions. By 2000, there were 50,000 documented cases of HIV infection in the Dominican Republic, with 7.6% of them assigned to homosexual/ bisexual contact (UAIDS, 2007)."[47] The HIV and AIDS pandemic led to the first persistent LGBTIQ+ institution-building with the emergence of ASA (Amigos Siempre Amigos) in 1989. ASA offered HIV prevention campaigns directed at gay men and men who had sex with men (MSM) and in many ways spearheaded a transformation that would lead to a significant increase of LGBTIQ+ organizations by 2005/2006, as discussed in the next chapter. ASA, along with Dominican artists and performers, clearly gave the sense that existing practices of relegating sexuality to a "private" matter were not only insufficient but profoundly injurious in the context of the HIV/AIDS pandemic.

Jáquez's "CERO," like "P.A.R.G.O.," has been staged both in New York and in the Dominican Republic as well as in various Latin American countries. "CERO" echoes some of "P.A.R.G.O."'s key characteristics and relies similarly on a series of short monologues by various characters directed at the audience; again, these monologues mix tales of loss and suffering with an irreverent humorous tone that emerges from the scripts' savvy verbal ploys and the characters' histrionic behavior as they re-tell their experiences. However, unlike "P.A.R.G.O.," which mainly employs just one actor (Jáquez himself), "CERO" featured in its first iteration alongside Jáquez two accomplished Dominican actresses, Carlota Carratero and María Castillo—the latter also had acted in *Puentes*—and the three take on a total of nine different characters. While in "P.A.R.G.O." the four characters' divergent lives intersect at an AA or NA-like support group meeting, in "CERO" the one aspect that all the characters share is an HIV positive status—either their own or a loved one's. In fact, rather than being in or from the same location, "CERO"'s characters are from various parts of Latinx America, including Mexico D.F., Santo Domingo, Puerto Rico, and New York. These characters' divergent places of origins, even if Dominican and Dominican-American characters predominate, as well as the notable differences in social class, occupation, and race, made visible by the fact that Jáquez is notably darker skinned than the two Dominican actresses, speaks to how the HIV virus affects Latinx Americans from all walks of life.

Among these characters are a Mexican wrestler, a Dominican teenager and her baby, a sex worker, a fortuneteller who left her husband and five children, an upper-class Dominican wife, a Puerto Rican musician, a Dominican gay man in Santo Domingo, a Dominican lesbian in New York, and, lastly, a Dominican poet. Through its range of characters, from the married wife from the upper echelons of society to the poor migrant sex worker, the play makes clear that in the context of HIV/AIDS the borders of respectability are irrelevant. Before each of the characters successively takes the stage for her or his monologue, all three actors are on stage for the opening lines that frame the play. This first scene is titled "Los trapos sucios se lavan en Casa" ("Dirty laundry is washed at home"), alluding to how things considered shameful or "dirty," including sexuality, are kept out of the public eye and dealt with privately. These "trapos sucios" are instead covered up, as the play's first lines declare, by "the same words as always," which means "speaking crap, filth, donkey's shit."[48] With these choice words the play suggests how what is spoken about publicly is a disservice to what is really happening privately and jolts the audience out of the complacency of living "as if nothing were happening."[49] The play thus speaks from its first lines to the urgency of creating a different and public discourse about HIV/AIDS and of interrupting a larger social reality that it describes as living in a "a bubble of lies," where the truth is hidden in privacy.[50]

In Jáquez's play the bubble of lies that it wants to burst, which includes stereotypes and prejudices about HIV/AIDS, and the different truths it wants to tell, are conveyed through the stories of these nine characters, beginning with Huracán García, a retired Mexican wrestler. This iconic Latin American male figure of physical prowess, now brought down by the virus, signals from the start how the virus affects not only marginalized subjects but anyone, whether male, female, rich, poor, old, young, heterosexual or homosexual. Each character is very different, evading any suggestion that HIV/AIDS follows necessarily a common pattern, or as Mark Padilla puts it, "defies the notion of a marked separation of homosexual and heterosexual [HIV/AIDS] epidemics"; instead, what these characters share are their "stories of pain that taste better with criollo seasoning."[51] This common denominator, this criollo seasoning, is "this thing what we Latin Americans do . . . we crap ourselves laughing while the devil takes us down."[52] Just as in "P.A.R.G.O.," humor is thus part of the affective arsenal through which Latinx American subjects face difficult realities. Yet, in "CERO" a darker tone predominates, and what functioned as a survival tactic in "P.A.R.G.O." becomes a gallows humor in this play. Thus, despite the play's humorous moments that the characters' hyperbole produces, its didactic intentions are clear: HIV and AIDS are no laughing matter, it declares, and it is time to wash the dirty laundry (sexuality) in public.

"CERO" forgoes pointing dogmatically to any single cause or principal culprits for the HIV/AIDS pandemic; instead, these Latinx American characters' HIV infections happen as much through sex work as through marriage, teenage love, and substance abuse. The play thereby brings the experience of HIV/AIDS close to the audience by conveying throughout that they could easily find themselves in one of the characters' positions no matter their own presumable "respectability." In fact, the play emphasizes the commonplace relations, both heterosexual and homosexual, that resulted in their infection rather than pointing to individual pathologies or failings—or suggestions that it is primarily transmitted through homo- or heterosexual relations. For the Mexican wrestler, the relation with his idolized lover Sobeyda leads to his infection. Sobeyda left for the U.S. seeking the "American dream" but had to turn to sex work to survive. She returns to Mexico infected with HIV and now Huracán declares, "she is dead and I am fucked."[53] While there are two other female characters for whom sex work led to their HIV infection, there are just as many characters in conventional heterosexual relations affected by the virus. For example, in the next scene it is the first love of a Dominican sixteen-year-old girl who leaves her "infected by this infectious love."[54] Two other women in the play, Lola and La señora con cartera Chanel, are also unsuspectingly infected by their husbands, showing how socially sanctioned relations are just as susceptible to HIV transmission, and social class does not protect one either. Again, as in "P.A.R.G.O." these subjects' stories are told in ways that foreground their relationalities, and despite the damaging, even deadly, effects of these relations these stories do not become denunciations of failed forms of self-protection and individual failings.

The play's rejection of pathologizing and exceptionalizing discourses is especially evident in the representation of the two explicitly non-heterosexual characters, La Vinicio, a Dominican gay man in Santo Domingo, and Marina la Positiva, a Dominican lesbian who lives in New York. In fact, La Vinicio does not tell of her own illness but mourns in her monologue the death from AIDS of her best friend, a married woman who worked as a sex worker abroad to support her family in the Dominican Republic. "CERO" thereby deftly connects these Latinx American lives to broader social, economic, and political patterns, including that of the uneven traffic between the North and the South of people, material goods, knowledge, and power. It is not primarily same-sex desire between men—it is not La Vinicio but her friend after all who died—but rather lasting structures of inequality, the racialized economies that underlie them, as well as unequal gender and sexual relations that help to sustain these that are the principal culprit.

This emphasis is in fact echoed in a key shift in focus in the organization ASA's (Amigos Siempre Amigos) approach to HIV/AIDS prevention. Initially, as Padilla describes, "the lack of a preexisting infrastructure organized around homoeroticism undoubtedly inhibited the development of intervention approaches based on local constructions of sexuality and identity, as well as the ability to advocate politically for such approaches."[55] An early focus on primarily gay men left out the many local men who had sex with men, including for pay, without claiming a "gay identity," and ASA adjusted its strategies over time; the organization's director, Leonardo E. Sánchez Marte, would come to foreground how "power relations and the lack of equity play a preponderant role in the risk that different populations run," and in recognition of this, ASA has "broadened its criteria facing HIV/AIDS, now we not only pay attention to risk behavior of individuals, but also immediate environmental and social factors that influence that behavior and the influence that family and the community have on the behavior of a person."[56] Jáquez's "CERO" points to the inadequacy of suggesting that the HIV/AIDS pandemic is primarily hetero- or homosexual and due to individual failings and a lack of morality as it is often represented in the mainstream imaginary and media representations.

Importantly, the play also steps back from the U.S. activists' responses that have developed in response to the HIV/AIDS pandemic, through the character of Marina. Marina is a Latinx lesbian living in New York City who rejects the commonplace discourses surrounding HIV/AIDS that she finds stifling. As she moves through some hallmark New York LGBTIQ+ spaces, including a bar and the LGBTIQ+ community center, she ardently resists these:

> when they come with the parsimony of solidarity, with the red solidarity ribbon, the testimonials, the AIDS quilts, the Central Park marches, I turn my back, because I don't want to be part of this, I am not the face of AIDS, I am Marina, getting on the subway, picking up my medicine, driving my cab from Brooklyn to Manhattan . . .[57]

Marina finds herself misapprehended by the standard HIV/AIDS activist discourses and practices. She rejects being "the face of AIDS," which would make it her identity; she also rejects her friends' "palabritas compasivas" ("compassionate little words") that make her a victim; instead, she shifts the emphasis to her successful survival for ten years. Indeed, contrary to assuming the position of a victim, she defiantly yells out upon entering a bar, "Soy Marina la Positiva" ("I am Marina the Positive one"); hence, she also does not remain silent about her HIV status. Her refusal to define herself through existing HIV/AIDS activist discourses and to inhabit her positive status in prescribed ways becomes in the plays' final monologue a broader critique of the exceptionalizing discourse surrounding HIV/AIDS that produce an "ocean of men, women, children and normal people that the world calls 'strange.'"[58]

The final monologue of the play is by the tellingly named Poeta del Sidario

("The AIDS Poet") who evokes and denounces the narratives that have been circulated about the virus in Latinx America, specifically to damaging effects: "you told me that it was all a lie . . . You said that the virus was a million dollar business to drive gay men away, an advertising trick of the first world countries . . . You told me not to worry. . . ."[59] There is much to unpack here; for one, this exclamation foregrounds the particularity of the Latinx American context where HIV and AIDS responses were shaped vis-à-vis the Global North; it suggests how the power inequalities that shape North-South relations lead to a defensive Latinx American standpoint where HIV/AIDS is suspiciously seen as part of a first-world economic interest (million dollar business) and viewpoints ("lie," "advertising trick") and "gay men" are exterior to this invoked Latinx American identity. The play ends by denouncing these willfully produced forms of "ignorancia" in media circuits and speaks of the Dominican Republic and how, "in the midst of this little Caribbean island, this tropical paradise where there is nothing to lose and so much to learn."[60] The play thereby effectively takes aim at the forms of "ignorance" that are willfully produced by defensive stances and stereotypes that (1) "gay men" are external to Latinx America, a tendency present in the Dominican Republic as well, where, as Mark Padilla and Daniel Castellano show, "discourses of homosexual invasion" brought on by globalization were prevalent in the early 2000s;[61] (2) by prefigured global Northern discourses on HIV/AIDS that foreground sexual preference—homosexuality—as a defining factor in infection patterns; and (3) by local forms of negotiating sexuality "en casa" as a private matter, or as Padilla puts it, where "both partners will participate in culturally informed patterns of sexual communication that is indirect and intuitive, rather than direct or rational" and where "*both partners participate in tacit agreements about how to interact with each other both socially and sexually*" often through "sexual silence," as echoed by Decena's discussion of the tacit.[62] In this context, "CERO" calls for a more open and explicit grappling with sexuality, challenging the boundaries of respectability, albeit without relying on prefigured LGBTIQ+ identity politics and HIV/AIDS activist discourses—a task that the Dominican activists and writers discussed in the following chapter take on with creative acuity and political urgency.

FOUR

Divagaciones 2006

New Directions in Dominican LGBTIQ+ Politics and Literature

THE LEONEL FERNÁNDEZ (PLD) PRESIDENCY ULTIMATELY BROUGHT little change for Dominicans in terms of political corruption, clientelism, and social inequality from 1996 to 2000. As a result, the main opposition party (PRD) was voted into power in 2000 with Hipólito Mejía as president. Mejía's more populist and more "traditional" Dominican presidential style, drawing from his rural background, was seemingly quite different from Fernández's overt ploy for modernity; yet it quickly became clear again that the new party in power and president would not change engrained political patterns and practices of corruption and significantly improve the lives of the majority of Dominicans. These political continuities, combined with an economic crisis, led to a return of Fernández to the presidency for two more terms, from 2004 until 2012. Dominicans' persistent political disenchantment existed alongside the increasing global interconnectedness in the economy and society, through tourism, the country's main industry, through international media, and especially through individuals' increasing access to cellphones and the internet in the 2000s. This conjecture—of having unmitigated access to information about LGBTIQ+ histories, practices, and organizing across the world, while knowing that political change from above, via the government, was unlikely— undoubtedly contributed to the notable expansion of LGBTIQ+ organizing in the country that greatly intensified in the 2005–2006 period.

Several scholars point to 2005–2006 as a key moment of burgeoning LGBTIQ+ organizing that I witnessed in Santo Domingo at the time as well;

Celiany Rivera-Velázquez, in her remarkably detailed report "Dominican Republic: LGBTT Landscape Analysis of Political, Economic & Social Conditions" (2017) for the ASTRAEA Lesbian Foundation for Justice, describes how "since the mid-2000s, there has been notable growth in the number of community-based organizations founded and the diversity of communities they seek to represent: lesbians, trans women and men, gay university students, and local LGBTT media-makers."[1] Daniel Castellanos, in his article "Santo Domingo's LGBT social movement: At the crossroads of HIV and LGBT activism" (2019) pinpoints how "a surge of LGBT collective actions between 2005 and 2006 increased the movement's visibility and encouraged its consolidation."[2] Castellanos offers several explanations for this surge: for one, he points to the emergence of a younger generation of activists: "By 2005, a great number of youths were visible in the Dominican LGBT movement. Colectiva Mujer y Salud and ASA, two health-focused organizations, had been producing cohorts of receptive young activists over many years."[3] While ASA, as discussed in the previous chapter, was focused on HIV/AIDS prevention, Colectiva Mujer y Salud was founded in 1984 as a women's organization, initially focused on health and reproductive rights. Castellanos emphasizes that though coming out of these long-standing organizations, "the new cohorts were, nonetheless, part of networks working on a variety of issues and more sympathetic to confrontational strategies such as public kiss-ins, demonstrations, boycotts and 'illegal' gatherings," and, unlike previous generations, "they had extensive electronic-based supportive networks."[4]

These "new cohorts" of LGBTIQ+ activists, connected by social media and with more confrontational public strategies, figure centrally in Lara's *Streetwalking* (2021), based on fieldwork undertaken between 2010 and 2013. Lara also argues that by the early 2000s "there had been an explicit shift in Dominican society," and "small groups of people began to walk the street while mobilizing LGBTQ political identities."[5] These ways of being out and about are what Lara terms "streetwalking," which she argues "break[s] with culturally acceptable tacit subjectivities."[6] Lara thereby pinpoints a change in the Dominican LGBTIQ+ landscape in the twenty-first century that was fully evident in 2005–2006 and had consolidated by the time of her 2010–2013 study. Yet, as we will see, these new "streetwalking" strategies did not simply replace other ways of negotiating same-sex desires and LGBTIQ+ identities more tacitly.

Alongside this local generational change noted by Lara, Castellanos, and

Rivera-Velázquez, certain global forces, namely a sudden increase of international HIV/AIDS funding, also served as a catalyst for the movement's renewed energy at the time.[7] As Castellanos describes, "The sudden influx of funding from 2005 to 2006 created opportunities for a surge in collective actions within the LGBT movement by existing groups. It also supported the emergence of two new LGBT groups associated with HIV prevention: REVASA (Red de Voluntarios de ASA) and Trans Siempre Amigas (TRANSSA)."[8] TRANSSA signaled the growing recognition and integration of trans women into the Dominican LGBTIQ+ movement.[9] The influx of international HIV/AIDS funding supported several public events in 2005 organized by ASA, some in conjunction with the short-lived but impactful (2004-2006) CAP LGBTIR (Comité de Acción Política de Lesbianas, Gays, Bisexuales, Transexuales, Transgéneros, Intersexuales, Raros y Raras)—whose meetings I attended occasionally as well.[10]

CAP was spearheaded by the aforementioned Jacqueline Jiménez Polanco, a Dominican political scientist, who in 2002 had returned to the Dominican Republic after many years working as a university professor in New York City.[11] In Santo Domingo, Jiménez Polanco was faculty and a subdirector at FLACSO (Facultad Latinoamericana de Ciencias Sociales) and organized with CAP the first academic "foro del movimiento de minorías sexuales" ("forum of the sexual minority movement") on February 23, 2005 at FLACSO.[12] This pioneering forum, in which I participated as well, resulted in a 2005 online issue of the FLACSO journal *Vértice*, which may well be the first scholarly publication on Dominican LGBTIQ+ issues largely by Dominican scholars and activists in Spanish, including Denise Paiewonsky, Yuderkys Espinosa, Ochy Curiel, Marianela Carvajal, Eddy Tejeda, Leonardo Sánchez Marte, Jacqueline Jiménez Polanco, Carlos U. Decena, and long-term resident Lorena Espinoza, as well as non-Dominican scholars Mark Padilla, Daniel Castellanos, and myself. Unfortunately, the contributions to the FLACSO forum that were published in this pioneering *Vértice* issue in Dominican LGBTIQ+ studies did not remain available online and have been largely lost to a broader public.

Not long after this first academic LGBTIQ+ forum, in June 2005, CAP collaborated with ASA in the organization of several events supported by the aforementioned international HIV/AIDS funding: an academic and art event was held at ASA, with an appearance by then New York State Senator Eric T. Schneiderman, who gave the event a formal (and "international") stamp of approval. There was also a "a public celebration at 'El Boulevard,' a pedestrian boulevard near a shopping area" that "attracted a crowd of close to 400 people"—myself included.[13] This impressive attendance, I suggest, was facilitated by its being a nighttime gathering in a public space with limited lit up areas, allowing attendees to negotiate in very concrete ways how visible or invisible they wanted to be, how tacit or explicit they wanted to make their affiliation with LGBTIQ+ identities, including to the media that were present. Yet the event caused tensions with police, and "while initially closing the area, the police allowed it, albeit without music, after the organizers mentioned that COPRESIDA sponsored the event as part of an HIV prevention effort."[14] The protective effect and financial support of COPRESIDA, a formal government initiative for HIV/AIDS prevention since 2001, signals the power that official political endorsement and government support could offer. This was important because the growing presence and visibility of LGBTIQ+ people alongside an ongoing concern with same-sex sex tourism, had led to a notable backlash in the Dominican public sphere at the time. As Padilla and Castellanos outline, around the same time, based on their media analysis from 2004 to 2007, there was a notable increase of "discourses of so-called homosexual invasion in the Dominican Republic ... by perverse outside influences."[15] As a result, there was a renewed policing of queer nightlife and gathering spaces, which repeatedly led "Dominican police to close gay bars in the Colonial Zone and arrest all patrons and employees found on site. This tactic has occurred periodically in the capital city for many years, but it was renewed in June 2005."[16] Indeed, not long after this LGBTIQ+ pride and protest gathering in June 2005 on the "Boulevard," the police closed down in November 2005 "Fritos Verdes," the food stand on the median where people gathered, and the space was lost as an informal public gathering spot for Dominican LGBTIQ+ people.

In this context, it is understandable that in making plans for the 2006 pride celebration, as Castellanos recalls, "the most influential LGBT leaders advocated for shifting strategies toward collaboration with COPRESIDA and realigning themselves more closely with HIV discourses to capitalise on the increased access to political elites and HIV."[17] As a result, in 2006, "sponsored by COPRESIDA and coordinated by ASA and REVASA," a forum on "Human Rights: Expression of Diversity" was held on June 23 at a hotel "with panelists from a variety of groups," including myself. Indeed, this forum at the hotel Clarion at Plaza Naco, a central commercial location, felt like a notable change from the previous year, when events were held at the modest ASA locale; the printed materials and catering accompanying the event also reflected this new influx of financial and institutional support by this COPRESIDA co-funded event.

This shift in strategy, however, did not agree with everyone, and the discontent ran largely along gender lines; as Castellanos describes, "some female leaders expressed concerns about the presence of HIV funding and governmental involvement and worried about co-optation, lack of intersectionality, and conservative strategies"; moreover "there were few lesbian leaders involved in the actual planning of the events, alienating and frustrating some of the remaining female activists."[18] These concerns about the influence of international funding and governmental co-optation foreshadow later debates about the impact of so-called global gay politics and agenda on the local activist context and creolized forms of queerness. Already in his discussion of a first impromptu "gay pride march" in Santo Domingo in 1999, Padilla voiced concerns about how "the unreflexive ways in which global models of gay social action were appropriated" ended up diluting "the expression of resistance against specific local practices."[19] However, such questions about the influence and impact of "global gay" agendas came most notably to a head later in 2013 when U.S. President Obama appointed the "out" gay and married diplomat James "Wally" Brewster as ambassador to the Dominican Republic. Rachel Afi Quinn has critiqued how Brewster's "push for gay civil rights, in line with the agenda of the US-based Human Rights Campaign, reflects a politics of LGBT identity that is embedded in whiteness, and class and gender privilege," and she argues that "this type of homonormativity obfuscates the poor and working-class LGBT and transnational feminist organizing taking place in the Dominican Republic."[20] This political framework has an impact on international funding, on who and what gets recognized and financially supported, which, again, helps give shape to and delimit local activist strategies. Quinn thus finds that "Brewster's homonormative performance as US ambassador highlights a problem faced by many queer Caribbean activists and organizers negotiating streams of funding that are tied to an individual rights framework and neoliberal ideologies of individual success for economic development rather than meeting collective concerns."[21] Lara similarly recognizes how Brewster's presence "enabled the neoliberal political development of the Dominican LGBT movement," and how his "presence served as a constant reminder of the potential mobilization of homonationalist forces in the service of empire."[22] Yet Lara more positively emphasizes local activists' "strategic" use of Brewster's support; "LGBT leaders who celebrated and built on their relationship with Brewster" were strategically engaging with a "universalized" concept of LGBT—which she terms their "strategic universalism"—which served to "make the movement legible to neoliberal international funding structures, human rights organizations, and networks"; moreover, Lara also notes how this usefully "renders a political subject category that can be made juridically legible both in national civic courts and international human rights platforms."[23] From these "strategically universalist" LGBTIQ+ organizers close to Brewster evoked by Lara, to the "poor and working-class LGBT and transnational feminist organizing" described by Quinn, we can see precisely the new multiplicity of strategies present in Dominican LGBTIQ+ activism in the twenty-first century.

This multiplicity became first strongly evident in 2006, when Castellanos and others, including Rivera-Velázquez, speak of both a new generational and a gendered rift in the Dominican LGBTIQ+ movement; according to Castellanos, "young leaders and lesbians working on other issues were dissatisfied with the strategies of collaboration with the state and with HIV as the focus of governmental responses to LGBT needs. Within this context, the generational and gender rifts among LGBT leaders became more evident."[24] In fact, a younger generation of activists, "dissatisfied with their inability to shape the direction of CAP and REVASA" would create "Los Muchachos and Muchachas de la Mesa de Atrás (MMMA, 'The boys and girls of the back table'), a tongue-in-cheek comment on their resentment of the lack of opportunities to participate in decision-making processes or positions of power in the movement."[25] Rivera-Velázquez similarly notes these divisions and concludes that "there is much disagreement among the leadership of LGBTT organizations about whether the programmatic and funding priorities of groups like ASA and REVASA represent the aims of the movement. The lack of trust within the movement manifests in a lack of strategic collaboration and support among some groups."[26] Hence, rather than coalescing, by 2006 the various LGBTIQ+-associated factions experienced their *divagaciones* or digressions. While this is described as a problematic fracturing of the movement, more positively, I find it also reflects the broadening of voices and viewpoints in the Dominican LGBTIQ+ movement at the time.

THESE POLITICAL AND ACTIVIST DIVAGACIONES, I ARGUE, WERE ALSO evident in the cultural and literary realm where new representations of Dominican queer lives emerged with the appearance of three new publications in 2006. These publications reflect the broadening in voices, perspectives, places, and strategies in representing Dominican LGBTIQ+ experiences. The contemporary writers, performers, and artists discussed in the previous two chapters, from Rita I. Hernández, Rey E. Andújar, Waddys Jáquez, Henry Mercedes, and Isabel Spencer to Francis Taylor, were interwoven in a dense network of countercultural and often queer relationalities centered in Santo Domingo with works produced in Spanish, even as several of them repeatedly left and returned to the island. Yet in 2006 there was an eruption of new voices and works largely from beyond these networks of relations that also shifted emphasis away from urban Santo Domingo as the center of Dominican LGBTIQ+ cultural expressions.

For one, Jiménez Polanco edited and published the anthology *Divagaciones bajo la luna: Voces e imágenes de lesbianas dominicanas*, a collection of largely autobiographic, poetic, and some fictional texts in both Spanish and English by Dominican and Dominican diaspora women who love women—including a text by Ana-Maurine Lara. The writer and scholar Lara in turn published her English-language novel *Erzulie's Skirt* in 2006, telling the story of the same-sex relationship of two rural women; and, lastly, the French writer Jean-Noël Pancrazi published in 2006 his French-language novel *Les Dollars de Sables* about the relation between a French long-term sex tourist and a young Dominican bugarrón in a northern beach town (Las Terrenas). The novel was translated into Spanish by a small alternative Dominican press in 2010, under the title *Dólares de arena*, and was the source for the eponymous feature-length movie *Sand Dollars* (2014) by the Dominican-Mexican director duo Laura Amelia Guzmán and Israel Cárdenas that I discuss later as well.

The anthology *Divagaciones* (2006) offers a key counterpoint to the previously discussed 2004 anthology *Antología de literatura gay en la República Dominican*. Unlike the 2004 anthology, for this collection, it was the declared sexual preference of the authors that brought together the varied writings; as the very first text by Yaneris González Gómes declares, "only a lesbian can write or produce lesbian writing."[27] Also, unlike the 2004 anthology, which came under critique for including excerpts from texts that they deemed "gay"-relevant without asking permission from the writers, the 2006 anthology came out of a long process of meetings and writing workshops organized by Jiménez Polanco for the express purpose of publishing this anthology. As Lara describes, she was invited "to join her and a group of young women at a monthly gathering in

Gazcue called Divagaciones bajo la luna," and "the stories we shared and wrote in that space" would later form the anthology.[28]

Hence, none of the texts reproduce the pitfalls of the 2004 anthology with its inclusion of homophobic texts simply because they mention same-sex desire. As a result, the texts in *Divagaciones* are largely written from an autobiographical perspective, and only about half the authors identify themselves as writers with previous publications in the included biographies. Also, unlike the 2004 anthology, about two-thirds of the contributors write from outside the Dominican Republic, many from the U.S., but also from Argentina and Mexico. Indeed, the anthology was funded by a grant from the ASTRAEA Lesbian Foundation for Justice in New York (which I helped Jiménez Polanco write). The funding and the gathering of authors reflected the LGBTIQ+ networks that the editor Jiménez Polanco formed part of in New York City and in the Dominican Republic and from which she drew for this anthology. The process of creating it had started, according to Jiménez Polanco, in 2002 and was inspired by similar anthologies published in the U.S., specifically Juanita Ramos's well-known anthology *Compañeras: Latina Lesbians* (1987).

The texts in the anthology almost all give a personal account, whether in the form of narrative or poetry, of how each woman arrived at a reckoning with their desire for women, the difficulties as they faced consternation from families, themselves, and others, and their relationship and sexual experiences with other women. In this way, these texts notably differ from Hilma Contreras's short stories and Rita I. Hernández's novels discussed in the previous chapters, where these desires were forestalled (Contreras) or interwoven into the rest of the narrative and more ancillary (Hernández). Notably, in these stories of sexual reckoning the approval or disapproval of mothers is often central (Glenda Hobal, Huracán, Mari Zabala, Dulce Reyes Bonilla, Jissel Ravelo, Lissette Norman), much more so than fathers, who are rarely mentioned. Mothers play a key role in the authors' grappling with their sexuality, and this emphasis on mother-daughter relationships and the family again differs from previous literary and theatrical works discussed in this book, where the family setting is rarely foregrounded; yet these texts thereby strongly reflect the prevalence of female-headed households in Dominican society and give glimpses into how knowledge about same-sex desire is negotiated between women in these predominantly female environments.

The centrality of family relationships in this anthology echoes Decena's findings in *Tacit Subjects*. However, in contrast to the Dominican men in Decena's study whose families tacitly "know" about their sexual preference but who they do not officially "come out" to, several of the women in *Divagaciones* emphasize the importance of speaking explicitly about their sexual preference with their mothers even as they face resistance. Glenda Hobal for example foregrounds this imperative in her account: "Officially I came out of the closet at 20 when I went to stay for a few weeks with my mom. Since I was in a relationship, I felt that it was necessary to tell my mom, I did not want to hide it nor lie about my life."[29] Others write of similar scenes of disclosures with their mothers that were anything but easy; Huracán writes, "almost three years after having affirmed, while looking into her eyes and terribly afraid, that, yes, I liked women and how sure I was of that, I continue to feel a bit bad about hurting my mother."[30] In "Letter to My Mother," Mari Zabala says, "Mother, I know that it is very difficult for you to understand me.... I still remember how you reacted the day that I told you that I am a lesbian.... but despite everything I know you love me and you know that I love you. Your mother's love is stronger than the hypocritical moral of the homophobic world that condemns me."[31] These repeated scenes of disclosure of same-sex desire reveal mother-daughter relationships that are tensed but not ruptured in the process.

I want to speculate here that this difference between these women's accounts of the "need to tell" and Dominican men's "need not to tell," recounted by Decena, indexes the gendered difference between Dominican men's and women's relationship to "privacy" and the right to keep one's sexuality a private matter as discussed in the first chapter; men can more readily claim privacy and keep their sexuality a topic of non-discussion, while women, whose sexuality is expected to happen within the confines of home and marriage, have their sexuality more closely scrutinized by family, neighbors, and the community. In fact, in the story of Huracán she recounts that she had to "come out" to her mother because of an anonymous call that informed her mother that she "was meeting with a woman" and "was very in love with her."[32] Her sexuality was thus a communal concern and policed by others who considered it important for her mother to explicitly "know" about it.

The "hurt" that Huracán's mother experiences because of her daughter, along with Mari Zabala's mother's reaction described above, index that these mothers' knowing does not mean an easy embrace of lesbianism; as Dulce Reyes Bonilla describes too, "Mom got obsessed:—'But where did you get this from?' . . . The knowledge of my sexuality was something that my aging mother, super religious and traditional, could not understand, nor could she recover from my decision to defy her and at twenty-five unexpectedly and surprisingly come out of the closet."[33] Indeed, in a text by Lissette Norman, her mother affirms decisively "mejor puta que pata," "better a whore than a lesbian."[34] As discussed in the second chapter, being called out as a "puta" is a key way of questioning a woman's sexual propriety and respectability; the derogatory "pata" also fixates on a women's sexuality but becomes an even graver offense here. Yet in the same story the mother's homophobic declaration coexists, just downstairs at a friend's house, with the tacit acceptance of a lesbian cousin and her same-sex partner by her family; when the partner comes to visit, unexpectedly for the narrator, "she wasn't sad, she was actually funny and joked with Liza's parents," indicating her being tacitly accepted and welcomed by them.[35] Importantly, in these varied stories of family acceptance, consternation, and refusal, there is no clear pattern to where the authors live—whether in the Dominican Republic, in the U.S., or elsewhere. Though some, such as Dulce Reyes Bonilla, suggest that immigration to the U.S. allowed them to live their sexuality perhaps more openly, as she states, "I was good or more than good . . . I asked myself constantly about destiny and what would have happened if I had stayed in Santo Domingo, if I hadn't emigrated with my mother at seventeen years old, how would I have dealt with my sexuality."[36] However, there are others who describe themselves as happily living with their long-term same-sex partner in the Dominican Republic (Elisa Morel and Erika Herfurth).

This focus on same-sex relationships is shared by the two novels published in 2006 as well, *Erzulie's Skirt* and *Dólares de arena*. The author of the first novel, the aforementioned, Ana-Maurine Lara (1975–), was born in the Dominican Republic and later migrated with her family to the U.S.; she completed degrees at Harvard and Yale University and is now a professor of anthropology at the University of Oregon. *Erzulie's Skirt* (2006) is her debut novel, and it tells the coming-of-age and relationship story of a Dominican woman of Haitian descent (Miriam) and a Dominican woman (Micaela). Both women are born into rural Dominican culture where the practice and culture of Vodoun/Vudú thrives and interweaves with Christianity—as reflected by the title of the book referring to the goddess Erzulie, "the great goddess of the sweet waters and ocean's wave."[37] In turn, Jean-Noël Pancrazi (1947–) is a well-established

French author who spent part of his childhood in Algeria, and who published several award-winning novels in France before *Dólares de arena* (2006). The novel is based on his own stays as a tourist in Samaná, on the northeast coast of the Dominican Republic, and tells the story of an older French writer and his relationship and sex-for-pay with a Dominican bugarrón (male sex worker), Noelí—as referenced by the novel title's "sand dollars."

As these brief summaries index, the two novels could not appear more different, as they indeed are, but nonetheless they coincide in two important divagaciones from previous LGBTIQ+ literary and artistic representations: (1) they make same-sex relationships the central raison d'être for their writing, and (2) they decenter Santo Domingo from its centrality in previous literary and cultural representations. Here LGBTIQ+ representations are extended into other, rural parts of the Dominican Republic, to the North coast and "El sur," the southern parts near the Dominican-Haitian border, specifically. This displacement raises interesting questions about how LGBTIQ+ lives and relationship are imagined in spaces where neither queer nightlife spaces (chapter 2) nor an abundance of queer-friendly cultural spaces (chapter 3) are as readily available.

LARA'S NOVEL IS FRAMED AS A STORY TOLD BY ERZULIE TO AGWE, "the great spirit of the ocean's depth," revealing how Miriam and Micaela's same-sex relationship is sanctioned by the Vodoun gods according to this narrative.[38] This openness to same-sex desire and gender nonconformity in Vodoun is alluded to at various points. For example, Micaela's father is a *brujo* who when he is possessed becomes "Anaísa," a goddess who was "beautiful, dressed in yellow satins and lace."[39] Such gender transgressions also take place in the reverse, from female to male: when Miriam is possessed, she becomes a male spirit and Micaela dances provocatively with her/him at a public ceremony, "she danced with him, excited by the feel of Miriam's breast pressed up against hers and the rum that laced their breaths like halos. She felt Miriam get excited."[40] The space for gender variance and same-sex desire in Vodoun in fact is documented in the work of various scholars, such as that by Omise'eke Natasha Tinsley, Roberto Strongman, and Lara herself. As Lara describes in *Streetwalking*, "in all my years working with and being 'in the life' with Dominican *servidores de misterios* and healers, everybody knew that I was gay. And nobody cared. In fact, there were a lot of 'us' in these communities."[41] In this way these "spaces of traditional ceremonies" very much differed from the active policing of gender and sexual difference in "public spaces" that she experienced and describes in her study.[42] Interestingly, her account also strongly evokes the workings of the "tacit," how "everybody knew" but "nobody cared," suggesting how sexual and gender difference is negotiated in religious communities not unlike in the familial and community settings described by Decena.

In Lara's novel Vodoun is presented as a central force in Dominican rural life, as much present in Miriam's family of sugar cane cutters of Haitian descent as in Micaela's rural Dominican peasant family. Beyond this continuity, however, the text emphasizes how Dominican history and society have created a deep wedge between their experiences. The 1937 massacre of thousands of Haitians and Dominicans of Haitian descent by the Trujillo dictatorship (1930–1961) features prominently in the novel. Miriam's parents lost six children in the massacre and many other family members; Miriam is unexpectedly born after the massacre. The harshness of work and life on the *batey*, the sugar plantation, marked by hunger and the injustice of landowners and merchants, is portrayed starkly in the novel. When Miriam migrates to Santo Domingo with her then husband and son to escape the brutal life of the batey, the novel describes the frequent police raids in the barrios to gather Haitians and Dominicans of Haitian descent, such as Miriam, to deport them violently back to Haiti. As someone who is perceived as being Haitian, the only work she can do is selling wares at the market or on the street, or braiding hair for tourists on the beach. While Micaela is also from a poor rural family, her family owned a house and some land where they grew food and herbs. As Micaela recognizes, "as a girl, she had never had to work for an unknown patron who unleashed his cruelty through his inhuman overseers. She had never suffered the pains of hobbled feet, changed by the sharp leaves of plantation rows and rocky paths. She had known hunger, but hunger had never etched itself onto her as it had . . . on Miriam."[43] This denunciation of the inequalities and discrimination that those of Haitian descent face in the Dominican Republic is a key point that the novel makes. Indeed, it is ultimately Miriam, driven by despair over the limited opportunities and fear of deportation that she and her son face for being perceived as Haitians that drives them together with Micaela to try to migrate in an illegal embarkation to Puerto Rico.

Their migration attempt ends tragically with Miriam's son dying during the crossing when they capsize, and Miriam and Micaela being held captive in a small room together and sex-trafficked. When they finally escape, through what seems like divine intervention by Vodoun gods, leaving with a large amount of dollars that are mysteriously scattered where they were held, they decide to return "home" to the Dominican Republic, rather than stay in Puerto Rico or make it to the mainland U.S. as was the original plan. They return not to the capital, but to the rural south where Miriam had grown up, to another batey, where they build and open up a small store, a *colmado*, with their sudden windfall of dollars. Though initially they are rejected by the community as *brujas*, in part because of Micaela's knowledge and use of herbs and potions, they are later accepted as an integral part of it. It is there that they die together a peaceful death seemingly of old age, attesting to the possibility of two women in a same-sex relationship growing old together in the Dominican Republic while being integrated into their community.

As much in the Santo Domingo urban barrio where Miriam and Micaela first met as on the batey in the rural South, their same-sex relationship is never addressed by neighbors, and it seemingly remains "invisible" to others throughout the story. The two women living together seems to awaken little suspicion or recognition, and they themselves never seem to worry about or address how their relationship may be perceived by others. In one scene in the barrio, a man, unaware of their relationship, proposes himself to Miriam. Miriam, in response, calls on her son to tell this man that "my mother already has a man in the house."[44] This evocation of gendered scripts, of all women needing a man in the house, is indicative of the gender divides that the novel describes throughout. However, at the same time, this offers a safe "cover" for Miriam and Micaela's long-standing relationship, which never seems to be questioned.

Gender inequalities in Dominican society and families are addressed at length through the story of Micaela who, unlike her brothers, was not allowed to go to school until a well-off aunt insisted on paying for her education. Micaela is expected to primarily help her mother in the household and care for her younger brother. Her father in contrast has little responsibility in the household, "most of the time he was in the town wandering about drinking rum, hanging out at the colmado with other men, or visiting other peoples' homes for consultations."[45] Her father's independence and the homosocial relations he is part of also give him the freedom to pursue same-sex encounters while married to Micaela's mother. As Micaela notices, other men's "eyes linger over her father's back muscles, his legs, and his gait as he walked away from them. Sometimes one of the men would follow her father, disappearing in la mata of the town where only men were allowed."46 Here the contrast between men and their access to public space, their right to pursue sexual relationships outside marriage, including with other men as long as it happens "discreetly" out of the public eye, contrasts with the experience of women for whom sexuality is restricted to the home, ideally to a formal husband, so that same-sex encounters remain invisible in the confines of the private space for women—echoing remarkably the much earlier writings of Pedro René Contín Aybar and Hilma Contreras, discussed in the first chapter.

Vis-à-vis the invisibility of Miriam and Micaela's relationship where visibility is never explicitly a question of concern, in *Dólares de arena* the potential visibility of the French gay writer's relation with Noelí, the young Afro-Dominican male sex worker, is a constant and ongoing concern for Noelí. While their sexual encounters are hidden in the privacy of the writer's hotel room in La Terrenas, a well-known beach town in Samaná, they are also out and about in public on the motorcycle that Noelí owns and go to restaurants and nightspots. Noelí is deeply embedded in a network of homosocial relations with other young Dominican men who hustle and try to succeed in the tourist economy just like him, including as motorcycle taxi drivers; sex work is an integral part of this economy, and securing the long-term financial support of a tourist is an important goal. However, while relationships with female tourists are celebrated—"Tony who was walking around proud for having won over Sweenie, the American woman staying at the [hotel] Atlantis"47—relationships with male tourists, or *pájaros* as they are derisively referred to, remain largely dissimulated and secretive. When Noelí provocatively dances with women, "he did because it was expected from him by the men from Sánchez ... to prove to them that he was not turning, because of hanging out with me, into a *pájaro*."48 Though Noelí enacts a starkly heteronormative masculinity, his relations with male tourists are not entirely invisible to others and lead to questions about his masculinity. Being publicly seen with the French writer, a pájaro, leads to gossip: "the rumor had begun to circulate, hadn't his wings come out, weren't his gestures more delicate."49 The rumor effectively effeminizes him, undermining the status of his masculinity in the eyes of others. These sexual rumors are a threat to his gender identity and standing in public.

At the same time, their relationship is also tacitly supported by others for its promise of economic benefit. For example, the writer describes how while he waits for Noelí each evening in front of his hotel, those who work there "seemed to encourage me, with friendly gestures, to love one of theirs—almost in secret, discreetly."[50] Indeed, when Noelí takes the writer to meet his mother in a show of commitment after he had disappeared for a while, the mother "seemed to tell me that it mattered little to her that I was a foreigner, a *pájaro* even, if I helped him."[51] The economic precarity and lack of opportunity for these poor rural families create an environment in which male sex work is tacitly accepted as a necessary strategy of survival: "to accept that he locked himself every afternoon in a hotel room with another man," they "ignored this different kind of love, thinking that maybe one day they would get something out of it."[52] This willful ignorance, these indirect ways of telling, and seeming forms of encouragement all reflect tacit negotiations of sexuality that are it seems strengthened in this globalized tourism economy. In fact, Padilla has pushed back against arguments that globalization will inevitably efface local "traditional" forms of gender and sexuality, instead arguing that "somewhat ironically, the global gay sex market seems to facilitate, rather than attenuate" a "particular expression of Dominican (hyper) masculinity that is also ... defined in opposition to a 'modern' gay identity."[53] By extension then, if the denial of being gay, or a pájaro, is central to this masculinity desired by sex tourists such as the French protagonist here, then the globalized sex industry also reinforces rather than weakens local practices of managing sexuality tacitly.

In the novel we only encounter the perspective of the narrator, the French writer, and not that of Noelí, the young Dominican male sex worker. The economic, social, racial, and age differences between the French writer and the humble origins of the Dominican Noelí, who is unable to read, are deep, and Noelí relies on the writer for daily financial support and for the hope of leaving the Dominican Republic for France with him, in exchange for sex and companionship. In *Erzulie's Skirt* the two main characters also live in great precarity, but they struggle through this as equals with reciprocal romantic feelings, reflected also in how both their lives and perspectives are shared in the novel. In this novel the French writer is deeply emotionally dependent on Noelí—"my preferred one for the rest of my life"[54]—but he can only speculate on the feelings he wants to think Noelí developed as well: "he looked at me a good while with a sort of surprised tenderness, ... as if it were possible for him to love me one day."[55] However, in the context of paying him for sex and affection, he can never be sure. And he remains, "trying . . . to know what he really thought, how he saw me exactly—like a 'kind' foreigner, as he said, who was not so bad, or simply as a 'savings bank.'"[56] This dynamic in same-sex sex tourism, particularly when longer-term relations are maintained between clients and the men they pay, is extensively described by Padilla. Padilla addresses the complicated question of "authenticity" of feelings in these contexts; he found in his study that long-term clients "often expect more 'authentic' expressions of affection from their partners" and sex workers are compelled to "perform romance"; while some sex workers do feel affection for their clients, Padilla rightfully notes how difficult it is "to understand the affective dimensions of these relationships, particularly when they are so fraught with differences of race, class, and nationality."[57]

In the novel, the unevenness of the protagonists' relationship in terms of economic, social, and racial privilege is certainly stark, as it is in the stories of two other gay foreign men (Michael and Paul) and their relations with a Dominican young man (Ricardo) and very problematically a young boy (Sili). The negotiating of sexual desire and "dollars" is constant, with each side struggling to get the most out of the relationship. For the foreign men this is sex, companionship, and affect, and for the Dominican young men and boys it is money and the possibility of leaving the country. In this context, unlike in *Erzulie's Skirt,* relationships are never certain to last, none of the characters die with their lovers of old age, but rather the relationships often end unexpectedly when money has run out, or as in the case of Paul and the French writer, when their Dominican lovers suddenly disappear. The writer is taken by surprise when the relationship, which he had hoped to last for several years, suddenly ends with Noelí's disappearance. After demanding a large sum of money from the writer, Noelí vanishes, for the writer to realize soon that he had used it for his illegal migration to Puerto Rico. "I had not wanted to understand—so that I could continue enjoying myself . . .—that he wanted to escape, as soon as possible, from his life in Las Majaguas, from his little shack, from the daily fight for bread, rice, the child support for his three children."[58] The writer had been unable to fathom the depths of Noelí's despair, as he thought him to be happy with their arrangement and life, gesturing to dimensions of Noelí's emotions and subjectivity that this one-sided novel cannot capture or comprehend, as the narrator to some degree recognizes himself. Here the two novels unexpectedly coincide again, both describing the difficult and deadly passage in a small boat from the Dominican Republic to Puerto Rico via the Canal de la Mona; and in both narratives this comes with great loss, as Miriam loses her son, and Noelí loses his best friend Lilo on a failed crossing.

At the very end of the novel, the French writer re-encounters the young boy Sili, now a man, who had been his deceased French friend's lover. Sili takes him for a ride on his motorcycle; "he said, while he drove under the last stars and brought my arms around his chest, toward his heart, when he accelerated or avoided a heap of sand: 'papa,' and I took that word for myself."[59] With this the novel suggests that Sili will be quickly replacing Noelí in the paid affections and desires of the French writer, a relation that the term "papa" covers under the mantel of familial relationships. The quick replacement of Noelí is accompanied by the declaration that "this is the great circuit of money in the tropics, the only proof, the only way of loving."[60] This dystopian proclamation that financially motivated "loving" is the *only* way of loving in the "tropics," is a bleak (and deeply reductive) account of affections that contrasts starkly with *Erzulie's Skirt*, where love is portrayed as outlasting poverty, racial discrimination, sexual trauma, and even death.

Erzulie's Skirt ultimately argues that creole queer love, and in particular love between two poor, rural Afro-Dominican women was always possible, long before the twenty-first century, and could survive, even at times thrive, during the most adverse circumstances. While this love had to remain largely invisible to others, making any public show of affection an impossibility, the women's sexual difference in some ways was also tacitly recognized and accepted, captured in their designation as *brujas*. In contrast, the novel *Dólares de arena* arguably can be summarized as a tale of uncertainty, of the agonizing emotional grappling of the French gay protagonist with the authenticity or lack thereof of Noelí's affections. Given that the novel is resolutely told from his perspective, albeit with many speculations about Noelí's motivations and possible feelings, the question of Noelí's view and emotions can never be answered.

I would argue that it is precisely the search of this Dominican side, of Noelí's perspective, that led the Dominican-Mexican director couple Laura Amelia Guzmán and Israel Cárdenas to turn this novel into a feature-length movie. *Dólares de arena* (2014) became one of the most internationally recognized Dominican movies perhaps not least because the directors were able to enlist Geraldine Chaplin as the main actress for the movie. In fact, it was Chaplin's interest in the story that led to the somewhat perplexing move to rewrite the story as the relation between two women, an older French woman and a young Dominican woman. This gender transposition makes this story quite a bit harder to believe, given that "lesbian" sex tourism has not been a prominent aspect of the sexual economy in the Dominican Republic (or elsewhere). Yet the movie offers something that Pancrazi's novel is unable to show: Noelí's perspective and emotional tribulations. While in the novel the male Noelí is part of a homosocial network of Dominican men who work in the tourism industry and roam the streets, the female Noelí here is shown as much more isolated, her main relationship being with her boyfriend, and she is often shown at home in their modest abode. This reflects key gender differences that do not give women the same access to street and public life that men have. In the movie the female and pregnant Noelí decides against going to France with her female client, and instead takes her passport and rides off on a motorcycle with her boyfriend and father of her unborn child. Ultimately, the directors Guzmán and Cárdenas thereby forcefully resist the dystopian ending of Pancrazi's novel, which declares that all love in the tropics is motivated by money. This ending in many ways conjures up a national romance that insists that love does exist beyond money for this soon-to-be young family; yet this national future is of course resolutely heterosexual, and there is no queer future imagined here. This future is also just as financially uncertain, if not more so, with a baby on the way; besides Noelí now having a passport, there is no suggestion how the couple will make do outside the sex tourism industry. Hence, while the movie recuperates an idea of (heterosexual) romance that is absent in the novel, it struggles to imagine a sustainable future for it.

In contrast, *Erzulie's Skirt* gently gestures to a possible queer future by having the two now old-aged women and lovers take on a young female apprentice, "Yealidad," a child whom they notice as "different" and to whom they pass on their knowledge of traditional healing deeply imbedded in their practice of Vodoun. Yet more than a queer future, the novel ultimately is about imagining a possible queer Dominican past, of two poor women of color loving each other in the Dominican Republic. However, in some ways the novel struggles to give this queer past a concrete historic and realistic outline. The time during which the story is set remains notably vague; we know that Miriam was born after the 1937 massacre when all her siblings were killed, presumably in the 1940s. She and Micaela both migrate as young adults to the capital, Santo Domingo, placing them in the 1960s, post-Trujillo, and the rest of their story would unfold mostly during the Balaguer years, with their deaths taking place in old age, likely past the 2000s. Yet, their environment even in old age seems strangely ahistorical and unconnected to "modern" life; when a much older Micaela finally meets her father again, she has to travel there in person, and no telephones, television, or any technology seem to exist at any point in the novel. The uncertainty about the historical and "real" life context in which their lives are placed contrasts with the certainty with which Vodoun is central to both their lives and as a framework for love, life, and death of these women-loving-women.

If Lara's 2006 novel offers an imaginary exploration of how two Afro-Dominican women loved each other in the past with some twists and turns and historical uncertainties that the freedom of fictions bestows, then her ethnographically based study *Queer Freedom: Black Sovereignty* (2020) grounds this exploration deeply in the realities and context of the Dominican Republic in the early twenty-first century. There Lara describes her interactions with "Dominican santería" and other Afro-Dominican religious practices as a queer Dominican woman through participation in religious ceremonies and formal and informal conversations with other practitioners, including many of the LGBTIQ+ community. Lara describes how various Dominican LGBTIQ+ peoples she knows and speaks to, some of them activists, are deeply informed by Afro-Dominican religious beliefs, at times while also being Catholics, and at times after finding Catholicism less welcoming to their gender and sexual variance. Here, as in *Streetwalking*, Lara is deeply critical of Catholicism and asserts the space that Afro-Dominican religion holds for gender and sexual variance. However, like other scholars who have written about gender and sexual variance in Afro-Caribbean religions, she also grapples with the ambiguities—as does Decena in his recent book *Circuits of the Sacred: A Faggotology in the Black Latinx Caribbean* (2023) in relation to Santería, and Omise'eke Natasha Tinsley in *Ezili's Mirrors: Imagining Black Queer Genders* (2018) in relation to Haitian Vodoun. In various scenes Lara describes moments in religious ceremonies that could be interpreted as expressions of homophobia, such as the outrage when during a ceremony another woman comes in contact with her, and it is stated that "We don't accept this kind of cosa aquí."[61] Lara grapples with the event and what it might mean but ultimately insists that it was the other woman's lack of following religious protocol, not necessarily homophobia, that was referred to. Decena and Tinsley and others, including Roberto Strongman, contend with this question about how open to gender and sexual variance Afro-Caribbean religions are or are not as well. While it is often thought that they are "more 'tolerant' of queer bodies," recent scholarship has complicated this view to some degree, differentiated between different practices, and as Decena concludes, "evidence in Santería suggests ambivalence."[62] Yet there is no question for Lara, Decena, and Tinsley that there are many practitioners with non-normative gender and sexualities in Afro-Caribbean religions, including themselves: Lara describing herself as a butch-presenting lesbian in *Streetwalking*, Decena describing his experience as an effeminate presenting male child and later gay man, and Tinsley calling herself a cisgender Black femme.

Moreover, even as they participate in different Afro-Caribbean religious traditions, notably Dominican, Cuban, and Haitian-rooted, their scholarly and personal paths intersect and inform each other in key ways, creating their own paths of queer relationality across academia and various Caribbean locations. Tinsley after all starts her book by acknowledging her debt to Lara's novel *Erzulie's Skirt*—she read an early unpublished version of the novel in 2005 and states "her [Lara's] vision of La Mar has colored my imagination ever since."[63] Decena was also struck by Lara's novel, which he in his own analysis of the work describes as "pioneering," for both the "explicitness" with which it addresses same-sex desire between women and its positive portrayal of "racialized, gendered subject formation."[64] It is not only Lara's creative work but also her organizational work that has lastingly shaped these scholars' trajectories. Both Decena and Tinsley attended the 2013 "Transnational Black Feminist Retreat" that Lara helped organize in Santo Domingo. Tinsley describes the personal importance of this event in her book's opening pages, as does Decena, for whom it had a transformative impact that ultimately led to his initiation as a Santería priest and to the writing of his book *Circuits of the Sacred*; as Decena acknowledges, "I credit and thank Ana-Maurine Lara and Alaí Reyes-Santos for the Transnational Black Feminist Retreat that changed everything for me."[65] While their three works diverge in key ways in their approaches, materials studied, and style of writing—wonderful material for some future in-depth analysis!—they create a web of queer Afro-Caribbean religious relationalities and densities that traces new and very old spiritual geographies and the queer lives rooted in them, gesturing to continuities from the past to the present that are difficult to reconstruct if one only goes by textual evidence and literary genealogies, as this study attests as well. Such intersections and affinities of the queer and Afro-Caribbean religions emerge not in academia alone, but also crucially emerge in the work of Dominican artists and writers; for example, the Dominican-American performance artist Nicolás Dumit Estévez has tellingly insisted that his "first introduction to the theme of queerness was at the Vodou altar" resulting in a "knowledge of the queer" that preceded his knowledge of queer theory.[66] Such experiences and assertions gesture to the depth, range, and vitality of a creolized queerness, also evident in the work of Rita Indiana Hernández and Johan Mijail, as I discuss now in the conclusion, that is hardly waning or being usurped by homonationalism and that warrants our ongoing critical attention.

CONCLUSION

Queer Dominican Genealogies

ALMOST A DECADE AFTER THE PLAY *PUENTES* WAS STAGED AT THE Dominican national theater, Rita Indiana Hernández returned to Santo Domingo to take the stage herself in another kind of creative collaboration. In March 2009, after living a few years in New York and Puerto Rico, she formed the band "Rita Indiana y Los Misterios" ("Rita Indiana and the Mysteries") with several Dominican musicians. After her initial forays into music with "Casifull," mostly as a performance art project in 2005, as described in chapter 3, and then briefly as the duo "Miti Miti" until 2008, Rita Indiana y Los Misterios quickly catapulted her to national fame. By the end of the year the band had played many sold-out concerts, including at the Santo Domingo Hard Rock Café; had opened for the renowned Scottish band "Franz Ferdinand"; and had been nominated for the most important creative industry prize, the Casandra, in the category "Revelation of the Year."

The meteoric rise of Rita Indiana y Los Misterios was driven by a sound that fused typical Dominican rhythms, especially merengue, with electronic music and by lyrics that thrived on Dominican vernacular expressions and colloquial language including a heavy nod to so-called Dominican Vodoun, or "Los Misterios," a key part of the band's name, aesthetic, and references. Just as described in the last chapter, we see a turn to Afro-Caribbean religious practices and beliefs, at first in Rita Indiana's music as well as later in her literary works, especially in *La mucama de Omicunlé* (2015). Dominican audiences embraced Rita Indiana y Los Misterios as deeply connected to and expressive of *dominicanidad* while the band also pushed Dominican music in new directions; the group not only sonically expanded boundaries but also did so visually by embracing a queer aesthetic centered on the androgynous look of Rita Indiana herself.

Without doubt Rita Indiana transgressed all norms for female performers in the Dominican Republic: in her concerts she was often, though not always, dressed androgynously and was in most songs flanked by two shirtless male dancers in spandex, while singing songs that often had sexually slippery lyrics and strong overtones of same-sex desire (such as "La Jardinera"). Sydney Hutchinson, who features Rita Indiana on the cover of *Tigers of A Different Stripe: Performing Gender in Dominican Music* (2016), offers a compelling musicological analysis of where the "queerness" of the sound can be located along with the singer's own presentation; similarly to how Rita Indiana's literary characters embrace a female appropriation of the normally male figure of the *tíguere*, as I show in chapter 2. Hutchinson also argues that Rita Indiana's "videos and bodily performances take tigueraje in a new direction, questioning its heteronormativity."[1] Verónica Dávila Ellis similarly argues that "Rita Indiana's exaggerated tíguere performances" provide "new ways of gender expression in and outside popular culture."[2] This again suggests how even seemingly heteronormative and homophobic local formations, such as the *tíguere*, leave room for reconfigurations and so-called forms of "queer embeddedness" with what may seem to be surprising levels of openness and acceptance for non-heteronormative subjectivities, as Rita Indiana's widespread national popularity attested to.

Nonetheless, when during her red-carpet entrance at the Casandra Awards on March 16, 2010, Rita Indiana held hands with her partner, now wife, and later shared a kiss, it caught the rabid attention of the Dominican press. This public display of same-sex affection caused public outrage and controversy, albeit without putting a dent into her popularity. Besides religious inspired comments about homosexuality being a sin, the most widely shared complaint was the public show of her non-heteronormative sexual preference instead of doing whatever she likes in "private." This shows how divisions between the public and the private continue to inform regulations of sexuality, where much is possible tacitly in public, but becomes scandalous when made explicit.

However, turning our attention forward, it was not long after the publicization of Rita Indiana's same-sex relationship that other performers were openly associated with the LGBTIQ+ community as well. Famously among them was La Delfi, a gay and cross-dressing dembow singer, who since 2012 was "queering dembow both sonically and esthetically [sic]," until her untimely death from health issues in 2020.³ In fact, Jennifer Mota, a public historian of dembow, who writes for the important Latinx digital publication REMEZCLA, argues that La Delfi "sparked the rise of queer dembow," and points to new trans stars such as La Shakatah Asota and La Kisty Rodriguez that followed in her steps.⁴ Then there is of course since 2018 the bisexual singer Tokischa, "la reina del dembow" who, as Elena Valdez argues, has taken things even further—"she adds a new step in the historic trajectory of female queer perreo that for her represents an aesthetic and a way of living."⁵ If Rita Indiana successfully put a highly visible female masculinity on stage, then Tokischa in turn has openly embraced the role of the "puta," which as we saw in chapter 2 has long served as an insult for women outside the bounds of respectability.

Also, with a very different sound from either of these queer dembow artists or Rita Indiana y Los Misterios, the band MULA emerged in 2015, formed by twin sisters Anabel and Cristabel Acevedo and Rachel Rojas, identified as a "trio of queer women."⁶ They also combine Dominican rhythms with electronic music, not unlike Rita Indiana, but the result is described as a "mix of whirring, featherlight beats and rapid-fire Dominican rhythms" that result in a music that is "playful, urgently feminine, and endlessly danceable."⁷ Their "urgently feminine" sound, quite different from Rita Indiana's, is also combined with an androgynous, albeit more punk, look of the women. I am not suggesting that these aforementioned performers' female masculinity, male effeminacy, and cross-dressing were inherently "new" to the Dominican public sphere. I have shown throughout this book how in fact men and women whose male effeminacy or female masculinity challenged gender norms, including in the public sphere, have long existed—one may think back to the first chapter's discussion of Pedro René Contín Aybar and the comedian Paco Escribano during the Trujillato; however, what is "new" here is the open association with LGBTIQ+ categories of identity with these performers. This is echoed by Dávila Ellis, who argues that Rita Indiana y Los Misterios and MULA both "are explicitly invested in a queer politics, not only due to the artists' open queerness, but because of their commitment toward representing lesbian love ethos in their music."⁸ At the same time, such a commitment is not simply a turn to a "gay market," as Hutchinson notes; in her conversation with Rita Indiana, the musician rejected this approach and instead argued for a broader critical project of wanting her audience to be "listening sideways," which "means accessing and interpreting music in a way that questions the assumptions upon which it is made."⁹ It is perhaps not incidental how this "listening sideways" carries echoes of Alison Donnell's argument for "feeling sideways" in the Caribbean and for a creolized queerness that needs to be understood on its own terms; though these musicians certainly tap into a legible globalized queerness, they also very much insist on "localized grammars and lexicons of Caribbean erotics" that deeply suffuse their lyrics and performance.¹⁰

POPULAR MUSIC HAS THE REACH AND ABILITY TO MAKE SOME ARTISTS household names in ways that other arts, such as visual arts or literature, rarely achieve. Yet in the realm of the visual arts we also see an increasing representation of explicitly LGBTIQ+ subjectivities, especially in the work of visual artist Carlos Rodríguez. Alongside exhibits of photographs of the annual Dominican pride march, Rodríguez also produced the documentaries, *Afuera hay aire* (2010) about the LGBTQ+ community and *Trans'it* (2015) about Dominican trans activists. The annual Dominican "outfest"—Festival Internacional de Cine GLBT—has helped since 2010 to create a regular forum and audience for such visual representations of Dominican LGBTIQ+ culture and undoubtedly fostered their creation, including the anticipated documentary *El Cocóro del Futuro* by Juanjo Cid that recovers the history of the gay disco "Penthouse" described in the second chapter.¹¹ Cid and Rodríguez also co-created in 2009 an organization, IURA, "Individuales Unidos por Respeto y Harmonía," to lead "media training workshops on how to cover LGBTQ issues respectfully and inclusively."¹² The emphasis is on "respect" here, shared by other LGBTIQ+ activists, such as well-known activist and former candidate for congress Deivis Ventura as well. These demands for "respect" for the LGBTIQ+ community are a purposeful and powerful reclaiming of so-called respectability culture with deep colonial roots that in the Caribbean and in Latin America has been a key way for regulating public expressions of gender and sexuality. As IURA and others insist, "respect" here is demanded for gender and sexual difference and works to counteract the at times ambivalent, at times stereotypical LGBTIQ+ representations found in the Dominican media that I described in chapter 3.

Rodríguez is also the founder of the widely popular "Draguéalo" parties, a sort of queer anything-goes party since 2013 that has taken Dominican queer nightlife into a new direction beyond the commercialized nightlife and "gay discotheque" spaces; these parties are in part inspired by New York's dragball scene, as the subtitle, "Santo Domingo is Burning," a play on the Jennie Livingston documentary *Paris Is Burning* about the New York City dragball scene, reveals. Yet, while deeply in conversation with now-globalized queer culture and histories, and while their activism is deeply embedded in a recognizable global LGBTIQ+ framework, Cid and Rodríguez in their work also insist on "a uniquely Dominican queer identity."[13] In fact, how these coexist and even cultivate each other, pushing back against assumptions that globalized forces inevitably erase localized expressions, was beautifully evident in the recent celebration of a Dominican drag ball. The house "Casa Atón" put on a ball on the telling date of October 12, 2024, dedicated to Dominican vodun or "Las 21 Divisiones," with competitions in the categories of "Rostro Erzulie" ("Erzulie's Face"), "Pasarela de Palo" ("Palo Music Runway"), and "Vogeando El Gagá" ("Voguing Gagá"). As Celiany Rivera-Velázquez describes in her essential history of Dominican and Puerto Rican drag balls, "since about 2017 and 2018—sizeable cuir kiki and ballroom communities have emerged and solidified across the Dominican Republic and Puerto Rico" and these "have blossomed into sanctuaries, nurturing autochthonous cuir Afro and indigenous expressions in the Dominican Republic."[14]

In comparison to these new musical, visual, and performative queer representations under the helm of LGBTIQ+ identifiers in the Dominican public sphere since 2010, Dominican literature is arguably more tentative in its explicit engagement with LGBTIQ+ culture and identities, even as there are long-standing representations of same-sex desires as I have shown throughout this book. Besides the writers discussed in this book, two Dominicans living abroad both published poetry/short narrative books that reflected back on their lives as gay men, including their same-sex desires and experiences: Nelson Ricart-Guerrero (1953–), living in France, whose homoerotic visual art exhibit "El doble" I address in chapter 3, and Jimmy Lam (1958–), living in the U.S., whose life experience in the Dominican Republic as a gay man in the '70s informs chapter 2. Ricart-Guerrero first published *Boca de tiempo roto* (2005), openly dedicated to his "compañero" Christian Vauzelle, followed by *Sólo quedan las palabras* (2009), with poetic evocations of Rey E. Andújar, and then the boldly titled, *Soy Leife, El pájaro malo* (2013). Jimmy Lam in turn published *Sexile=Sexilio* in 2017, a compilation of short texts and poems with explicit descriptions of same-sex desires. That same year, on the island, Karol

Starocean (1981–), who now goes by Damien Starocean, published the short story collection *Dramamine* (2017), where both opposite and same-sex desires are described. As with other writers discussed in this book, literature was not Starocean's only genre of creative expression, and their sketchbooks, writing, and drawings were part of the national visual arts competition of the Centro León Jimenes in 2016 and even won the main prize (shared with two other artists).

However, I would argue Dominican literature's queer reckoning came with the return of Afro-Dominican writer and performance artist Johan Mijail (pronouns she/her) after an eight-year stay in Chile in 2019. Mijail (1990–) published a short text collection *Metaficciones* in 2011, and then *Pordioseros del Caribe* in 2014, both republished by Miguel D. Mena's key publishing venture Cielonaranja in 2018, which also published Mijail's first novel *Chapeo* in 2021. In 2016 Mijail cowrote and published with the Chilean Jorge Díaz *Inflamadas de retórica: Escrituras promiscuas para una tecno-decolonialidad*, and in 2018 she published *Manifiesto antirracista: escritura para una biografía inmigrante*. Not long after her return to Santo Domingo, she published *Santo Domingo is Burning*, a so-called zine with her own new publishing venture Catinga Ediciones, and which was republished as well by the Argentine Lumpen editorial. Catinga Ediciones is described by Mijail as "a publishing project based in the Dominican Republic specializing in writings by Black and/or Afro-descendant people from the LGBTQI+ community."[15] Catinga Ediciones published in 2020 four short "fanzines," besides Mijail's, including Juan Valdez's "Mariconfianza," Agatha Brooks's "Agatha Brooks," Ju Puello's "Ju Puello," and Cesar Peralta's "Entre pieles de negro, un amanecer," all written explicitly from Afro-Dominican LGBTIQ+ perspectives.

In addition, Mijail shortly after her return to the Dominican Republic organized a series of at least five readings along with some performances by queer authors and creatives called "Lecturas Cuir" from 2019 until 2020, in the café, gallery, and bookstore Mamey in the colonial center of Santo Domingo. This series of readings brought out an astonishing number of "cuir" Dominican writers, twenty-five in the first five editions, who read their works in public, along with some performances and visual works. Thus, unquestionably, Mijail almost single-handedly created a public LGBTIQ+ Dominican literary scene, whose only antecedent was the collective "Divagaciones bajo la Luna," organized by Jacqueline Jiménez Polanco in the early 2000s, as discussed in chapter 4; but while some of the contributors to "Divagaciones" had met in person, this was not mainly done in the kind of public-facing form in which "Lecturas Cuir" took place at a key alternative cultural space such as Mamey.

The Hispanophone spelling of "queer" as "cuir" in this event series reflects Mijail's critical engagement with Global Southern perspectives and challenges to globalized Northern LGBTIQ+ expressions. During her time in Chile she was deeply engaged with avant-garde Chilean culture, visual and performance art, and, as her co-written book *Inflamadas de retórica: Escrituras promiscuas para una tecno-decolonialidad* reflects, she was committed to thinking about sexual and gender difference from a specifically Global Southern and Latin American viewpoint.

Mijail's first two collections of texts, republished as *Escrituras del otro cuerpo* (2018), as well as her novel *Chapeo* (2021) attest to how as a fiction writer she is embedded in contemporary Dominican literature and in conversation with key writers such as Frank Báez and Rita Indiana Hernández. Mijail's writings share their urban scenarios and traversing of the city of Santo Domingo while making critical observations about Dominican history, politics, and a stifled national culture. Her texts also portray, like Hernández's texts, a localized queer landscape, of *travestis, maricones* and *bugarrones,* and *muchachas que son muchachos*.[16] Indeed, Mijail includes in *Pordioseros del Caribe* a text that is an explicit play on Hernández's second novel *Papi,* titled "Juego con Papi" ("Play on/with Papi"), and includes a footnote that makes this link explicit.

The footnote by Mijail describes Hernández's novel *Papi* as the "delirious" telling of a girl's relationship with her father, a "neomacho del trópico," and includes a long paragraph of the novel describing the hyperbolic figure of Papi. This paragraph is framed with Mijail's own short text that is also a "delirious" or surreal-seeming recounting of the day of the funeral of Afro-Dominican politician José Francisco Peña Gómez. The scene describes how everything is turning off (*se apaga todo*), the bridges falling, the colonial zone having been abandoned, along with other surreal-seeming happenings. Peña Gómez, of course, was one of the most important Dominican political figures in the late twentieth century, whose presidential campaign was smeared by racist commentary about his Haitian ancestry, and who not long after died of cancer. The pairing of *Papi* with Peña Gómez is suggestive here; it intermixes the denunciation of the "neomacho" with a critique of Dominican racism, which viciously prevented Peña Gómez from becoming the "father" a.k.a. president of the nation. Mijail thus conjugates Hernández's critique of masculinity with a critique of racism and suggests how these both de-realize and distort Dominican reality and society. Mijail thereby presses *Papi* toward a reckoning with race and Afro-Dominicanidad.

Not many pages after this play on *Papi*, Mijail then engages with what is arguably Dominican writer Frank Báez's most well-known text, "La Marilyn Monroe de Santo Domingo." This poem is included in a collection of writings titled *Postales* (2008) but is most well-known for being Báez's most famous poem when he performs as part of "El Hombrecito," a spoken word group with fellow Dominican writer Homero Pumarol and several musicians. The poem is written from the perspective of a trans woman who injects hormones but hasn't had the money for a sex-change operation, and who as the "Marilyn Monroe of Santo Domingo" moves through Santo Domingo, other parts of the country, and then through New York City, until she gets deported back to Santo Domingo. Mijail's text is a close re-telling in prose of the poem, with some telling changes that emphasize the very real dangers trans women face; in fact, the text is titled "Una de las *Postales* mentía" ("One of the *Postales*/ *Postcards* lied"), suggesting that her text offers a correction of Báez's "Marilyn Monroe de Santo Domingo." Mijail's text pushes back against the mythized representation of Dominican trans life in Báez's standout poem, which does not represent fully its difficulties and hardships. I discuss Mijail's "play" on Hernández's writing and "correction" of Báez's writing here at greater length, because they pinpoint key aspects of Mijail's ongoing critical preoccupations in her writing: her ardent defense in the face of stark racism of Afro-Dominican and by extension Afro-Caribbean bodies and cultures both in the Dominican Republic and in Chile, and her identification with trans subjectivities. These critical preoccupations are elaborated further in her more essayistic writings in the co-written *Inflamadas de retórica: escrituras promiscuas para una tecno-decolonialidad* (2016), *Manifiesto antirracista: escrituras para una biografía inmigrante* (2018), as well as in *Santo Domingo is Burning* (2020). These preoccupations are then brought to life in Mijail's first novel *Chapeo* (2021), where, as Danny Méndez describes, "the characters embrace and celebrate their trans black bodies ... these are bodies that stubbornly insist on being seen and recognized and, in this way, forge new possibilities for existing as Dominicans in this space" for which they "draw inspiration from political theology of Afro-Dominican religion."[17]

Hand-in-hand with this embrace and celebration of Afro-Dominican religion and Black trans subjects is Mijail's strong rejection of masculinity, "Mi interior dice y se enuncia así: EN ESTA INCERTIDUMBRE INDENTITARIA LO UNICO QUE SE ES QUE HOMBRE NUNCA HE SIDO" ("My inside says and declares this: IN THIS IDENTITARIAN UNCERTAINTY THE ONLY THING I KNOW IS THAT I HAVE NEVER BEEN A MAN").[18] For Mijail, here and in many other places in her writing, the questioning of masculinity, and heteromasculinity in particular, is central; Mijail's and Díaz's articulation of "sexual dissidence" as well as "decoloniality" take this interrogation of masculinity as a point of departure. For me this harks back in key ways to a colonial past and legacy where the affirmation of one's heteromasculinity was central within the racial politics of empire as a precondition for racialized subjects to assert themselves as colonial subjects with rights and later as citizens—this highlights the deep colonial imbrication of race, gender, and sexuality that need to be unraveled in any attempt at decolonization.

Mijail's critical decolonial project comes from a decidedly South-South perspective in which gaining "representation" is insufficient for decolonizing knowledge, and there is a healthy skepticism of globalized Northern LGBTIQ+ agendas. Mijail is critical of "una agenda global lgbtqia+, por sus matices neoliberales y racistas 'gay power'" ("a global lgbtqia+ agenda, because of its neoliberal and racist 'gay power' nuances") and questions a gay politics focused on the right to marry.[19] In *Inflamadas de retórica,* Mijail and Díaz's notion of sexual dissidence further questions the idea of "una verdad sexual que deba develar, así que no confía en el clóset como experiencia" ("a sexual truth that has to be revealed, and hence it does not trust in the closet as an experience.")[20] Despite such critiques, they do engage deeply with U.S. queer scholarship and cite the work of José E. Muñoz, Jack Halberstam, and Shulamith Firestone.[21] However, their critical and political articulations are most directly influenced by Latin American writers and thinkers; as Mijail's public series of "Lecturas Cuir," suggests, it is a decidedly Latin American/Hispanophone conjugation of the queer. Indeed, according to them, central for their aesthetic and their "letra anarcobarroca" ("anarcho-baroque writing") are "the Chilean Pedro Lemebel, the Argentine Néstor Perlongher and the Cubans Virgilio Piñera and José Lezama Lima."[22] Mijail's critical perspective reveals a South-South genealogy that, while informed by European (Guattari) and U.S. theorists as discussed above, is rooted and routed primarily in and through the South Americas and a tradition of Latin American *cuir* thought. In this way, Mijail's work and return to Santo Domingo opened up, one may argue, a third way, between localized queer Dominican expressions and globalized LGBTIQ+ formations; he evokes a critical framework from "down south" that he brings back from Chile.

Interestingly, Mijail's South-South critical move in many ways lands him in a place similar to that of a very different writer: Rafael S. Morla. Morla, primarily known as a playwright, actor, and now director of the National School of Theatre in Santo Domingo, and whom I mention in the introduction, published in 2018 the provocative collection of stories *Saunatopía: Mariconería y domesticidad en un rincón caribeño*. I discuss Morla's stories, set in a Dominican gay sauna, at length elsewhere, but here I want to emphasize Morla's politicization of the *culo* ("ass") in the tellingly titled story "Liberen al culo!" ("Liberate the Ass!"). Morla declares that "deseaba liberar a mi culo de la tiranía del pene. Era era la verdadera revolución" ("I wanted to liberate my ass from the tyranny of the penis. That was the true revolution.")[23] In a closely related vein, Mijail in his works celebrates the *ano,* the anus; like Morla he is critical of how those who practice anally receptive sex are more stigmatized in the LGBTIQ+ community, and in his perhaps most famous performance Mijail inserted a tree branch into his anus while rolling on the ground in pursuit of what he terms "amor vegetal."[24] These critical anal redemptions are key overlaps between Mijail and Morla, whose own book is strongly influenced by the Spaniard Paul B. Preciado's work on "pornotopías," which also has its mention in Mijail's texts. Both Mijail and Morla take aim at the phallus, or a masculinized value system—though Morla can't deny his erotic attraction to some of it. Mijail describes an urgent need to confront "al tiguerajε como cultura hegemónica de lo local" ("being a *tíguere* as local hegemonic culture.")[25] The consistent feminization of the male narrative voices in the gay sauna, by using female names and pronouns, in Morla's texts, and the *travesti* positionality inhabited by Mijail, along with the embrace of the anal as the obverse of the phallic, reflects their critique of heteropatriarchal Dominican society and the pressures it puts on masculinity to conform to and perform its mandates. For this critique they draw from and redeploy theories from elsewhere, not to simply apply them, but for a self-conscious theorizing from and of their Dominican experience. Between Mijail's return to Santo Domingo and Morla's sexual boundary-pushing *Saunatopía,* both in early 2019, along with the rise of *Tokischa* since 2018 and the Dominican drag ball scene fully emerging around the same time, one might well argue, as does Rivera-

Velázquez, that at that time a "significant shift" was taking place "that marks a considerable expansion in the dynamics of cuir spectularity."[26]

Queer genealogies were yet again reconfiguring, which is reflected in the publication of the second iteration of the lesbian anthology *Divagaciones*. However, if the anus and its radical potential and politics are foregrounded by Mijail and Morla, this collection gestures to other possible points of departure: 2023 saw the publication of *Divagaciones II: Un antología de mujeres dominicanas lesbianas, bisexuales y queer,* edited by Jacqueline Jiménez Polanco and Jenny Marbelle Marte Chalas, broadening the initial scope of "lesbian writing" of the first anthology discussed in the last chapter. This anthology stands out for giving voice to women of many generations, which is reflected in its being co-edited by Jiménez Polanco together with Marte Chalas, who also designed the cover. With some repeat authors and many new voices, they foreground some new themes: one of the most notable new themes is the inclusion of parenting stories and having and raising children as queer women. The very first narrative, "Annie Tiene Dos Mamis," by Ana García as well as the second one, "Andrógina" by Liberka Reyes Banks, foreground these as joyful experiences, as well as describing the pushback by family and by the community. These queer families all have to face conventional assumptions about who has children and who should parent them. Notably, in these family dynamics the authors' mothers continue to play a key role, as much in "Annie Tiene Dos Mamis," as in Liberka Reyes Banks's poem "Carta a mi Madre" and the text "Always Present Necessity" by Sarahí Yajaira Almonte Caraballo, who refers to her mother as "Commander-in-Chief."[27] We thus continue to see how female-headed households and family structures ground these queer women's lives in powerful even if not always easy ways. We see a profound grappling with the web of relationalities that these authors are inscribed in and both their enabling and constraining dimensions.

As in the first anthology, many accounts refer to the turmoil and intensity of first attractions to other women, as in J. M. Marte's "Cuentos de amor, pérdida y erotismo," or Lissa Aimet's "Entre cacao, plátanos, mangos y mandarinas," as well as histories of disappointments, pain and loss, as in Deyanira García's poem "Creando nuevas memorias," or Edli Acevedo's poem "Insensata," Lissa Aimet's poem "En un jardín," Micheline Nuñez's poem "Defeated," and Yaras' poem "Te Guardo." Yet, alongside these there are also enthusiastic celebrations of eroticism and love, as in J. M. Marte's poem "Piel de Otoño," Laura Márquez's poem "Prometo," Liberka Reyes Banks's poem "Movimiento," Mar en Calma's poem "Hilos de Plata," and Jacqueline Jiménez Polanco's text "Alice: mi diosa safista." These texts thereby create a complex and nuanced portrayal of same-sex love between women that does not shy away from describing the challenges as much between lovers as in relation to family and the community. In this way *Divagaciones II* creates a rich tapestry of queer women's voices that weaves a rich and varied account of what it means to love a woman as a Dominican woman, laying out current and future paths for thinking and writing queer Dominican genealogies that yet remain to be traced and that without doubt are multiple.

NOTES

INTRODUCTION | QUEER DOMINICAN GENEALOGIES

1 All translations are mine unless otherwise noted.
2 LGBTIQ+ is the most recent acronym employed by several (but not all) Dominican activist groups and by the annual pride celebrations in 2024, and it is the term that I will use throughout the book.
3 Donnell, *Creolized Sexualities*, 11–12.
4 Duggan, "The New Homonormativity."
5 La Fountain-Stokes, "Remembering Jean Franco," 207.
6 Tinsley, *Ezili's Mirrors*, 3–4.
7 Donnell, *Creolized Sexualities*, 16.
8 De Moya, "Juegos de guerra." ". . . de interés primordial . . . estudiar cómo, por ejemplo la esclavitud y el colonialismo ha impactado a toda la población caribeña"; "a entender mejor lo que parece ser una sexualidad distinta, compleja y contradictoria, un ser-y-no-ser."
9 Padilla, *Caribbean Pleasure Industry*, 136; Decena, *Tacit Subjects*, 7.
10 Decena and Portorreal Liriano, "*Saberes raros,*" 164.
11 De Moya, "La constante homoerótica," 2. "la condición principal para que esto ocurra parece ser que se haga un voto de secreto entre los participantes, una especie de 'ley de silencio.'"
12 De Moya, "La constante homoerótica," 2. "El bardaje es una persona de 'doble espíritu' (masculino y femenino) o un andrógino ritual: un varón criado como hembra, o una hembra criada como varón."
13 Garza Carvajal, *Butterflies Will Burn*, 139, 139–40.
14 Garza Carvajal, *Butterflies Will Burn*, 157, 156, 157.
15 Garza Carvajal, *Butterflies Will Burn*, 159.
16 Garza Carvajal, *Butterflies Will Burn*, 159.
17 Foucault, *History of Sexuality*, 6.

18. Foucault, *History of Sexuality*, 9, 17, 24.
19. Foucault, *History of Sexuality*, 35.
20. Stoler, *Race and the Education of Desire*, 26.
21. Stoler, *Duress*, 309. I thank Professor Irina R. Troconis for helpfully pointing me to this book.
22. Stoler, *Race and the Education of Desire*, 128–29.
23. King, *Island Bodies*, 10, 69.
24. Decena, *Tacit Subjects*, 112.
25. Decena, *Tacit Subjects*, 36.
26. Decena, *Tacit Subjects*, 36, 18.
27. Decena, *Tacit Subjects*, 19.
28. Padilla, *Caribbean Pleasure Industry*, 126.
29. King, *Island Bodies*, 63, 64, 65.
30. King, *Island Bodies*, 65.
31. King, *Island Bodies*, 73.
32. King, *Island Bodies*, 86. Decena delves into this dynamic further: "[c]onventional views of *coming out* in the United States celebrate the individual, the visible, and the proud. Given the growing legitimacy of predominantly white and middle-class lesbian and gay men in this country and of models that presume and uphold individual decision making, refusals of speech, pride, and visibility have been generally interpreted as suspect, as evidence of denial or internalized homophobia, or as outright pathology." *Tacit Subjects*, 18.
33. Quiroga, *Tropics of Desire*, 15–16.
34. Decena, *Tacit Subjects*, 71.
35. King, *Island Bodies*, 86.
36. Lara, *Streetwalking*, 84.
37. Lara, *Streetwalking*, 15.
38. Lara, *Streetwalking*, 22.
39. Lara, *Streetwalking*, 22.
40. Indeed, Rachel Afi Quinn echoes this with her finding that "Dominican visual artists, musicians, dancers, writers, and theater directors are actively responding to the contemporary moment in the Dominican Republic with new works that engage with the reality of Dominican queerness not highlighted by Pride festivals." Afi Quinn, "Dominican Pride and Shame," 142.
41. Negrón-Muntaner, "Can You Imagine?" 349, 350.
42. Gill, *Erotic Islands*, 11; Donnell, *Creolized Sexualities*, 2.

ONE | DICTATORSHIP AND SAME-SEX DESIRE

1 There are certainly many other possible starting points; for one, de Moya highlights the pre-Columbian indigenous visual and artistic artifacts representing indigenous same-sex desire before colonization. "La constante homoerótica en la historia de América," 2. Then there are a range of Spanish colonial texts from the sixteenth century onward that describe and denounce same-sex practices among Indigenous peoples as well as cases of "sodomitic" practices of some of the Spanish colonizers. De Moya, "La constante homoerótica," 6.
2 Mena, "Letras saliendo del closet," 27. Mena points to these two authors as those who made "the first wager for the truth of a condition and situation" ("la primera apuesta por la verdad de una condición y una situación").
3 Mena, "Letras saliendo del closet," 27. Mena emphasizes "how difficult it was to proclaim to search for homoerotic subjectivities," when "the subject's body was the body of the tyrant" ("Bajo semejantes condiciones hay que imaginarse lo difícil que era el proclamar la búsqueda de sujetividades homoeróticas"; "el cuerpo del sujeto fue el cuerpo del tirano").
4 Collado, *Anécdotas y crueldades,* 82. "Acuda a mí cuando usted encuentre en la prensa de Estados Unidos un artículo en el que se diga que Rafael Leonidas Trujillo Molina es un maricón!"
5 De Moya and García, "AIDS and the Enigma of Bisexuality," 123.
6 Derby, *The Dictator's Seduction,* 136–38.
7 Paulino Ramos, "Mecanismos de Trujillo." "Cuando se quería asociar a alquien con la homosexualidad, la correspondencia llevada al periódico iba firmada a nombre de 'Pajarito Pichón'"; the author here cites Dominican historian Orlando Inoa, *Historia dominicana.* (Letragráfica, 2013), 631.
8 De Moya and García, "AIDS and the Enigma of Bisexuality," 123.
9 De Moya and García, "AIDS and the Enigma of Bisexuality," 123.
10 Gill, *Erotic Islands,* 1.
11 Manley, *The Paradox of Paternalism,* 25.
12 Derby, *The Dictator's Seduction,* 167.
13 Museo Memorial de la Resistencia Dominicana, "Homofobia, represión y resistencia," 32. "pues muchas familias . . . estaban formadas por varias generaciones de mujeres, abuelas, hermanas, tías, hijas, nietas que convivían en una misma residencia." This indicates the greater "permissiveness for the cohabitation of women in our society, and during the dictatorship it was considered part of social life" ("La convivencia de mujeres tiene mayor permisividad en nuestra sociedad, y en la dictadura se entendía como parte de la vida social").
14 Museo Memorial de la Resistencia Dominicana, "Homofobia, represión y resisten-

cia," 32. "la búsqueda de mujeres lesbianas que vivieron la dictadura de Trujillo . . . una tarea muy difícil."

15 Museo Memorial de la Resistencia Dominicana, "Homofobia, represión y resistencia," 33. "a pesar de esta cierta invisibilidad, existían los chismes y rumores sobre ciertas mujeres que eran calificadas como 'machorras' y de femininidad dudosa."

16 Museo Memorial de la Resistencia Dominicana, "Homofobia, represión y resistencia," 33. "en el Foro Público se utilizaron algunos calificativos que cuestionaban la reputación de mujeres intelectuales o las que eran oposistoras al regimen para 'desacreditarlas' y afectar con ello su integridad profesional y personal pues la sociedad condenaba y satanizaba todo tipo de manifestación de lesbianismo entre las mujeres."

17 Mayes, "Why Dominican Feminism Moved to the Right," 361.

18 Mayes, "Why Dominican Feminism Moved to the Right," 361; Museo Memorial de la Resistencia Dominicana, "Homofobia, represión y resistencia," 42.

19 Museo Memorial de la Resistencia Dominicana, "Homofobia, represión y resistencia," 51. "contenían prohibiciones expresas y sanciones para las personas que sostuvieron relaciones sexuales con otras del mismo sexo."

20 Collado, "Don Paco Escribano." "una de las figuras públicas renombradas de la radiodifusión, que batió records de audiencia en la República Dominicana en las décadas de los cuarenta y cincuenta, lo fue don Paco Escribano, el Archipámpano de la Carcajada, Rey del Disparate y Rey de la Alegría, locutor, humorista, actor teatral y peculiar homosexual que se travestía de bailarina cupletera y que gustaba pregonar su condición." Paco Escribano was especially known for his daily radio show "La Hora de la Alegría," and Collado speaks admiringly of "the mark he made, his brilliant blunders, his exceeding intelligence, his exaggerated humoristic capacity, his street language, sometimes with intellectual touches, his daring jokes with double meanings and political risk" ("su impronta, sus repentismos geniales, su sobrada inteligencia, su exagerada capacidad humorística, su lenguaje callejero, a veces con dejos intelectuales, sus atrevidos chistes de doble sentido y riesgo político").

21 Pérez, "El Foro Público." "La homosexualidad era yerro y a ninguno de estos se les permitía el pavoneo desenfadado. . . . Pero había una excepción. . . . un disimulado gay de reconocida solvencia trujillista y aceptación pública casi obligada dentro y fuera de los corrillos permitidos durante la era del Jefe."

22 "Paco Escribano: The King of Nonsense," Videocine Palau. "Se reconoce que era homosexual, él no hablaba, . . . pero sus adamanes, su manera, sus amistades lo denotaban."

23 Decena, *Tacit Subjects*, 19.

24 Decena, *Tacit Subjects*, 19, 22.

25 Decena, *Tacit Subjects*, 29.

26 "Paco Escribano," Videocine Palau. "Era un hombre muy digno, no era un hombre que andaba exhibiendo cosas desagradables ni mucho menos, pero era evidente que era homosexual."
27 "Paco Escribano," Videocine Palau. "El manejaba todo con respeto y dignidad y por eso muchas personas visitaban la casa de Paco Escribano sin importar los prejuicios que existían en esta época en contra de la homosexualidad."
28 "Homosexualidad: Verdades, Mitos y Leyendas—Paco Escribano," *Gaytimes RD*. The video claims "Don Paco Escribano es el padre del transformismo dominicano."
29 Decena, *Tacit Subjects*, 28.
30 King, *Island Bodies*, 65, author's emphasis.
31 King, *Island Bodies*, 93.
32 King, *Island Bodies*, 102, my emphasis.
33 Barrios Rosario, *La ventana al silencio*, 24.
34 Barrios Rosario, *La ventana al silencio*, 24.
35 Mayes, "Why Dominican Feminism Moved to The Right," 353.
36 Mayes, "Why Dominican Feminism Moved to The Right," 353, 354.
37 Barrios Rosario, *La ventana al silencio*, 25. "El doctor Contreras envía a la educadora Ercilia Pepín para acompañar a Hilma."
38 Mayes, "Why Dominican Feminism Moved to The Right," 369.
39 Barrios Rosario, *La ventana al silencio*, 28.
40 Horn, *Masculinity after Trujillo*, 87–89.
41 Barrios Rosario, *La ventana al silencio*, 26. "Definitivamente Hilma Contreras no apoyó el régimen dictatorial de Rafael Leónidas Trujillo."
42 Rueda, "Pedro René Contín Aybar," 79.
43 Mena, "Letras saliendo del closet," 28.
44 Mena, "La literatura dominicana en el contexto caribeño," 54. "Los fundamentos del canon literario dominicano se establecieron durante la Era de Trujillo (1930–1961), a raíz de la celebración del Centenario de la República en 1944. Sus creadores serían Pedro René Contín Aybar—con su Antología poética dominicana—y Manuel Arturo Peña Batlle—con sus dos volúmenes de Antología de la literatura dominicana."
45 Nacidit-Perdomo, "Melba Marrero de Munné." "víctima de la misoginia de Pedro René Contín Aybar"; "asimilado como 'intelectual de primera' al servicio de la dictadura de Trujillo, se prestó contra Melba, a la mayor perversidad que un 'crítico' puede hacer: por encargo de María Martínez de Trujillo." This history recently became officialized when the Dominican government in 2019 ordered a renaming of a street after Melba Marrero de Munné, making reference to how Trujillo's wife ordered Contín Aybar to critique her "acerbamente" ("bitterly"). This 2019 Ordenanza also decrees another street to be named after Hilma Contreras. "Ordenanza No. 12/2019."
46 García Cuevas, *Poesía moderna*, 43. "Valga recordar . . . que LPS [La Poesía Sorpren-

dida] compone de un colectivo de poetas que agrupa bajo una misma publicación, a los poetas Franklin Mieses Burgos, Mariano Lebrón Saviñón, Manuel Rueda, Freddy Gatón Arce, Antonio Fernández Spencer, Rafael Américo Henríquez, Aída Cartagena Portalatín, Manuel Velario, Manuel Rueda [sic], Manuel Llanes, Juan Manuel Glass Mejíak al chileno Alberto Baeza Flores y al español Eugenio Fernández Granell."

47 García Cuevas, *Poesía moderna*, 45. "otro grupo de poetas e intelectuales, que liderado por Pedro René Contín Aybar fundan, con apoyo oficialista del régimen trujillista, los Cuadernos Dominicanos de Cultura."

48 Alvarez, "Un siglo de literatura," 539. "la represión apretaba las garras y *La Poesía Sorprendida* había desaparecido, [*Cuadernos*] abrió sus páginas a escritores que en los primeros años habían sido excomulgados, como fueron los propios sorprendidos"; "en diversas ocasiones tanto Contín Aybar como Incháustegui Cabral y Manuel Arturo Peña Batlle sirvieron de escudo para escritores que por alguna razón eran mal vistos o vigilados por el régimen."

49 Rueda, "Pedro René Contín Aybar," 79. "una figura de excepción"; "su opinion no dejó de ser oída con reverencia y era tal la notoriedad que alcanzó . . . que sus excentricidades fueron aceptadas como algo natural hasta el punto de que se hizo de él un mito, una de esas figuras que dictaminan el valor de los demás, sin tener que situarse a sí mismo."

50 Rueda, "Pedro René Contín Aybar," 79. "postura elegante que subrayaba el aletear de un abanico perfumado."

51 Nacidit-Perdomo, ed. *Hilma Contreras: Diario íntimo*.

52 Nacidit-Perdomo, Prefacio, 12. "vistió 'de hombre en París'"; "por prejuicios, por estereotipos y temor a la censura de su madre."

53 Andrés L. Mateo quoted in De Camps and García, *Antología de la literatura gay*, 300.

54 Decena, *Tacit Subjects*, 3.

55 Decena, *Tacit Subjects*, 2.

56 Decena, *Tacit Subjects*, 2–3.

57 Decena, *Tacit Subjects*, 1.

58 Andrés L. Mateo quoted in De Camps and García, *Antología de la literatura gay*, 300. "Contín Aybar arrojó un provocación histórica sobre la sociedad dominicana de entonces, que no estaba preparada para asimilar la ruda franqueza desnuda del amor homosexual."

59 Mena, "Letras saliendo del closet," 28. "Años después de la muerte del crítico y poeta, Antonio Fernández Spencer, en una de aquellas mesas míticas de la Cafetera El Conde, hablaría de Biel como uno de los amantes del poeta, que vivía en Borojol, y de quien el poeta no quería zafarse."

60 Contín Aybar, "Biel, el marino," 301. "olía a libertad"; "era un canto vibrante y amplio. Como el mar."

61   Contín Aybar, "Biel, el marino," 302. "aquella criatura, semisalvaje, me atraía por su candor y por su fortaleza. Carne donde morder y campo para sembrar."
62   Contín Aybar, "Biel, el marino," 306, 309.
63   Contín Aybar, "Biel, el marino," 310. "respetuoso de nuestra distancia, agrandada, quién sabe, por una especie de admiración a ese mundo distinto donde yo me movía, lejos de sus alcances."
64   Contín Aybar, "Biel, el marino," 310. "capaz de darle a Biel lo que no estaba en su poder ofrecerle."
65   Contín Aybar, "Biel, el marino," 303. "jóvenes como él y como él audaces, ligeros y vibrantes."
66   Contín Aybar, "Biel, el marino," 304. "sordas preocupaciones estériles, libre de estúpidos convencionalismos."
67   Contín Aybar, "Biel, el marino," 311. "Me placía olvidar las preocupaciones de la Guerra, lo estúpido,—inevitable!—y cotidiano, de mi trabajo para ganarme un mendrugo, un ramo de rosas y conquistarme un puesto donde, al verme tomando el sol, dijeran:—Tienes ideas raras."
68   Contín Aybar, "Biel, el marino," 305. "¿Por qué no podía yo reclinar su cabeza sobre hombro allí, en medio a todos, sin escándalo de nadie, y acariciar en su frente los sueños que aquella escenas producían en su alma?"
69   Contín Aybar, "Biel, el marino," 312. "Cada ola es un pensamiento. Cada pensamiento es un deseo. Todos mis deseos convergen hacia un punto. Y, sin pensar siquiera, estoy lleno de ti, Amor."
70   Contín Aybar, "Biel, el marino," 313.
71   Contín Aybar, "Biel, el marino," 312. "Estoy rodeado de personas tan desemejantes a mí."
72   Agard-Jones, "What the Sands Remember," 334, 336.
73   Tinsley, *Thiefing Sugar*, 211.
74   Indeed, the collection includes the aforementioned story "La Ventana" from Contreras's first short story collection from 1953 and published in the journal *Cuadernos dominicanos de cultura* as well.
75   Mena, "Letras saliendo del closet," 27.
76   Mijail, "Retazo cimarrón de promiscuidad." "Una madre cuir para la nación."
77   Contreras, *Between Two Silences*, 43.
78   Decena, "Multiplying Archives," 183.
79   Contreras, *Between Two Silences*, 41.
80   Contreras, *Between Two Silences*, 43.
81   Contreras, *Between Two Silences*, 43.
82   Contreras, *Between Two Silences*, 43.
83   Contín Aybar, "Biel, el marino," 304. "un silencio lleno de sugerimientos, de sol y de aires marinos."

84 Lugo-Ortiz, "Community at Its Limits," 129, 131.
85 Contreras, *Between Two Silences*, 41.
86 Decena, "Multiplying Archives," 181.
87 Contreras, *Between Two Silences*, 43.
88 Contreras, *Between Two Silences*, 43.
89 Contreras, *Between Two Silences*, 43.
90 Contreras, *Between Two Silences*, 35.
91 Contreras, *Between Two Silences*, 35.
92 Contreras, *Between Two Silences*, 37.
93 Contreras, *Between Two Silences*, 35.
94 Contreras, *Between Two Silences*, 37, my emphasis.
95 Contreras, *Between Two Silences*, 37.
96 Contreras, *Between Two Silences*, 37.
97 Contreras, *Between Two Silences*, 37, emphasis in original.
98 Contreras, *Between Two Silences*, 37.
99 Contreras, *Between Two Silences*, 37.
100 Contreras, *Between Two Silences*, 39.
101 Contreras, *Between Two Silences*, 39.
102 Contreras, *Between Two Silences*, 39.
103 Contreras, *Between Two Silences*, 39.

TWO | QUEER NIGHTLIFE DURING THE BALAGUER YEARS IN THE NOVELS OF RITA I. HERNÁNDEZ (1977–) AND REY E. ANDÚJAR (1977–)

1 Betances, *State and Society*, 118. "The Balaguer regime was the product of the U.S. invasion."
2 Betances, *State and Society*, 119. "When Balaguer took power on 1 July 1966 the first item on his political agenda was to provide 'order' and 'social peace,' in other words, to destroy the popular movement. The Dominican security forces terrorized those who had participated in or sympathized with the revolution, targeting organized labor, student organizations, and leftist political parties as enemies of the state. State-sponsored terrorist groups secretly killed hundreds and jailed thousands during Balaguer's twelve years in office."
3 Hartlyn, *The Struggle for Democratic Politics*, 101.
4 Indeed, according to sociologist Emelio Betances, "the emergence of a dependent financial and industrial bourgeoisie was the most important development of the Balaguer administration." Betances, *State and Society*, 122.
5 See Elizabeth S. Manley's book *Imagining the Tropics* (2025) for a history of how tourism in the Caribbean developed from the early to the late twentieth century with a particular eye toward the role of women.

6 Elizabeth S. Manley not only graciously reminded me of this history but also generously shared scans of *Spartacus* from her archival research. *Spartacus*, 152.
7 Lam, *Sexile=Sexilio*, 80. "hubo una bonanza en los sitios de encuentro para los gay," "en esos tiempos, la homosexualidad continuaba siendo un tabú ya que la sociedad dominicana no aceptaba ni remotamente la vida gay y, hasta cierto punto, ser homo públicamente, era como sufrir una muerte social."
8 Lam, *Sexile=Sexilio*, 80. "la emergente clase media dominicana."
9 Lam, *Sexile=Sexilio*, 79. "hubo una cierta explosión de la vida gay en cuanto a clubes se refiere."
10 Lam, *Sexile=Sexilio*, 81. "Había una discoteca en la Avenida Winston Churchill (presidida por una loca fabulosa, la famosa Perfumista) y llamada apropriadamente, Infinito. Otra por la 17 que terminó llamándose el Pent-House pero que inicialmente la llamaban el Bochinche ... Ya para mediado de los 70 los clubes gays se había 'desarrabilizados' pues había otras dos discotecas, una en la calles Lope de Vega (Cinema) y otra en la Avenida Abraham Lincoln (Zardoz) y, bueno desde siempre existió Marte en Gazcue, que no era oficialmente 'gay' pero adonde solo íbamos los pájaros."
11 Lam, *Sexile=Sexilio*, 81. "aquella vida estrictamente nocturna"; "no había centros comunalees, ni organizaciones, ni grupose de apoyo a nada, ni mucho menos aliados. Las discotecas eran los únicos establecimiento donde uno podía demonstrar su mariconería."
12 Lam, *Sexile=Sexilio*, 80. "Los únicos pájaros públicos eran los que yo había bautizado como pájaros de profesión.... O sea, que en la RD de los desdichados años 70, pájaros eran solo los bailarines, los coreógrafos, los diseñadores de moda y de interiores y los peluqueros ... El resto de los gays y lesbianas estábamos en el closet."
13 Betances, *State and Society*, 124. "Middle-class organization, organized labor, and student associations began to reorganize after the crushing defeats of the early 1970s and to hold demonstrations and strikes. Police repression could not stop the rising protests, and by 1978 large segments of the peasantry had joined the opposition led by the PRD."
14 Mena, *Poética de Santo Domingo II*, 10. "la revolución de la nocturnidad"; "espacio para el consumo, y tambien para la constitucion de nuevas subjetividades."
15 "Los creadores de imagen," *Listín Diario*.
16 "Anuncian espectáculo," *El Pregonero*.
17 Padilla, *Caribbean Pleasure Industry*, 8. "ASA is a not-for-profit organization based in Santo Domingo, with institutional roots in the late 1980s, and has received considerable funding from the United States Agency for International Development (USAID) and other international donor agencies to provide HIV-related services to gay identified men in the Dominican Republic." And up until the early 2000s, ASA was "the country's only legally incorporated organization run by and for gays."

18 Hernández, "Discurso inaugural," "... comenzé a frequentar la discoteca gay 'Disco Free' ... En 'Disco Free' ... el cuerpo ... era el protagonista ... al ámparo de la música disco sobrevivía una población de seres de la noche dedicados a explotar en mil pedazos cualquier suposición de la heternormatividad. Allí se celebraba la diferencia, la espectacularidad y el desenfado. El transformismo fuera de la seguridad de la discoteca era un acto suicida."
19 Valdez, *Las ciudades del deseo*, 2. "subjetividades *queer* que se leen como un síntoma del fracaso de los proyectos politicos nacionales heteronormativos."
20 Mena, "Letras saliendo del closet," 28.
21 Mena, "Letras saliendo del closet," 28. "en los años 80 y en casi todos los 90s hubo una ausencia de esta temática"; "a finales de los noventa, en *La estrategia de Chochueca* (2000), de Rita Indiana Hernández (1977)."
22 Mena, "Ciudades revisadas," 353. "la gran sorpresa de las últimas promociones literarias"; "los canónes establecidos del sentido común insular."
23 Valdez, "Masculinities in Crisis," 126. Elena Valdez reads these two Dominican novels side-by-side as well in her essay "Masculinities in Crisis," where she argues that both novels "put into crisis" their protagonists' "virile and feminine images, problematize their sexualities, and transform them into sexually ambiguous beings."
24 Hernández, *La estrategia de Chochueca*, 32. "el infame cabalgar de la gente, gente sola que no va a ninguna parte, que coinciden meneando la cabeza con la gran sinfonía del desencanto y el escándalo."
25 Hernández, *Chochueca*, 18. "arriba para abajo, hacienda bulla, bebiendo, fumándonos entre diez un cigarro"; "siempre acababan echándonos de todos lados, ... era algo en la forma de sonreír, como si con nosotros y nuestro entrar en los baños en tres en tres, nuestro besarnos en la boca hombre y mujeres, nuestro reír con la boca llena, salpicarámos a los que nos miraban con una sustancia insoportable."
26 Hernández, *Chochueca*, 16. "Lorena vivía en Naco en un apartamentazo ... allí celebraba unos bonches apoteósicos que siempre terminaban en desastre, una riquita intoxicada vomitando por la nariz sobre un violador de quince años que soba a su amigo dormido por el Lorazepan y el Brugal."
27 Hernández, *Chochueca*, 39–40. "en un bonche en casa de Franco ... nos recibió con los ojos pintados y una faldita de chifón verde. ... Ya en la madrugada era más placentero verlo con el maquillaje vuelto sopa, la ropa deshecha, y la risa de Marlene Dietrich, eso cuando no lloraba y te abrazaba y te quería y te hacía meterte con él varios gramos de perico y te contaba como su ultimo amor le metía pedazos de manguera o linternas por el culo."
28 Hernández, *Chochueca*, 35. "Se presentó y me sonrió con una mariconería aprendida. Ya se lo habría metido, porque Franco era tenaz y había dos manchas pegajosas en el cubrecama. Leo, ... tenía dieciséis años y en Ciudad Nueva, una noviecita ... Franco ... le acariciaba la cabeza como a un perrito de peluche."

29 Padilla, *Caribbean Pleasure Industry*, 32.
30 Padilla, *Caribbean Pleasure Industry*, 11.
31 Padilla, *Caribbean Pleasure Industry*, 11.
32 Padilla, *Caribbean Pleasure Industry*, 20.
33 Hernández, *Chochueca*, 66. "La música estaba brutal,... el dj y su zug zigui zug.... Ven, vamos a movernos un poco, me decía Amanda... y cuando me tocaba era una ducha tibia que me subía... Amanda Amanda Amadísima, le decía yo y le besaba los labios con paciencia."
34 Palacios, "Actos peatonales, actos de consumo," 566. "la queerificación del espacio en *La Estrategia de Chochueca*"; "la dimensión interpersonal *queer* de la novela se articula fuera de la esfera privada dominicana, forjando una intimidad a contracorriente que altera al alcance normativa de la organización social dominicana."
35 Valdez, *Las ciudades del deseo*, 13. "una forma de relación *queer* que supera el poder regulatorio"; "como contranarrativa a la memoria y el archivo oficiales."
36 Hernández, *Chochueca*, 67. "un moreno con una gorra de los Mets que trata de imitar el acento Boricua cuando habla, toda la pinta de los prostitutos que van al Pent House."
37 Padilla, *Caribbean Pleasure Industry*, 11.
38 Padilla, *Caribbean Pleasure Industry*, 33, 32.
39 Padilla, *Caribbean Pleasure Industry*, 65.
40 Valdez, "Masculinities in Crisis," 125.
41 Hernández, *Chochueca*, 43, 44. "¿Qué tú haces con esta tipa?"; "que yo era una puta, que yo era una tecata, que yo era unaunauna, ya no sabía que más decir."
42 Padilla, *Caribbean Pleasure Industry*, 64.
43 Hernández, *Chochueca*, 46. "me había disfrazado [de Octaviano]..., pero no es fácil ser el Octano, hace falta cojón, falta una amnesia absurda y consecuente, hace falta way para ponérsele al lado en su mundo de él, habría que ser Chochuceca."
44 Padilla, *Caribbean Pleasure Industry*, 133, 134–35.
45 Andújar, *El hombre triángulo*, 13. "te enganchas porque estás cansado de que la policía te joda en la calles.... Porque si eres morenito y la ropa no te ayuda te jode que no te dejen entrar... o te digan 'Lo sentimos, fiesta privada.'"
46 Andújar, *El hombre triángulo*, 14. "Y ya el gusanito de la hombría y el maldito machismo-heterodominicano se te van inflando."
47 Andújar, *El hombre triángulo*, 14. "E que el mariconcito se cree poeta"; "pues you le voy a enseñar a redactor un informe como un hombre."
48 Andújar, *El hombre triángulo*, 24. "un civil en ropa de military, un hombre atormentado."
49 Padilla, *Caribbean Pleasure Industry*, 84.
50 Padilla, *Caribbean Pleasure Industry*, 63, 57. "male sex workers are highly mobile, often moving between various bars, *discotecas,* restaurants, and other businesses," 63.

51 Andújar, *El hombre triángulo*, 26. "lo que me vuelve loco Rotunda son tus vellos de hombre que nunca te me afeites las piernas Rotunda nunca te me afeitas tus bigotitos naturales y tu voz ronca ronquísima."
52 Andújar, *El hombre triángulo*, 36. "siempre estaba lleno de maricones, aunque la música era buena, los tragos eran baratos . . . esas eran las buenas excuas para sentarse de vez en vez en Parada 77, el bar donde hasta el diablo bota la ropa después de las tres de la mañana."
53 Andújar, *Saturnario*, "Aquella noche, aquel beso," 65–66; "Superaquello," 86.
54 Andújar, *El hombre triángulo*, 22. "creo que puedo quererte."
55 Andújar, *El hombre triángulo*, 25. "Trago a trago, pensó en sus ojos, su agonía, ese hombre, ese hombre tan desnudo, tan bien formado, tan limpio para ser un vagabundo."
56 Andújar, *El hombre triángulo*, 27. "su piel estaba nítidamente suave."
57 Andújar, *El hombre triángulo*, 39. "pestañas falsas de sentimientos verdaderos de hombre deseando hombre, carne, sudor, agua dulce."
58 Andújar, *El hombre triángulo*, 36.
59 Andújar, *El hombre triángulo*, 43. "entre tanta mierda, con tanto maricón alrededor, maldito tectao, crakero de mierda. Tanta palabra bonita y tanta vaina pendejo maricón de mierda coño."
60 Andújar, *El hombre triángulo*, 45. "esos ojos marrones y envolverse en la crespura de ese pelo negro, ser levantado hasta la eternidad por esos brazos morenos, ser bendecido por esas manos grandes y duras, quedarse con él, en él."
61 Andújar, *El hombre triángulo*, 46. "Se abrazaron. Pérez tenía razón al decir que aquella piel era suave, pero ahora todo era diferente, ahora estaba sintiendo esa piel, que vibraba bajo sus manos. Un abrazo, fuerte, un cruce de caras, un roce muy ligero, casi imperceptible, después: el beso."
62 Andújar, *El hombre triángulo*, 50. "Sangre: lo que brotaba de la boca de Baraka después de los puñetazos que Pérez le propinó por esa falta de respeto. Coño, qué es eso, un hombre besando a un guardia."
63 Andújar, *El hombre triángulo*, 50. "una de las locas lo empujaba y le gritaba desde la puerta: Acéptalo, admítelo coño que tú también eres maricón buena mierda, abusador coño."
64 Indeed, in both novels, as De Maesener and Bustamante in their essay "Cuerpos heridos en la narrativa de Rita Indiana Hernández, Rey Emmanuel Andújar y Junot Díaz," point out, injured bodies are central, even as they stylistically differ in many ways. De Maeseneer and Bustamante, "Cuerpos heridos," 410. "Hernández emphasizes the description of the wound through a visual poetic which, through spectacularizing and parodies of audiovisual strategies of science fiction, produces a total distancing from the injured body. In turn, in the texts by Andújar the question centers not on how wounds are inflicted but rather on what they generate, or what

they imply, so that the relation with the injured body triggers an internal drama in the individuals, enveloped in a serious and anguished tone." ("Hernández enfatiza la descripción de la herida bajo una poética visual que, a través de la espectacularización y parodias de estrategias audiovisuales propias de la ciencia ficción, produce un distanciamiento total del cuerpo herido. En cambio, en los textos de Andújar la pregunta no se centra en cómo son infligidas las heridas, sino más bien en qué generan, o qué implican, por lo que la relación con el cuerpo herido desencadena un drama interno en los individuos, envuelto en un tono de seriedad y angustia").

65   Andújar, *El hombre triángulo*, 65. "qué será de él en un mundo tan straight."
66   Notably, in Andújar's following novel, *Candela* (2006), which again features a police lieutenant who, however, remains resolutely heterosexual, homoeroticism is addressed through two male bisexual characters (Lubrini and Gustaff), who, like Hernández's characters, do not struggle with anxieties and traumas relating to their same-sex desires. This pattern of male bisexual characters who are writers/intellectuals (like Lubrini) and reject Dominican mainstream society and readily move between heterosexual and homosexual encounters, in fact, becomes a prevalent representation in Andújar's later stories, including in the stories "Monociclo," "Aquella noche, aquel beso," and "Superaquello," in the collection *Saturnario* (2011). Notably, the latter two stories both feature the same bar, Parada, in the Zona Colonial, as in *El hombre triángulo*.
67   Adeyemi, Khubchandani, and Rivera-Severa, *Queer Nightlife*, 2.

THREE | WADDYS JÁQUEZ'S THEATER, TRAVESTIS, AND HIV/AIDS IN THE NEW DEMOCRATIC ERA

1   Parts of this chapter were previously published in *Studies in Twentieth and Twenty-First Century Literature*, as "Passion Plays: The Dominican Diaspora in Waddys Jáquez's *P.A.R.G.O.*" *ST&TCL* 32, no. 2 (Summer 2008): 342–58.
2   Castillo, "Proceso de expansion de la comunidad homosexual," 13. "Para mediados del año 1997, ya los diarios dominicanos se atrevían a presentar informes estadísticos y analíticos, sin ningún pudor sobre las preferencias sexuales íntimas de los homosexuales."
3   Tallaj, "Desde la Orilla," 221–22. Francisco Castillo lists the following TV personalities: "varios hombres, abiertamente homosexuales se incorporan a los programas de farándula y moda. Tal es el caso del Sr. Jary Ramírez, de Telemicro Canal 5, Francisco Sanchíz, de Producciones Borea en Santiago de los Caballeros, Alex Macía, de la Red Nacional de Noticias y el popular travesti por todos conocido como 'Chachita' en Amé 47 y actualmente en Telesistema en la co-producción de un programa con el presentador Henry Brito." "Proceso de expansión," 14. ("various openly homosexual men have become part of entertainment and fashion TV programs. This is the case

of Sr. Jary Ramírez, of Telemicro Channel 5, Francisco Sanchíz, from Borea Productions in Santiago de los Caballeros, Alex Macía of the National News Web and the popular travesti known by everyone as 'Chachita' in the program Amé 47 and currently with Telesistema in a co-produced program with the presenter Henry Brito.")

4 Tallaj, "Desde la Orilla," 222.
5 Encarnación, "Tratamiento del personaje homosexual," 13. "la presencia del tema de la homosexualidad y de lo personajes pertenecientes a ésta orientación sexual, es escasa y que el mínimo tratamiento que en esos filmes se ofrece a ambos elementos los presenta como risibles, vituperables, latosos y socialmente inaceptables." Encarnación's findings are based on an analysis of the following Dominican movies: *Nueba Yol: Por fin llegó Balbuena* (1995), Dir. Angel Muñiz; *Perico ripiao* (2003), Dir. Angel Muñiz; *Negocios son negocios* (2004), Dir. Joppe de Bernardi; *La Cárcel de la Victoria: el cuarto hombre* (2004), Dir. José Enrique Pintor; *El sistema* (2006), Dir. Humberto Espinal; *Sanky Panky* (2007), Dir. José Enrique Pintor; *Ladrones a domicilio* (2008), Dir. Angel Muñiz; *Al fin y al cabo* (2008), Dir. Alfonso Rodríguez; *Santi Cló: la vaina de la navidad* (2008), Dir. José Enrique Pintor. "Tratamiento del personaje homosexual," 101-2.
6 De Camps Jiménez, "Interview with Mabel Caballero." "Quienes han abordado el tema."
7 Tallaj, "Desde la Orilla," 226.
8 Lam, "¿Existe una literatura gay en República Dominicana?" n.p. "Una magnífica recopilación"; "una necesaria y mínima coherencia ... en cuanto al contenido de las obras allí presentada."
9 Lam "¿Existe una literatura gay en República Dominicana?" n.p. "Sin modestia."
10 De Camps, "Interview." De Camps Jiménez also made it be known that there is no link between his own sexuality and the theme of the anthology; he declares himself securely anchored in his own heterosexual identity and notes, "I know my sexuality and because of that I do not have to question it." The project, on de Camps Jiménez's part at least, did not emerge out of his strong link with the Dominican LGBTIQ+ community and their concerns, but followed the prompts of a globalized and commercialized LGBTIQ+ culture (the other editor, Mélida García, unfortunately passed away not long after the publication of this anthology, and she did not give, as far as I am aware of, such public rationales for her involvement in this project).
11 This raises the question if *any* form of public circulation of the global symbols and discourses of LGBTIQ+ culture and politics in the Dominican Republic, including through this anthology, is necessarily a positive development for Dominican LGBTIQ+ communities and subjects. Lam cautiously considers what the positive benefits of this anthology might be despite its obvious shortcomings: "despite the substantial homophobia in the majority of the texts its publication *could* promote a greater acceptance of a gay minority in Quisqueya by presenting publicly emotions,

celebrations, rituals, sexual relations and images of our alternative culture" ("a pesar de la sustancial homofobia en la mayoría de los textos su publicación *podría* promover el avance de la aceptación de la minoría gay en Quisqueya al presentar públicamente emociones, celebraciones, rituales, relaciones sexuales e imágenes de nuestra cultura alternativa"). "¿Existe una literatura gay," n.p. While some texts in the anthology point toward this alternative culture, a much larger number of texts in the anthology, at best, can be said to obscure the lived social reality of queer Dominicans, and in the worst cases, simply echo and reinforce existing homophobic views.

12 Glave, *Our Caribbean*, 13.
13 Glave, *Our Caribbean*, 14, 16. The Spanish original is from De Camps and García, *Antología de la literatura gay*, 50, 51, 53.
14 Méndez, "De travestismos sospechosos," 523. "el travestismo se utiliza . . . como un elemento alusivo a una sexualidad entendida siempre como 'anormal' o pertubadora."
15 Méndez, "De travestismos sospechosos," 526, 524. "los personajes travestis de los cuentos son un elemento grotesco"; "no proponen un compromiso directo con la elaboración de una identidad gay positiva."
16 Lora, "La Zona Colonial."
17 Lara, *Streetwalking*, 7.
18 Quinn, "Dominican Pride and Shame," 142.
19 Horn, "Queer Caribbean Homecomings," 361–81.
20 Ramos et al., *Gráfica Independiente Dominicana*, 65–68.
21 Volonteri, "P.A.R.G.O., o la irrupción de la verdad," n.p. "hijo pródigo del teatro dominicano." For example, in 2004 the Dominican critic Marivell Contreras affirmed emphatically: "I say without fear of doubt that Dominican theatre has revived in the last three years thanks to the ingenuity and the staging of the works of this Dominican actor and dramaturge living in the United States" ("Lo digo sin temor a dudas que el teatro dominicano se ha avivado en los últimos 3 años gracias al ingenio y a las puestas en escena de las obras de este actor y dramaturgo dominicano residente en los Estados Unidos"). "Waddys, 'una ausencia llena de presencia,'" n.p. The well-known Dominican writer and radio personality Carmen Imbert Brugal similarly finds that in the country "the survival of theater has the name of Waddys Jáquez" ("La pervivencia del teatro tiene el nombre Waddys Jáquez"). "Waddys Jáquez: contundente," n.p.
22 Jáquez contributes to the Dominican cultural, and specifically theatrical landscape, in other ways too. He regularly directs or acts in plays and musicals staged in the Dominican Republic, many of them at the national theater in Santo Domingo, and he is currently a judge on *Dominicana's Got Talent* and hence a formidable public presence.

23 Muñoz, "Waddys vuelve con Cero." "In 1999 he left his anonymity with his montage of 'Yerbamala,' which obtained the maximum applause during the 'May-Month of theatre' of that time period" ("En 1999 dejó el anonimato con el montaje de 'Yerbamala,' que obtuvo los máximos aplausos 'del Mayo Teatral' de esa época").
24 Lissette Rojas, "Waddys: Para morirse de la risa." "Nadie supone lo que es ser marica en un pueblo chico. Ay Loma Alta, pueblito insignificante, . . . si pudiera escupiría fuego sobre ti."
25 Volonteri, "P.A.R.G.O., o la irrupción de la verdad." "El público respondió, soportó las historias, disfrutó," n.p.
26 Martínez Tabares, "Caribbean Bodies, Migrations, and Spaces of Resistance," 26.
27 Stevens, *Aquí and Allá*, 95.
28 Jáquez, "P.A.R.G.O." "Buenas noches compañeros de P.A.R.G.O., para los que no me conocen mi nombre es Pasión, Pasión Contreras es mi nombre. Tengo un año y medio en la organización. Ex-adicta, ninfómana y alcohólica debido a la soledad según dice mi siquiatra. Latina por descendencia, pero nacida y criada en Nueva York, así que yo soy del grupo de los que ellos dicen que no somos de ningún sitio. Noticia curiosa, un pequeñito detalle, mi mai me parió varón aunque usted no lo crea. Y fui bautizada y todo bajo el nombre de Ramón, Ramón que nombre tan bello. Pero a los 19 años hice mi cross-over hacia el sexo femenino, soy operada de mi parte, transexual es el término medico de mi condición actual. Yo me hice los pómulos y los senos con inyecciones y años más tarde cuando salieron los implantes yo me aumenté dos tallas para ir a la vanguardia con la tecnología."
29 Volonteri, "P.A.R.G.O., o la irrupción de la verdad," n.p. "humanización del travesti."
30 Acevedo, "La metamorfosis de Waddys," n.p.
31 Ronzino, "'Letal' arriba a la Sala Ravelo," n.p. "la obra cuenta varias historias enlazadas por el sensacionalismo."
32 Rivera, "La caligrafía del alma," 68.
33 Rojas, "IV Festival de Teatro," 170.
34 Volonteri, "Puentes sobre tierras turbulentas," n.p. "los personajes se entrecruzan, se conectan, se tocan, narran, viven, mueren y resucitan."
35 Rojas, "IV Festival Internacional de Teatro," 170. "una compleja realidad nacional afectada por el consumismo, el turismo sexual, la droga, la pobreza, la invasión de productos internacionales y el control de poderes hegemónicos nacionales e internacionales."
36 Rojas, "IV Festival Internacional de Teatro," 171. "Ante un inminente huracán, 'una madre sale a buscar sus hijos-perros rialengos para protegerlos,' pero ellos se rebelan y la devoran."
37 Volonteri, "Puentes sobre tierras turbulentas," n.p. "la melancolía del pasado"; "la tragedia del presente."

38 Baud, "Realidades e ideologías de la modernidad," 40. "A pesar de las promesas del gobierno sobre la reforma de educación y políticas sociales, una gran parte de los gasto público fueron destinados a obras públicas. Se han hecho muchas críticas, por ejemplo, en contra de la construcción de los elevados y túneles en la Capital."
39 Centro Cultural de España Santo Domingo, "Varones." "romper con los prejuicios que existen dentro de la sociedad en torno al género, la sexualidad, el amor y las relaciones humanas"; "Un canto a la libertad liderado por miembros de la comunidad LGBT."
40 Cielo Naranja, "Tony Capellán."
41 Garrido Castellano et al., "Inside and Outside the Exhibition Space," 32.
42 Garrido Castellano et al., "Inside and Outside the Exhibition Space," 52.
43 Ramos, Rosario, and Sánchez, *Gráfica Independiente Dominicana*, 65–68.
44 Stevens, *Aquí and Allá*, 218.
45 More recently, Carlos Ortiz/Soriano participated with his short films in 2012 and 2013 at the Festival Internacional de Cine GLBT.
46 Such wounding and vulnerability of the heart is a theme that also emerges in Noa María Batlle's drawings, where the main female figure is almost always accompanied by a disembodied heart.
47 Castellanos, "Santo Domingo's LGBT Social Movement," 965.
48 Jáquez, "CERO." "con las mismas palabras de siempre"; "hablando pupú, bazofia, cagá de burro."
49 Jáquez, "CERO." "Como si pasara nada."
50 Jáquez, "CERO." "burbuja de mentira."
51 Padilla, *Caribbean Pleasure Industry*, 177. "historias de dolor que con el sazón criollo saben mejor."
52 Jáquez, "CERO." "esa vainita que tenemos los latinoamericanos . . . que nos cagamos de la risa aunque nos esté llevando el Diablo."
53 Jáquez, "CERO." "ella está muerta y yo jodido."
54 Jáquez, "CERO." "Infectada de este amor infeccioso."
55 Padilla, *Caribbean Pleasure Industry*, 202.
56 Sánchez Marte, "Empoderamiento de hombres gay," 23. "Las relaciones de poder y la falta de equidad social desempeñan un papel preponderante en el riesgo en el cual incurren las diferentes poblaciónes"; "Por estas y otras razones hemos ampliado el criterio frente al VIH/SIDA y, ahora no sólo prestamos atención al comportamiento de riesgo de los individuos, sino también a los factores ambientales y sociales inmediatos que influyen en dicho comportamiento y a la influencia que la familia y la comunidad ejercen sobre el comportamiento de la persona."
57 Jáquez, "CERO." "cuando me vienen con toda la parsimonia de la solidaridad, el lacito rojo, los testimonials, la manta de honor a los desaparecidos y la marchas en Central Park, respond poniendo el pecho donde tengo la espalda, porque no quiero

ser parte de la comparsa, porque yo no soy la cara del SIDA, soy Marina la, montándose en el subway, haciendo mi laundry, buscando mi medicina, manejando mi taxi de Brooklyn hasta Manhattan..."
58 Jáquez, "CERO." "un mar de hombres, mujeres, niños y gente normal que el mundo llama 'Rara.'"
59 Jáquez, "CERO." "Me dijiste que todo era mentira... Dijiste que el virus era un negocio de millones para ahuyentar maricones, un truco publicitario de países desarrollados... Tú me dijiste que no me preocupara."
60 Jáquez, "CERO." "en medio de esta islita del Caribe, este paraíso tropical donde no hay nada que perder y mucho que aprender."
61 Padilla and Castellanos, "Discourses of Homosexual Invasion," 32.
62 Padilla, *Caribbean Pleasure Industry*, 180.

FOUR | DIVAGACIONES 2006

1 Rivera-Velázquez, "Dominican Republic: LGBTT Landscape Analysis," 12.
2 Castellanos, "Santo Domingo's LGBT social movement," 963.
3 Castellanos, "Santo Domingo's LGBT social movement," 967.
4 Castellanos, "Santo Domingo's LGBT social movement," 967.
5 Lara, *Streetwalking*, 22.
6 Lara, *Streetwalking*, 26.
7 Castellanos, "Santo Domingo's LGBT social movement," 965. "In June 2004, the Dominican Republic received a 5-year grant from the Global Fund to Fight HIV/AIDS, Tuberculosis, and Malaria, including US$48.5 million for HIV/AIDS. Developed by the Presidential Commission on AIDS (COPRESIDA) in collaboration with other NGOs, the proposal included funding for men who have sex with men and required a strategy to create a political environment that favoured human rights for the prevention and treatment of STDs (Global Fund, 2004, 2015). Lagging behind in the implementation of this project, in early 2005 Global Fund officials increased the pressure on COPRESIDA to speed up the implementation of the five-year project (personal communication). As a result, COPRESIDA dramatically increased AIDS related spending around June 2005, close to a year after the approval of the proposal (Global Fund, 2015)."
8 Castellanos, "Santo Domingo's LGBT social movement," 968.
9 As Castellanos describes, "transgender women had become more and more integrated within the movement as inter-personal violence, sex work, and needle use for hormones were integrated within the broader view of HIV prevention for sexual minorities." "Santo Domingo's LGBT social movement," 972.
10 Castellanos, "Santo Domingo's LGBT social movement," 968.
11 Jiménez Polanco, "Lesbianas y gays. Llegó la hora," 29.

12 Valera, "Presentación," 3.
13 Castellanos, "Santo Domingo's LGBT Social Movement," 969.
14 Castellanos, "Santo Domingo's LGBT social movement," 969.
15 Padilla and Castellanos, "Discourses of Homosexual Invasion," 32.
16 Padilla and Castellanos, "Discourses of Homosexual Invasion," 36.
17 Castellanos, "Santo Domingo's LGBT social movement," 969.
18 Castellanos, "Santo Domingo's LGBT Social Movement," 969.
19 Padilla, *Caribbean Pleasure Industry*, 88.
20 Quinn, "Dominican Pride and Shame," 133.
21 Quinn, "Dominican Pride and Shame," 132.
22 Lara, "Strategic Universalisms," 106.
23 Lara, "Strategic Universalisms," 111.
24 Castellanos, "Santo Domingo's LGBT social movement," 970.
25 Castellanos, "Santo Domingo's LGBT social movement," 970.
26 Rivera-Velázquez, "Dominican Republic: LGBTT Landscape," 14.
27 González Gómez, "Una escritura lésbica/A Lesbian Writing," *Divagaciones*, 1. "solo una lesbiana puede escribir o producir una escritura lésbica."
28 Lara, *Streetwalking*, 1.
29 Hobal, "Mi vida como lesbiana," *Divagaciones*, 16. "Oficialmente salí del closet a los 20 cuando fui a quedarme por unas cuantas semanas con Mami. Ya que estaba en una relación sentí que era necesario decírselo a mami, no quería esconderle ni mentirle sobre mi vida."
30 Huracán, "Una salida del closet y vivir tipo huracán," *Divagaciones*, 20. "a casi 3 años de haberle afirmado, mirándolo a los ojos y con un terrible miedo, que sí me gustaban las chicas y de lo segura que me sentía sigo sintiendo algo de pena por herir a mi madre."
31 Zabala, "Carta a mi Madre," *Divagaciones*, 23. "Madre, yo sé que es muy difícil para ti comprenderme... Aún recuerdo cómo reaccionaste el día que te dije que soy lesbiana.... Mas, a pesar de todo y de todos sé que me amas y sabes muy bien que te amo. Tu amor de madre sobrepasa la hipócrita moral del mundo homofóbico que me condena."
32 Huracán, "Una salida del closet y vivir tipo Huracán," *Divagaciones*, 23. "que yo estaba encontrándome con una mujer y que andaba muy enamorada de ella."
33 Reyes Bonilla, "Pero m'ija, y de dónde sacáte 'eso'?" *Divagaciones*, 41. "Mami se obsesionó:—Y de dónde saca'te 'eso'?... El conocimiento de mi sexualidad era algo que mi madre envejeciente, super religiosa y tradicional no lograba entender, ni de lo que podía recuperarse tras mi decisión de desafiarle al salirle, a mis veinticinco años, inesperada y sorprendentemente del closet."
34 Norman, "Mejor Puta que Pata," *Divagaciones*, 132.
35 Norman, "Mejor Puta que Pata," *Divagaciones*, 134.

36 Reyes Bonilla, "Pero m'ija, y de dónde sacáte 'eso'?" *Divagaciones*, 47. "yo estaba bien o más que bien... Me preguntaba constantement acerca del destino y qué hubiera pasado si hubiera aún estado en Santo Domingo, si no hubiera emigrado a los E.E.U.U. a los dieciseite años junto a mi madre, cómo hubiera bregado con mi sexualidad."
37 Lara, *Erzulie's Skirt*, xiii.
38 Lara, *Erzulie's Skirt*, xiii.
39 Lara, *Erzulie's Skirt*, 65.
40 Lara, *Erzulie's Skirt*, 121.
41 Lara, *Streetwalking*, 3.
42 Lara, *Streetwalking*, 4.
43 Lara, *Erzulie's Skirt*, 215–16.
44 Lara, *Erzulie's Skirt*, 123.
45 Lara, *Erzulie's Skirt*, 62.
46 Lara, *Erzulie's Skirt*, 62.
47 Pancrazi, *Los dólares de arena*, 53. "Tony, que andaba orgulloso de haber conquistado a Sweenie, la americana del Atlantis."
48 Pancrazi, *Dólares de arena*, 61. "lo hacía porque era lo que esperaban de él los hombres de Sánchez... para probarles que no se estaba convirtiendo, a fuerza de andar conmigo, en un *pájaro*."
49 Pancrazi, *Dólares de arena*, 61. "el rumor que había empezado a circular, que no le habían salido alas, que sus gestos no eran más delicados."
50 Pancrazi, *Dólares de arena*, 9. "parecían alentarme, con sus gestos amistosos, a amar uno de los suyos–casi en secreto, discretamente."
51 Pancrazi, *Dólares de arena*, 38. "parecía decirme que poco importaba que yo fuera gringo, *pájaro* si lo quería, si lo ayudaba."
52 Pancrazi, *Dólares de arena*, 95. "Para que aceptaran que se encerrara con un hombre, todas las tardes, en una habitación en un hotel de Las Terrenas"; "ignoraban un amor diferente, pensando tal vez les tocaría, un día, una tajada."
53 Padilla, *Caribbean Pleasure Industry*, 207.
54 Pancrazi, *Dólares de arena*, 31. "mi preferido para toda la vida."
55 Pancrazi, *Dólares de arena*, 11. "me miraba un buen rato con una especie de ternura sorprendida,... como si le hiciera possible amarme un día."
56 Pancrazi, *Dólares de arena*, 13. "tratando... de saber lo que él pensaba realmente, cómo me veía exactamente—como un extranjero 'amable,' como él decía, que no estaba tan mal, o como una simple '*caja de ahorros*.'"
57 Padilla, *Caribbean Pleasure Industry*, 149, 152, 152–53.
58 Pancrazi, *Dólares de arena*, 109. "No había querido entender—para seguir disfrutando,...—que quería escaper, lo antes possible, de su vida en Las Majaguas, de la *ca-*

sita, de la batalla cotidiana para conseguir el pan, el arroz, la *'pensión'* para mantener a sus tres hijos."
59 Pancrazi, *Dólares de arena,* 122. "decía, mientras conducía bajo las últimas estrellas y llevaba mis brazos a su pecho, hacia su corazón, como cuando aceleraba o esquivaba un montículo más alto de arena: *'papá,'* y yo tomaba esa palabra para mí."
60 Pancrazi, *Dólares de arena,* 55. "ese era el gran circuito del dinero en el trópico, la única prueba, la única forma de querer."
61 Lara, *Queer Freedom: Black Sovereignty,* 37.
62 Decena, *Circuits of the Sacred,* 14.
63 Tinsley, *Ezili's Mirrors,* ix.
64 Decena, "Multiplying Archives," 186, 187.
65 Decena, *Circuits of the Sacred,* xi.
66 Dumit Estévez, "Artistic Transfiguration."

CONCLUSION | QUEER DOMINICAN GENEALOGIES

1 Hutchinson, *Tigers of a Different Stripe,* 209.
2 Dávila Ellis, "Uttering Sonic Dominicanidad," 120.
3 "La Delfi."
4 Mota, "Si Tu Quiere Dembow."
5 Valdez, "Suciedad divina," 167, 170. "Agrega un nuevo escalón en la trayectoria histórica del perreo queer femenino que para ella significa una estética y un estilo de vida."
6 Villa, "Pabllo Vitar, Esteman, MULA."
7 Villegas, "MULA Draws with Every Color."
8 Dávila Ellis, "Uttering Sonic Domicanidad," 100.
9 Hutchinson, *Tigers of a Different Stripe,* 207.
10 Donnell, *Creolized Sexualities,* 13.
11 Cid, *El Cocoró del Futuro.*
12 Villegas, "Underground Santo Domingo Parties."
13 Villegas, "Underground Santo Domingo Parties."
14 Rivera-Velázquez, "Caribbean Kiki," 244.
15 Mijail, "Catinga Ediciones." "un proyecto editorial con base en República Dominicana especializada en escrituras que promueven producciones realizadas por personas negras y/o afrodescendiente de la comunidad LGBTQI+."
16 Mijail, *Escrituras del otro cuerpo,* 25, 28, 89, 35.
17 Méndez, "Chapeo Consciousness," 30.
18 Mijail, *Santo Domingo is Burning,* 41.
19 Mijail, *Santo Domingo is Burning,* 49, 117.

20 Díaz and Mijail, *Inflamadas de retórica*, 156.
21 Díaz and Mijail, *Inflamadas de retórica*, 93, 174, 175.
22 Díaz and Mijail, *Inflamadas de retórica*, 154. "el chileno Pedro Lemebel, el argentino Néstor Perlongher y los Cubanos Virgilio Piñera y José Lezama Lima."
23 Morla, *Saunatopía*, 94.
24 Mijail, *Santo Domingo is Burning*, 32.
25 Mijail, *Santo Domingo is Burning*, 48.
26 Rivera-Velázquez, "Caribbean Kiki," 253.
27 Almonte Caraballo, "Always Present Necessity," 64.

BIBLIOGRAPHY

Acevedo, Abdía. "La metamorfosis de Waddys se posa sobre papel." *El Caribe* (Santo Domingo), Feb. 24, 2004.
Adeyemi, Kemi, Kareem Khubchandani, and Ramón Rivera-Severa, eds. *Queer Nightlife*. University of Michigan Press, 2021.
Agard-Jones, Vanessa. "What the Sands Remember." *GLQ: A Journal of Lesbian and Gay Studies* 18, no. 2–3 (2012): 325–46.
Alcántara Almanzar, José. "Lulú o la metamorphosis." In *Antología de la literatura gay en la República Dominicana*, edited by Miguel de Camps Jiménez and Mélida García. Editora Manatí, 2004.
Alcántara Almanzar, José. "Lulú or the Metamorphosis." In *Our Caribbean: A Gathering of Lesbian and Gay Writing from the Antilles*, edited by Thomas Glave. Duke University Press, 2008.
Almonte Caraballo, Sarahí Yahaira. "Always Present Necessity: A Monologue." In *Divagaciones II: Una antología de mujeres dominicanas lesbianas, bisexuales y queer/An Anthology by Dominican Lesbian, Bisexual and Queer Women*, edited by Jacqueline Jiménez Polanco and Jenny Mabelle Marte Chalas. New York, 2023.
Alvarez, Soledad. "Un siglo de literatura." In *Historia de la República Dominicana Vol II*, coordinated by Frank Moya Pons. Academia dominicana de la historia/Ediciones Doce Calles, 2010.
Andújar, Rey Emmanuel. *Candela*. Alfaguara, 2006.
Andújar, Rey Emmanuel. "Ciudadano Cero." In *El Factor Carne*. Editores Isla Negra, 2005.
Andújar, Rey Emmanuel. *El hombre triángulo*. Editores Isla Negra, 2005 [2003].
Andújar, Rey Emmanuel. *Saturnario*. Editora Nacional/Ministerio de Cultura, 2011.
"Anuncian espectáculo 'Los Creadores de Imágenes Visión 2020.'" *El Pregonero* (Santo Domingo), Mar. 12, 2020. https://elpregonerord.com/anuncian-espectaculo-los-creadores-de-imagenes-vision-2020/.
Arenas, Reinaldo. *Antes que anochezca*. Tusquets Editores, 1992.

Báez, Frank. *Postales*. Editorial Universidad de Costa Rica, 2008.
Barrios Rosario, Sheila. *La ventana al silencio: La narrativa de Hilma Contreras*. Isla Negra Editores, 2011.
Baud, Michel. "Realidades e ideologías de la modernidad en la República Dominicana del siglo XX." *Revista Estudios Sociales* 34, no. 124 (2001): 9–50.
Bergmann, Emilie L., and Paul Julian Smith, eds. *¿Entiendes? Queer Readings, Hispanic Writings*. Duke University Press, 1995.
Betances, Emelio. *State and Society in the Dominican Republic*. Westview Press, 1995.
Cárdenas, Israel, and Laura Amelia Guzmán, dirs. *Dólares de arena/Sand Dollars*. Aurora Dominicana/Canana/Rei Cine, 2014.
Castellanos, Daniel H. "Santo Domingo's LGBT Social Movement at the Crossroads of HIV and LGBT Activism." *Global Public Health* 14, no. 6–7 (2019): 963–76.
Castillo, Francisco. "Proceso de expansión de la comunidad homosexual en la sociedad dominicana en los últimos 30 años." Thesis, Universidad Apec, Santo Domingo, 2004. http://www.monografias.com/trabajos17/homosexuales-dominicana/homosexuales-dominicana.shtml.
Centro Cultural de España de Santo Domingo. "Varones." https://ccesd.org/evento/el-patio-de-butacas/.
Cid, Juanjo, dir. *El Cocoró del Futuro: Capítulo Penthouse*. Posted Oct. 25, 2017, by MrCid86. YouTube, 18 min., 54 sec. https://www.youtube.com/watch?v=7Vwz69feDbQ.
Cielonaranja. "Tony Capellán: Exposiciones y Colectivas." http://www.cielonaranja.com/tcexpos.htm.
Collado, Lipe. *Anécdotas y crueldades de Trujillo*. Editora Collado, 2002.
Collado, Lipe. "Don Paco Escribano en mis recuerdos infantiles y juveniles." *Acento* (Santo Domingo), Nov. 6, 2016. https://acento.com.do/opinion/don-paco-escribano-en-mis-recuerdos-infantiles-y-juveniles-8356465.html.
Contín Aybar, Pedro René. "Biel, el marino." In *Antología de la literatura gay en la República Dominicana*, edited by Miguel de Camps Jiménez and Mélida García. Editora Manatí, 2004.
Contreras, Hilma. *Between Two Silences/Entre dos Silencios*. Translated by Judith Kerman. Mayapple Press, 2013.
Contreras, Marivell. "Waddys, 'una ausencia llena de presencia.'" *Hoy* (Santo Domingo), Jan. 11, 2004.
"'Los creadores de imagen,' hoy en el ensanche Paraíso." Entrenemiento, *Listín Diario*, Mar. 13, 2020, https://listindiario.com/entretenimiento/2020/03/13/608129/los-creadores-de-imagen-hoy-en-el-ensanche-paraiso.html.
Dávila Ellis, Verónica. "Uttering Sonic Dominicanidad: Women and Queer Performers of Música Urbana." Dissertation, University of Illinois-Evanston, 2020. https://doi.org/10.21985/n2-3tk9-gf60.
De Camps Jiménez, Miguel. Interview with Mabel Caballero. *El Caribe* (Santo Domingo), Feb. 16, 2004.

De Camps Jiménez, Miguel, and Mélida García, eds. *Antología de la Literatura Gay en la República Dominicana*. Editora Manatí, 2004.

Decena, Carlos U. *Circuits of the Sacred: A Faggotology in the Black Latinx Caribbean*. Duke University Press, 2023.

Decena, Carlos U. "Multiplying Archives." *Small Axe: A Caribbean Journal of Criticism* 20, no. 3 (2016): 179–88.

Decena, Carlos U., and Fátima Portorreal Liriano. "*Saberes raros* and Postdictatorial Empiricism: A tribute to E. Antonio Yaguarix De Moya." *Small Axe: A Caribbean Journal of Criticism* 56 (2018): 161–74.

Decena, Carlos U. *Tacit Subjects: Belonging and Same-Sex Desire among Dominican Immigrant Men*. Duke University Press, 2010.

De Maeseneer, Rita, and Fernanda Bustamante. "Cuerpos heridos en la narrativa de Rita Indiana Hernández, Rey Emmanuel Andújar y Junot Díaz." *Revista Iberoamericana* 79, no. 243 (2013): 395–14.

De Moya, E. Antonio, and Rafael García. "AIDS and the Enigma of Bisexuality in the Dominican Republic." In *Bisexualities and AIDS: International Perspectives*, edited by Peter Aggleton. Taylor & Francis, 1996.

De Moya, E. Antonio. "La constante homoerótica en la historia de América." Unpublished Manuscript.

De Moya, E. Antonio. "Juegos de guerra: El enfoque genérico-cultural de la respuesta al VIH-SIDA." Talk at conference "Estudios de Género al Inicio del III Milenio," FLACSO/INTEC, Santo Domingo, July 3–4 2003.

Derby, Lauren. "The Dictator's Seduction: Gender and State Spectacle during the Trujillo Regime." *Callaloo* 23, no. 3 (2000): 1112–146.

Derby, Lauren. *The Dictator's Seduction: Politics and the Popular Imagination in the Era of Trujillo*. Duke University Press, 2009.

Díaz, Jorge, and Johan Mijail. *Inflamadas de retórica: Escrituras promiscuas para una tecnodecolonialidad*. Editorial Desbordes, 2016.

Donnell, Alison. *Creolized Sexualities: Undoing Heteronormativity in the Literary Imagination of the Anglo-Caribbean*. Rutgers University Press, 2022.

Duggan, Lisa. "The New Homonormativity: The Sexual Politics of Neoliberalism." In *Materializing Democracy: Toward a Revitalized Cultural Politics*, edited by Russ Castronovo and Dana Nelson. Duke University Press, 2002.

Dumit Estévez, Nicolás. "Artistic Transfiguration: An Interview with Marcial Godoy-Anativia." https://multimedio.hemi.press/nicolas-dumit-estevez/qa-nicolas-and-marcial/.

Durban, Erin L. *The Sexual Politics of Empire: Postcolonial Homophobia in Haiti*. University of Illinois Press, 2023.

Encarnación, Aimée. "Tratamiento del personaje homosexual en el cine dominicano, año 1988–2008." Thesis, Departamento de Comunicación Social, Pontificia Universidad Católica Madre y Maestra, Santo Domingo, 2006.

Foucault, Michel. *History of Sexuality: An Introduction.* Vol. 1. Vintage, 1990.
García Cuevas, Eugenio. *Poesía moderna dominicana del siglo XX y los contextos internacionales (Estudios sobre La Poesía Sorprendida).* Editora Nacional, 2011.
Garrido Castellano, Carlos, et al. "Inside and Outside of the Exhibition Space: The Poetics and Politics of Colectivo Quintapata." *Small Axe: A Caribbean Journal of Criticism* 24, no.3 (2020): 31–52.
Garza Carvajal, Federico. *Butterflies Will Burn: Prosecuting Sodomites in Early Modern Spain and Mexico.* University of Texas Press, 2003.
Gill, Lyndon K. *Erotic Islands: Art and Activism in the Queer Caribbean.* Duke University Press, 2018.
Glave, Thomas, ed. *Our Caribbean: A Gathering of Lesbian and Gay Writing from the Antilles.* Duke UP, 2008.
González Gómez, Yaneris. "Una escritura lésbica/A Lesbian Writing." In *Divagaciones bajo la luna: voces e imágenes de lesbianas dominicanas/Musing under the Moon: Voices and Images of Dominican Lesbians,* edited by Jacqueline Jiménez Polanco. Idegraf Editora, 2006.
Hartlyn, Jonathan. *The Struggle for Democratic Politics in the Dominican Republic.* University of North Carolina Press, 1998.
Hernández, Rita Indiana. "Azúcar." In *Cuentos y poemas (1998–2003).* Ediciones Cielonaranja, 2017.
Hernández, Rita Indiana. "Discurso Inaugural: Skaters y Dragqueens: Ecología Cultural Dominicana DIY." Tilting Axis 4 en Colaboración con Curando Caribe 3. Posted June 19, 2018, by Centro León. Youtube, 13 min., 39 sec. https://www.youtube.com/watch?v=O6jpS696TfM.
Hernández, Rita Indiana. *La estrategia de Chochueca.* Editores Isla Negra, 2003 [2000].
Hernández, Rita Indiana. *La mucama de Omicunlé.* Editorial Periférica, 2015.
Hernández, Rita Indiana. *De nombres y animales.* Editorial Periférica, 2013.
Hernández, Rita Indiana. *Papi.* Ediciones Vértigo, 2005.
Hobal, Glenda. "Mi vida como lesbiana." In *Divagaciones bajo la luna: voces e imágenes de lesbianas dominicanas/Musing under the Moon: Voices and Images of Dominican Lesbians,* edited by Jacqueline Jiménez Polanco. Idegraf Editora, 2006.
"Homosexualidad: Verdades, Mitos y Leyendas—Paco Escribano." Posted July 27, 2013, by Gaytimes RD. Youtube, 3 min., 26 sec. https://www.youtube.com/watch?app=desktop&v=ztyA1oWza8Y.
Horn, Maja. *Masculinity after Trujillo: The Politics of Gender in Dominican Literature.* University Press of Florida, 2014.
Horn, Maja. "Queer Caribbean Homecomings: The Collaborative Art Exhibits of Nelson Ricart-Guerrero and Christian Vauzelle." *GLQ* 14, no. 2–3 (2008): 361–81.
Horn, Maja. "*Saunatopía:* Theorizing Sexual Freedom in the Dominican Republic." *CENTRO Journal* 36, no. 2 (2004): 131–42.
Huracán. "Una salida del closet y vivir tipo huracán." In *Divagaciones bajo la luna: voces e*

imágenes de lesbianas dominicanas/Musing under the Moon: Voices and Images of Dominican Lesbians, edited by Jacqueline Jiménez Polanco. Idegraf Editora, 2006.

Hutchinson, Sydney. *Tigers of a Different Stripe: Performing Gender in Dominican Music*. University of Chicago Press, 2016.

Imbert Brugal, Carmen. "Waddys Jáquez: contundente." *Clave Digital* (Santo Domingo), Oct. 10, 2006.

Jáquez, Waddys. "La Cabeza del Rey," unpublished play, 2009.

Jáquez, Waddys. "CERO," unpublished play, 2005.

Jáquez, Waddys. "Letal, televisión en vivo," unpublished play, 2004.

Jáquez, Waddys. "P.A.R.G.O.: Los Pecados Permitidos," unpublished play, 2001.

Jiménez Polanco, Jacqueline, ed. *Divagaciones bajo la luna: voces e imágenes de lesbianas dominicanas/Musing under the Moon: Voices and Images of Dominican Lesbians*. Idegraf Editora, 2006.

Jiménez Polanco, Jacqueline. "Lesbianas y gays: llegó la hora. Un relato de mi experiencia en el movimiento LGBTIR dominicano." *Vértice: Revista de Ciencias Sociales, FLACSO* 3, no. 1 (2005): 25–30.

Jiménez Polanco, Jacqueline. "The Lesbian and Gay Movement in the Dominican Republic: A Historical and Sociological Approach." Global Gayz. http://www.globalgayz.com/domrep-JP-news.html (page no longer available).

Jiménez Polanco, Jacqueline, and Jenny Mabelle Marte Chalas, eds. *Divagaciones II: Una antología de mujeres dominicanas lesbianas, bisexuales y queer/An Anthology by Dominican Lesbian, Bisexual and Queer Women*. New York, 2023.

King, Rosamond S. *Island Bodies: Trangressive Sexualities in the Caribbean Imagination*. University Press of Florida, 2014.

King, Rosamond S., and Angelique V. Nixon. "About the Caribbean IRN." *Caribbean IRN Blog*. https://caribbeanirn.blogspot.com/p/about-caribbean-irn.html.

"La Delfi." Gran Varones, Mar. 26, 2020. https://granvarones.com/la-delfi/.

La Fountain-Stokes, Lawrence. *Queer Ricans: Cultures and Sexualities in the Diaspora*. University of Minnesota Press, 2009.

La Fountain-Stokes, Lawrence. "Remembering Jean Franco." *Revista Hispánica Moderna* 76, no. 2 (2023): 206–9.

Lam, Jimmy. "¿Existe una literatura gay en República Dominicana?" Cielonaranja. http://www.cielonaranja.com/jimmylamantologia.htm.

Lam, Jimmy. *Sexile=Sexilio*. Xlibris, 2017.

Lara, Ana-Maurine. *Erzulie's Skirt*. Redbone Press, 2006.

Lara, Ana-Maurine. *Queer Freedom: Black Sovereignty*. State University of New York Press, 2020.

Lara, Ana-Maurine. "Strategic Universalisms and Dominican LGBT Activist Struggles for Civil and Human Rights." *Small Axe: A Caribbean Journal of Criticism* 56 (2018): 99–114.

Lara, Ana-Maurine. *Streetwalking: LGBTQ Lives and Protest in the Dominican Republic*. Rutgers University Press, 2020.

Lora, Elvira. "La Zona Colonial entre velos rosa." *Clave* (Santo Domingo), June 15, 2006, p. 34.
Lugo-Ortiz, Agnes I. "Community at Its Limits: Orality, Law, Silence, and the Homosexual Body in Luis Rafael Sánchez's 'Jum!'" In *¿Entiendes? Queer Readings, Hispanic Writings*, edited by Emilie L. Bergmann and Paul Julian Smith. Duke University Press, 1995.
Manley, Elizabeth S. *Imaging the Tropics: Women, Romance, and the Making of Modern Tourism*. Rutgers University Press, 2025.
Manley, Elizabeth S. *The Paradox of Paternalism: Women and the Politics of Authoritarianism in the Dominican Republic*. University Press of Florida, 2017.
Martínez Tabares, Vivian. "Caribbean Bodies, Migrations, and Spaces of Resistance." *TDR: The Drama Review* 48, no. 2 (2004): 24–32.
Mayes, April J. "Why Dominican Feminism Moved to the Right: Class, Colour and Women's Activism in the Dominican Republic, 1880s–1940s." *Gender & History* 20, no. 2 (2008): 349–71.
Mena, Miguel D. "Ciudades revisadas: La literatura pos-insular dominicana (1998–2011)." *Revista Iberoanericana* 79, no. 243 (2013): 349–69.
Mena, Miguel D. "Letras saliendo del closet: Literatura Homoerótica en la República Dominicana." In *Antología de la literatura gay en la República Dominicana*, edited by Miguel de Camps Jiménez and Mélida García. Editora Manatí, 2004.
Mena, Miguel D. "La literature dominicana en el contexto caribeño: ¿Cómo seguir pensando los inicios de las vanguardias?" *Mitologías hoy: revista de pensamiento, crítica y estudios literarios latinoamericanos* 12 (2015): 253–55.
Mena, Miguel D. *Poética de Santo Domingo II*. Ediciones Cielonaranja, 2003.
Méndez, Danny. "Chapeo Consciousness: On Blackness, Queerness, and Marronage in Johan Mijail's Chapeo (2021)." *Review: Literature and Arts of the Americas* 56, no. 1 (2023): 24–31.
Méndez, Danny. "De Travestismos sospechosos y seducciones peligrosas: La identidad sexual en dos cuentos de José Alcántara Almánzar." *Revista Iberoamericana* 79, no. 243 (2013): 523–33.
Mijail, Johan. "Catinga Ediciones: Poéticas para imaginaciones negras y sexo-género disidentes." *NGRXSMGZ black activism magazine*. https://www.negrxs.com/n11/2020/7/10/catinga-ediciones-poticas-para-imaginaciones-negras-y-sexo-gnero-disidentes.
Mijail, Johan. *Chapeo*. Elefanta del Sur, 2021.
Mijail, Johan. *Escrituras del otro cuerpo*. Ediciones Cielonaranja, 2018.
Mijail, Johan. *Manifiesto antirracista: escrituras para una biografía inmigrante*. Los Libros de la Mujer Rota, 2018.
Mijail, Johan. "Retazo cimarrón de promiscuidad escritural." Más: Movimiento Afrolatino Seattle, Mar. 8, 2024. https://movimientoafrolatino.org/2024/03/08/retazo-cimarron-de-promiscuidad-escritural/.
Mijail, Johan. *Santo Domingo is Burning*. Catinga Ediciones, 2021.

Molloy, Sylvia, and Robert McKee Irwin, eds. *Hispanisms and Homosexualities.* Duke University Press, 1998.

Morla, Rafael Stalin. *Saunatopía: Mariconería y domesticidad en un rincón caribeño.* Circulo Rojo, 2019.

Mota, Jennifer. "Si Tu Quiere Dembow: How La Delfi Sparked the Rise of Queer Dembow," *Remezcla*, Feb. 13, 2020. https://remezcla.com/features/music/si-tu-quiere-dembow-la-delfi-queer-superstar/.

Muñoz, Luis Alberto. "Waddys vuelve con Cero." *El Caribe* (Santo Domingo), Sept. 29, 2006.

Museo Memorial de la Resistencia Dominicana. "Homofobia, represión y resistencia durante la dictadura de Rafael Trujillo en República Dominicana y sus efectos en la Sociedad Actual," coordinated by Kary Colón. International Coalition of Sites of Conscience, 2020, 1–65. https://www.sitesofconscience.org/member_resources/homofobia-represion-y-resistencia-durante-la-dictadura-de-rafael-trujillo-en-republica-dominicana-y-sus-efectos-en-la-sociedad-actual/.

Nacidit-Perdomo, Ylonka, ed. *Hilma Contreras: Diario íntimo de su amistad con Segundo Serrano Poncela,* 2007. https://ylonkanaciditperdomo.wordpress.com/wp-content/uploads/2007/10/diario-intimo-hilma-contreras.pdf.

Nacidit-Perdomo, Ylonka. "La joven Hilma Contreras: Notas a su biografía." In *La carnada* by Hilma Contreras. Letra gráfica, 2007.

Nacidit-Perdomo, Ylonka. "Melba Marrero de Munné, sepultada dos veces." *Acento* (Santo Domingo), Nov. 07, 2016. https://acento.com.do/cultura/melba-marrero-munne-sepultada-dos-veces-8363582.html

Nacidit-Perdomo, Ylonka. Prefacio to *Cuentos completos: Hilma Contreras,* edited by Miguel d. Mena. Ediciones Cielonaranja, 2021, 9–17.

Negrón-Muntaner, Frances. "'Can You Imagine?': Puerto Rican Lesbian Activisms, 1972–1991." *Centro Journal* 30, no. 2 (Summer 2018): 348–77.

Norman, Lissette. "Mejor Puta que Pata." In *Divagaciones bajo la luna: voces e imágenes de lesbianas dominicanas/Musing under the Moon: Voices and Images of Dominican Lesbians,* edited Jacqueline Jiménez Polanco. Idegraf Editora, 2006.

"Las Noches Reprimidas." *Clave* (Santo Domingo), June 15, 2006.

"Ordenanza No. 12/2019." Ayuntamiento del Distrito Nacional. Despacho del Presidente, Santo Domingo, R.D. https://adn.gob.do/wpfd_file/ordenanza-12-2019/.

"Paco Escribano: The King of Nonsense." Posted Jan. 6, 2021 by Videocine Palau. Youtube, 11 min., 53 sec. https://www.youtube.com/watch?v=u_iYl9ijhP8.

Padilla, Mark. *Caribbean Pleasure Industry: Tourism, Sexuality, and AIDS in the Dominican Republic.* University of Chicago Press, 2007.

Padilla, Mark, and Daniel Castellanos. "Discourses of Homosexual Invasion in the Dominican Global Imaginary." *Sexuality Research & Social Policy* 5, no. 4 (2008): 31–44.

Palacios, Rita M. "Actos peatonales, actos de consumo: La *queerificación* del espacio en *La estrategia de Chochueca* de Rita Indiana Hernández." *Hispania* 97, no. 4 (2014): 566–77.

Pancrazi, Jean-Noël. *Los dólares de arena*. Translated by David Puig. Ediciones De a Poco, 2010.

Paulino Ramos, Alejandro. "Mecanismos de Trujillo para la represión política: Un 'Foro público' para perseguir, difamar y destruir moralmente." *Acento* (Santo Domingo), May 5, 2019. https://acento.com.do/cultura/mecanismos-de-trujillo-para-la-represion-politica-un-foro-publico-para-perseguir-difamar-y-destruir-moralmente-18-8678549.html.

Pérez, Pedro Julio. "El Foro Público." *Acento* (Santo Domingo), Dec. 17, 2012. https://acento.com.do/opinion/el-foro-publico-207272.html.

Puentes, written by Rita Indiana Hernández, dir. Henry Mercedes and Jorge Pineda/Teatro Simarrón, Teatro Nacional, Santo Domingo, 2003.

Quinn, Rachel Afi. "Dominican Pride and Shame: Gender, Race, and LGBT Activism in Santo Domingo." *Small Axe: A Caribbean Journal of Criticism* 22, no. 2 (2018): 128–43.

Quiroga, José A. *Tropics of Desire: Interventions from Queer Latino America*. NYU Press, 2000.

Ramos, Juanita. *Compañeras: Latina Lesbians/Lesbianas Latinoamericanas*, 2nd ed. Latina Lesbian History Project, 2004.

Ramos, Rossy, Ángel Rosario, Maurice Sánchez. *Gráfica Independiente Dominicana 2000–2010*. Capital Books, 2013.

Reyes Bonilla, Dulce. "¿Pero m'ija, y de dónde sacáte 'eso'?" In *Divagaciones bajo la luna: voces e imágenes de lesbianas dominicanas/Musing under the Moon: Voices and Images of Dominican Lesbians*, edited by Jacqueline Jiménez Polanco. Idegraf Editora, 2006.

Ricart-Guerrero, Nelson. *Boca de tiempo roto*. Editorial Letra Gráfica, 2005.

Ricart-Guerrero, Nelson. *Sólo quedan las palabras*. Editorial Isla Negra, 2009.

Ricart-Guerrero, Nelson. *Soy Leife, El pájaro malo*. Erizo Editorial, 2013.

Rivera, Claudio. "La caligrafía del alma." *Conjunto: revista de teatro latinoamericano* 123 (2001): 66–69.

Rivera-Velázquez, Celiany. "Caribbean Kiki: The Cuir Irreverence of Puerto Rican LaBori-Vogue and Dominican Draguéalo." *Centro: Journal of the Center for Puerto Rican Studies* 36, no.2 (Summer 2024): 241–74.

Rivera-Velázquez, Celiany. "Dominican Republic LGBTT: Landscape Analysis of Political, Economic & Social Conditions." ASTRAEA Lesbian Foundation for Justice, 2017.

Rojas, Lissette. "Waddys: Para morirse de la risa." *El Caribe* (Santo Domingo), Oct. 5, 2005.

Rojas, Mario A. "IV Festival Internacional de Teatro de Santo Domingo: Un modelo de políticas culturales de producción y recepción teatral." *Latin American Theatre Review* 37, no. 2 (Spring 2004): 159–76.

Ronzino, Maickel. "'Letal' arriba a la Sala Ravelo." *El Caribe* (Santo Domingo), Sept. 14, 2004.

Rueda, Manuel. "Pedro René Contín Aybar (1907–1981)." In *Dos siglos de literatura dominicana (S. XIX-XX) Poesía II*, edited by Manuel Rueda. Colección Sesquicentenario de la Independencia Nacional Vol. X. Editora Corripio, 1996.

Sánchez Marte, Leonardo E. "Empoderamiento de hombres gay y hombres que tienen sex con otros hombres." *Vértice: Revista de Ciencias Sociales, FLACSO* 3, no. 1 (2005): 20–24.

Spartacus: International Gay Guide, ed. John D. Stamford. Amsterdam, The Netherlands, 1982.

Starocean, Karol. *Dramamine*. Ediciones Cielonaranja, 2017.

Stevens, Camilla. *Aquí and Allá: Transnational Dominican Theatre and Performance*. University of Pittsburgh Press, 2019.

Stevens, Camilla. "The Politics of Abjection in *P.A.R.G.O.: Los pecados permitidos* by Waddys Jáquez." *Symposium* 61, no.4 (2008): 255–65.

Stoler, Ann Laura. *Duress: Imperial Durabilities in Our Times*. Duke University Press, 2016.

Stoler, Ann Laura. *Race and the Education of Desire: Foucault's* History of Sexuality *and the Colonial Order of Things*. Duke University Press, 1995.

Tallaj, Angelina. "Desde la Orilla: Fighting for a Queer Identity in the Dominican Republic." In *Queer Identities/Political Realities*, edited by Bruce Drushel and Kathleen German. Cambridge Scholars Publishing, 2009.

Tinsley, Omise'eke Natasha. *Ezili's Mirrors: Imagining Black Queer Genders*. Duke University Press, 2018.

Tinsley, Omise'eke Natasha. *Thiefing Sugar: Eroticism Between Women in Caribbean Literature*. Duke University Press, 2010.

Valdez, Elena. *Las ciudades del deseo: Las políticas de género, sexualidad y espacio urbano en el Caribe Hispano*. Purdue University Press, 2023.

Valdez, Elena. "Masculinities in Crisis: A Tíguere, A Military Figure, and a Sanky-Panky as Three Models of Being a Man in The Dominican Republic." In *Queering Iberia: Iberian Masculinities at the Margins*, edited by Josep M. Armengol-Carrera. Peter Lang, 2012.

Valdez, Elena. "Suciedad divina: provocaciones *queer* y Resistencia en la música de Tokischa." *CENTRO: Journal of the Center for Puerto Rican Studies* 36, no. 2 (Summer 2024): 165–91.

Valera, Cheila. "Presentación." *Vértice: Revista de Ciencias Sociales, FLACSO* 3, no. 1 (2005): 3.

Varones, written by Rafael Morla, dir. by Isabel Spencer, Teatro Maleducadas, Casa de Teatro, Santo Domingo, 2018.

Villa, Lucas. "Pabllo Vitar, Esteman, MULA + More Queer Latin Acts for your Pride Playlist." *Mitú*, June 2, 2021. https://wearemitu.com/crema/pride-playlist-2021-8-latin-acts/.

Villegas, Richard. "MULA Draws with Every Color in the Dominican Crayon Box on New Album 'Aguas.'" *Remezcla*, Mar. 13, 2017. https://remezcla.com/features/music/mula-aguas-interview/.

Villegas, Richard. "These Underground Santo Domingo Parties Are Shattering Gender Norms and Celebrating Queer History." *Remezcla*, Dec. 27, 2017. https://remezcla.com/features/culture/queer-nightlife-santo-domingo-dominican-republic/.

Volonteri, Mónica. "Pargo, o, la irrupción de la verdad." *Aguapintada*, Dec. 12, 2022. https://monicavolonteri.wordpress.com/2008/12/22/pargo-o-la-irrupcion-de-la-verdad/.

Volonteri, Mónica. "Puentes sobre tierras turbulentas." *Aguapintada*, Dec. 21, 2008. https://monicavolonteri.wordpress.com/2008/12/21/puentes-sobre-tierras-turbulentas/.

Zabala, Mari. "Carta a mi madre." In *Divagaciones bajo la luna: voces e imágenes de lesbianas dominicanas/Musing under the Moon: Voices and Images of Dominican Lesbians*, edited by Jacqueline Jiménez Polanco. Idegraf Editora, 2006.

INDEX

Acevedo, Anabel, 101
Acevedo, Cristabel, 101
Acevedo, Edli, 109
Acosta, Mariluz, 63
Afro-Dominicans: police force and, 50, 55; racism and, 106; religious beliefs, 96, 106; same-sex desire, 37, 50, 94, 96, 104; social class and, 50, 55
Afuera hay aire (2010), 102
Agard-Jones, Vanessa, 2, 31
"Agatha Brooks" (Brooks), 104
Aimet, Lissa, 109
Albelo, Juan Carlos, 41
Alcántara Almánzar, José, 58–59, 66
Allen, Jafari S., 9
Almonte, Eliú, 70
Almonte Caraballo, Sarahí Yajaira, 109
Alvarez, Soledad, 26
Andújar, Rey E.: *Candela*, 123n66; *Ciudadano Cero*, 70–71; performance art, 70–71; post-insular writing, 44; queer relationalities, 84; same-sex desires, 37; *Saturnario*, 51, 123n66; theater groups, 67
Andújar, Rey E. *El hombre triángulo*: injured bodies in, 53, 122n64; masculinity and, 50–54; on privileges of masculinity, 49–50; queer nightlife and, 13, 42–44, 50–53; racial and social class in, 50, 53–55; same-sex desire in, 51–54; sexual ambiguity and, 50, 120n23; sexual geographies in, 51–52
Antes que anochezca (Arenas), 31
Antología de la literatura dominicana (Contín Aybar), 25
Antología de la literatura gay en la República Dominicana (de Camps Jiménez and García), 4, 57–59, 84
Antología poética dominicana (Contín Aybar), 25
Aquí and Allá (Stevens), 71
Arenas, Reinaldo, 4, 31
Arte-Estudio, 70
Arte para llevar exhibition, 70
Arts and artists: activism, 11–12, 72, 102–3, 112n40; alternative cultural spaces, 61–62; countercultural critiques, 69–71; on Dominican heteronormativity, 70; identity frameworks, 12; international events, 62; LGBTIQ+ subjectivities, 102–3; performance art, 70–72, 99; queerness and, 60–61, 100–101, 112n40; relationalities, 69, 71–72, 84; visual art collectives, 69–70; wounding and vulnerability of the heart, 72, 127n46. *See also* Music and musicians
ASA (Amigos Siempre Amigos): HIV/AIDS prevention campaigns, 41, 59, 72, 75–76, 119n17; LGBTIQ+ activism, 41, 79, 81, 83; USAID funding, 119n17
Astraea Lesbian Foundation for Justice, 79, 85
Aybar, Lina, 70

Báez, Frank, 44, 105–6
Balaguer, Joaquín, 4, 38, 56
Balaguer regime: financial and industrial bourgeoisie, 38, 118n4; mass migration and, 38–39, 41; queer nightlife during, 13, 39–40, 42–43, 54; repression of political dissidents, 38, 118n2; return to power, 41–42, 56; U.S. involvement in, 38, 118n1
Bardaje, 6

Bar-Gallery Patín Bígotes, 61
Bar-Gallery Tamaño, 61
Barrios Rosario, Sheila, 25
Batlle, Noa Maria, 70, 127n46
Beaches, 12, 29–32, 36, 84, 91
Bergmann, Emilie L., 3
Betances, Emelio, 118n4
Boca de tiempo roto (Ricart-Guerrero), 103
Bosch, Juan, 24, 38
Brand, Dionne, 31
Brewster, James "Wally," 82–83
Brito, Henry, 124n3
Brooks, Agatha, 104
Bugarrones: Dominican nightlife and, 45–46; hyper-masculinity and, 46, 92; male prostitution, 13–14, 42–43, 45–46; social class and, 47–48; tensions with gay men, 47–48
Butterflies Will Burn (Garza Carvajal), 6

Cabral, Incháustegui, 26
Cabrera, Lydia, 31
Caminero, Clara, 70
Camps Jiménez, Miguel de, 4, 57–58, 124n10
Capellán, Tony, 69
CAP LGBTIR (Comité de Acción Política de Lesbianas, Gays, Bisexuales, Transexuales, Transgéneros, Intersexuales, Raros y Raras), 80, 83
Cárdenas, Israel, 14, 84, 94–95
Caribbean: Afro-Caribbean religions, 96–99; developmental narratives, 2–3, 9; feeling sideways, 2, 102; female same-sex desire in, 22–23, 31; Hispanophone, 1, 3–4, 42, 107; LGBTIQ+ activism, 82; LGBTIQ+ discourse and culture, 2–3; LGBTIQ+ literature and drama, 3–4; LGBTIQ+ studies, 107; literature and performance, 1, 3–4; male visibility, 22; migration from, 64; queer embeddedness in, 12, 18, 20; respectability culture, 102; same-sex desire in, 9–10, 13, 23, 31; secreto abierto and, 9–10, 22; sexual rights activism, 3, 10–11; tourism industry, 118n5
Caribbean International Research Network (Caribbean IRN), 10
Caribbean Pleasure Industry (Padilla), 5, 31, 46
Caribbean queerness: collective understandings, 10; colonial concerns with, 6–7, 102; gender and, 22–23, 32; homoerotic encounters at beaches, 29–32; Indigenous male same-sex practices, 5–6; masculinity and, 5; non-heteronormative public figures, 9; silence and discretion, 4, 8–9. *See also* Dominican queerness
Caribbean women: beaches and same-sex desires, 31; female cohabitation, 18–19, 34, 37; invisibility tropes, 22–23. *See also* Women
Carratero, Carlota, 73
Cartagena Portalatín, Aída, 24–25, 32
Carvajal, Marianela, 80
Casa de Bastidas, 61
Casa de Francia, 61, 69
Casa de Teatro, 61–63, 71
Casa de Tostado, 71
Casal, Julián del, 4
Casas, Bartolomé de la, 6
Casifull, 71
Castellanos, Daniel, 72, 77, 79–83, 128n9
Castillo, Caryana, 70
Castillo, Francisco, 56
Castillo, María, 73
Castillo, Máximo del, 70
Castro, Carlos, 67
Catholic Church: artist critique of, 69; denouncement of homosexuality, 19, 59–60, 69, 96; heteronormative values and, 44; LGBTIQ+ identity and, 96; political rhetoric and, 38–39
Catinga Ediciones, 104
Ceballos, Fermín, 70
Centro Cultural de España, 61, 69–71
Centro León Jimenes, 42, 61, 104
Chachita, 124n3
Chaplin, Geraldine, 94
Chapuseaux, Manuel, 67, 71
Chin, Matthew, 10
ChocoPOP, 62, 70–71
Cid, Juanjo, 42, 102–3
Circuits of the Sacred (Decena), 96–97
Clave, 39
Cliff, Michelle, 31
Colectiva Mujer y Salud, 79
Colectivo de Teatro Maleducadas, 68
Colectivo Shampoo, 69–70
Collado, Lipe, 16–17, 20, 114n20
Colonialism: creolized queerness and, 3; gender discourse, 6–8; heteromasculinity discourse, 8, 107; Indigenous heteropatriarchy and, 6;

racialized subjects, 107; respectability culture, 102; sexuality discourses, 6–8, 102, 113n1
Compañeras (Ramos), 11, 85
Contín Aybar, Pedro René: beach idyll, 30–31; editorships, 25–26; literary criticism by, 25–26; non-heteronormative life, 12, 16, 26–28; public role of, 25–28; secreto abierto, 9; support of Trujillo women, 25–26, 115n45
Contín Aybar, Pedro René. "Biel, el marino": anthologization, 58; autobiographical elements, 28–31; escape from society in, 29–30; fear of public scandal, 32; homoerotic encounters at beaches, 29–32, 36; homoerotic writing, 28–30; homosociality, 33; public/private life and, 30, 32; silence and discretion, 32–33; tacit same-sex desire in, 32, 36–37
Contreras, Darío, 23–24
Contreras, Hilma: ambiguities of sexuality, 27; attempted seduction by Cartagena Portalatín, 32; critique of Trujillo, 24–26; early life and education, 23–24; homoerotic encounters in private sphere, 31; La Poesía Sorprendida, 24–26; non-heteronormative life, 26–28; public role of, 24–25, 28; recognition of, 115n45; same-sex desire in stories by, 12, 16, 27–28, 31–32; surveillance of behavior, 27
Contreras, Hilma. "La espera" ("The Wait"): anthologization, 58; attempted seduction in, 31–34; domestic/private space surveillance, 36–37; fear of public scandal, 32; female masculinity in, 33–34, 37; patriarchal surveillance in, 32; tacit same-sex desire in, 32–34, 37
Contreras, Hilma. Works: *4 Cuentos*, 25; "Canícula" ("Dog Days"), 34–37; *Entre dos silencios*, 31, 34, 37, 117n74; "La Ventana," 117n74
Contreras, Marivell, 125n21
Contreras, Rosa Julia, 26
Creadores de Imágenes, 41
Creadores de Imágenes Visión 2020, 41
Creolized queerness: Afro-Caribbean religions, 96–98; coloniality and, 3; Dominican cultural production, 2–3, 98, 105; genealogies of, 3–4, 107–9; LGBTIQ+ studies, 107–8; LGBTIQ+ subjectivities, 43, 98; musical groups, 98, 102; public/private nightlife, 54; respectability and discretion, 3; same-sex love and, 94. *See also* Dominican queerness
Creolized Sexualities (Donnell), 2

Cross-dressing, 20, 41
Cuadernos de cultura, 26
Cuadernos dominicanos de cultura, 26, 117n74
Cuba, 4, 9, 31, 42
Cuentos completos (Nacidit-Perdomo), 27
Curiel, Ochy, 80

Dávila Ellis, Verónica, 100, 101
Decena, Carlos U., 2, 5, 8–10, 15, 20–21, 28, 32–33, 60, 77, 80, 86, 97, 112n32
Derby, Lauren, 17–18
Díaz, Elvin, 70
Díaz, Jorge, 104, 107
Dicent, Juan, 44
Disco Free, 42
Divagaciones, 11–12
Divagaciones bajo la luna (Jiménez Polanco), 14, 70, 84–86, 104
Divagaciones II: Un antología de mujeres dominicanas lesbianas, bisexuales y queer (Jiménez Polanco and Marte Chalas), 109–10
Dólares de arena (Sand Dollars) (2014), 14, 84, 94–95
Dominicana's Got Talent, 62, 125n22
Dominican media: cross-dressing, 20, 41; HIV/AIDS discourse, 72, 74–76; homophobic discourse, 17, 19, 57; homosexual themes/characters, 13, 57, 59, 123n3, 124n5; LGBTIQ+ issues, 59–60, 78; queer entertainers, 20–22, 25, 41; stereotypical representations in, 57–63, 67, 102; tacit homosexuality in, 20–22, 114n20; training for respectful coverage, 102
Dominican National Theatre, 1, 61–62
Dominican queerness: arts and, 61; creolized, 2–4, 74, 82; cultural genealogies, 15, 40–42, 60–61, 83–84, 88; gay tourism, 31, 39, 46, 88, 91–94; local subjectivities, 10, 13, 40, 42–43, 75, 77, 92, 105; nightlife and, 39–40, 42, 47; relationalities, 69, 71–72, 75, 84; stereotypical representations, 57–59, 61–63, 67. *See also* Creolized queerness
Dominican Republic: anti-Haitian racism/violence, 89, 105–6; democratic government in, 13, 15, 38, 56, 60; economic crisis, 42; female-headed households, 18–19, 37, 85, 109; gender norms in, 13, 18, 33, 44–45, 48, 90; homophobic discourse, 16–19, 81; masculinity in, 5, 10, 16–17; migration to the U.S., 38–39, 41, 87;

Dominican Republic (*continued*)
neoliberal economic policies, 12, 56, 60, 82–83, 107; PRD years, 40–41, 78, 119n13; queer embeddedness in, 20, 27–28, 30, 37, 40, 60; sex work in, 42–43, 46, 51; social inequities in, 12–13, 47, 78, 89; social norms in, 44–45, 48–49; tourism industry, 39, 56, 78, 89, 95, 119n6

Donnell, Alison, 2, 4, 12, 18, 102

Drag queens: cross-dressing, 20, 41; cuir kiki and ballroom communities, 103, 108; Draguéalo parties, 102–3; *travestis/tranformistas*, 66; Trujillo dictatorship, 20; visibility in media, 57, 66, 123n3. *See also* Travestis/tranformistas

Dramamine (Starocean), 104

Duggan, Lisa, 3

Dumit Estévez, Nicolás, 98

Durban, Erin L., 10

Duress (Stoler), 7

El Boulevard, 60, 80–81

El Caribe, 17

El Cocóro del Futuro, 102

El Hombrecito, 106

El hombre triángulo (Andújar), 13

El Parque Duarte, 60

El Último Show, 41

Encarnación, Aimée, 57

Encuentro Artesanal, 61

Encuentros Internacionales de Performance—ChocoPOP, 62, 70–71

¿Entiendes? Queer Readings, Hispanic Writings (Bergmann and Smith), 3

"Entre pieles de negro, un amanecer" (Peralta), 104

Errores Imperdonables (Taylor), 72

Escribano, Paco (Paquita): privacy and, 21–22; as radio and television personality, 20, 25, 114n20; *secreto abierto* and, 9, 20–22; tacit understandings of homosexuality, 20–22

Espinosa, Yuderkys, 80

Espinoza, Lorena, 80

Ezili's Mirrors (Tinsley), 96

Femininity: challenge to gender norms, 13, 33, 48–49; homosexuality and, 19, 50–51, 54, 91, 97, 101; hyper-masculinity and, 50, 54; music and, 101; perceptions of sexuality, 19, 48–49, 120n23; performances of, 65; public spaces and, 13, 48; women's same-sex desires, 19, 48. *See also* Women

Fernández, Elena, 71

Fernández, Leonel, 56, 78

Fernández, Ricardo, 71

Festival Internacional de Cine GLBT, 68, 102

Festival Internacional de Teatro, 62

Firestone, Shulamith, 107

FLACSO (Facultad Latinoamericana de Ciencias Sociales), 11, 80

Foucault, Michel, 6–7

IV Bienal del Caribe, 62

IV Festival Internacional de Teatro de Santo Domingo, 67

Galería Modafoca, 61

García, Ana, 109

García, Deyanira, 109

García, Mélida, 4, 57, 124n10

García, Rafael, 17

García Cuevas, Eugenio, 26

Garrido Castellano, Carlos, 69

Garza Carvajal, Federico, 6–7

Gatón Arce, Freddy, 25

Gaylesdom: Colectivo de Gays y Lesbianas Dominicanas, 59

Gay men: beaches and homoerotic encounters, 12, 29–32, 36, 91; Dominican immigrants, 5, 8, 21; globalized and local repertoires, 10; HIV/AIDS discourse, 75–77; HIV-related services, 82, 119n17, 128n7; masculinity and, 5, 8, 92; public roles of, 20, 39–41; queer nightlife and, 39–41; social class and, 47–48; tensions with *bugarrones*, 47–48; tourism, 31, 39. *See also* Bugarrones; Male sex workers

Gayumba, Teatro, 67

Gender: challenges to norms, 11, 13, 48–49, 69; colonial discourses, 6–8; divides in perception, 18; heteronormative, 68; homoerotic encounters and, 12, 31–32; Indigenous practices, 6; LGBTIQ+ identity, 82–83; musical groups, 100; normative masculinity, 8, 33, 53; policing of, 89; private spaces and, 14, 22, 31, 86; public spaces and, 12–14, 31, 40, 44–45, 54–55, 89; same-sex desire and, 5, 15, 22, 31, 33, 37, 40, 48, 55, 86, 89, 95, 105; *secreto abierto* and, 23; sexuality and, 8, 13; tacit in, 23, 37; women's restriction mechanisms, 32, 54. *See also* Masculinity

Gender nonconformity: cultural spaces for, 60; networks of surveillance and, 34; public spaces and, 8, 48; queer nightlife and, 42–43, 45, 48; same-sex desire and, 48–50, 88; Vodoun and, 88
Gill, Lyndon K., 10, 12, 18
Ginebra, Freddy, 61
Global Fund to Fight HIV/AIDS, Tuberculosis, and Malaria, 128n7
Global South, 9, 105
González, Viena, 67
González Gómes, Yaneris, 84
Gráfica Independiente Dominicana 2000/2010, 70
Guadeloupe, 9
Guloya, 67
Guzmán, Laura Amelia, 14, 84, 94–95
Guzmán, Sayuri, 70

Haiti and Haitians: Afro-Caribbean religions, 97; discrimination and violence against, 38, 60, 89, 105; LGBTIQ+ activism, 10; Vodoun and, 87, 96
Halberstam, Jack, 107
Hartlyn, Jonathan, 38
Henríquez Ureña, Max, 26
Herfurth, Erika, 87
Hermann, Sara, 61–62
Hernández, Rita Indiana: creolized queerness, 98–100; critique of masculinity, 49, 106; demand for public space, 49; Divagaciones writing group, 11; female masculinity, 100–101; on listening sideways, 101–2; literary influence of, 105–6; musical groups, 1, 71, 99–100; performance art, 70–71, 99; post-insular writing, 44; on queer nightlife, 42; queer relationalities, 84; Rita Indiana y Los Misterios, 1, 71, 99–100; tíguere performances, 100
Hernández, Rita Indiana. *La estrategia de Chochueca*: anthologization, 58; on bugarrones and prostitution, 45–48; Dominican social norms in, 44–49; injured bodies in, 47, 122n64; norms of femininity in, 48–49; public space and masculinity, 48–49; queer urban nightlife in, 13, 42–48, 53; same-sex desire in, 47–49, 53; sexual ambiguity and, 120n23; sexual geographies in, 51–52; social class and, 45–48, 53–54
Hernández, Rita Indiana. Works: *De nombres y animales*, 49; *Impotencia*, 71; *La mucama de Omicunlé*, 49, 69, 99; *Nadie va al Padre si no através de mi*, 71; *Papi*, 49, 71, 105–6; *Puentes (Bridges)*, 1–2, 13, 67–68, 99; *Ready y los Niños Envueltos*, 71; *Rumiantes*, 43
Heteronormativity: critique of, 2, 68, 70, 100; Dominican society and, 44, 63, 70; gender norms, 33; homophobic discourse, 63; masculinity and, 16, 91; queer subjectivities and, 42, 100; Trujillo dictatorship, 12, 16, 18, 21–22, 26, 28, 37
Hispaniola, 7
Hispanisms and Homosexualities (Molloy and Irwin), 3
History of Sexuality, The (Foucault), 6
HIV/AIDS crisis: ASA services, 41, 59, 72, 75–76, 119n17; challenges to media discourse, 72, 74–77; Dominican theater and, 62, 72–77; Global North narratives, 77; international funding for, 80–82, 119n17, 128n7; LGBTIQ+ activism, 41, 59, 68, 72–73, 76, 81–82; Mercedes and, 1–2, 68; power relations and risk, 76–77; prevention campaigns, 68, 72, 75–76, 80–81; sexuality and, 55, 72–73; stereotypical representations, 74; transgender women and, 128n9
Hobal, Glenda, 85–86
Homonationalism, 82, 98
Homonormativity, 3, 82
Homophobic discourse: Catholic Church and, 19; Dominican police force and, 51–54; heteronormativity and, 63; media and, 17, 19, 57; military and, 19; mother-daughter relationships, 86–87; portrayals of the Caribbean, 3; Trujillo regime and, 16–19, 36; Vodoun ceremonies, 96; women's gender performance, 19
Homosexuality: anti-gay policies, 51; effeminacy and, 50; Hispanophone literary and cultural studies, 1, 3, 5; HIV/AIDS discourse, 72, 74, 76–77; Indigenous practices, 6; invasion discourse, 77, 81; male practices and desires, 5–6; public figures and, 9, 20, 40; silence and discretion, 3, 5–6, 8, 39; social capital and, 22; social control of, 17–19; tacit understandings, 8–10, 20–22, 72; Trujillo regime sanctions, 16–19; visibility in media, 57, 60, 123n3. *See also* Creolized queerness; Dominican queerness; Gay men; Lesbians; LGBTIQ+ identity
Hostos, Eugenia María de, 23
Hungría, Oscar, 70

Huracán, 85–86
Hutchinson, Sydney, 100–101

Imagining the Tropics (Manley), 118n5
Indigenous, 5–6, 113n1
Inflamadas de retórica (Mijail and Díaz), 104–7
Inoa, Orlando, 113n7
Instituto Cultural Dominicano Americano, 70–71
Irwin, Robert McKee, 3
Island Bodies (King), 8
Isla Negra Editores, 44
IURA (Individuales Unidos por Respeto y Harmonía), 102

Jamaica, 10, 31
Jaqueca, 67
Jáquez, Waddys: *Dominicana's Got Talent* judging, 62, 125n22; HIV/AIDS subjects, 62; homosexual themes/characters, 63–65; impact on Dominican theater, 62–63, 125n21, 125n22; popularity of, 62–63, 126n23; Premio Casandra prize, 62; queer relationalities, 84; Resurección cycle, 62; trans subjects, 62
Jáquez, Waddys. *Cero:* audience-directed monologues in, 73, 76–77; awards for, 62; HIV/AIDS crisis in, 13, 72–77; homosexual themes/characters, 73–74; humor in, 74; Latinx American representation in, 73, 77; rejection of pathologizing discourse, 72, 74–77; relationalities in, 75; sexuality and, 77
Jáquez, Waddys. *P.A.R.G.O.:* audience-directed monologues in, 64–66; awards for, 62; humor in, 63–66, 74; marginalized characters in, 63–66, 73; nonstereotypical representations, 63–65; relationalities in, 75; trans subjectivity in, 13, 63–66
Jáquez, Waddys. Works: *La Cabeza del Rey,* 69; *Letal, televisión en vivo,* 67; *Requiem por la Damián,* 63; *Yerba Mala,* 63, 126n23
Jarné, Ricardo Ramón, 61
Jesús Candelier, Pedro de, 51
Jiménez, Arlyn (Buloya), 70
Jiménez, Pery, 70
Jiménez Polanco, Jacqueline: CAP LGBTIR and, 80; *Divagaciones bajo la luna,* 14, 70, 84–86, 104; *Divagaciones II,* 109–10; FLACSO and, 11, 80; on LGBTIQ+ organizations, 41, 59
"Ju Puello" (Puello), 104

Katarsis, 67
King, Rosamond S., 2, 8–10, 22–23

Las ciudades del deseo (Valdez), 42
La Delfi, 100–101
La Fountain-Stokes, Lawrence, 3, 9
La Kisty Rodriguez, 101
La loca, 13
Lam, Jimmy, 39–40, 58, 103, 124n11
"La Marilyn Monroe de Santo Domingo" (Báez), 106
Lancaster, Roger, 9
La Poesía Sorprendida (The Surprised Poetry), 24–26
Lara, Ana-Maurine: on homonationalism, 82; on queer nightlife, 52; on strategic universalism, 83; on streetwalking, 10–11, 15; on Vodoun and gender variance, 88–89, 96–97
Lara, Ana-Maurine. *Erzulie's Skirt:* economic precarity in, 92; gender inequality in, 90–91; invisibility of same-sex desires, 90–91; massacre of Haitians and descendants, 89; queer love and affection, 90, 94–96; queer relationalities, 97; rural same-sex desires in, 14, 84, 87–91; Vodoun in, 14, 88–90, 95
Lara, Ana-Maurine. Works: *Divagaciones bajo la luna,* 84–85; *Queer Freedom,* 96; *Streetwalking,* 10–11, 51, 60, 79, 88, 96–97
La Sedería, 69–70
La Shakatah Asota, 101
Latin America: *cuir* thought, 108; HIV/AIDS crisis, 73, 77; LGBTIQ+ studies, 3–4, 9, 107–8; masculinity and, 74; non-heteronormativity in, 9, 23, 30; respectability culture, 102
La Vaina, 69
La Voz Dominicana, 25
Lemebel, Pedro, 107
León, Derissé De, 70
Leonardo, Engel, 70
Lesbians: artists and performers, 60; Dominican writing collections, 11–12, 70, 84–86, 109–10; explicit same-sex desire, 86; female-headed households, 18–19, 37, 85, 109; invisibility of same-sex desires, 22–23, 90–91; LGBTIQ+ activism, 41, 59, 79–80, 82–83; mother-daughter relationships, 85–87, 109; musical groups, 99–101; queer nightlife and, 39–40; relationalities, 109; social control of, 19; streetwalking, 15;

tacit understandings, 23; writing groups, 11, 14. See also LGBTIQ+ identity; Women
Lezama Lima, José, 107
LGBTIQ+ activism: artist participation, 11–12, 72, 102–3, 112n40; Caribbean, 3, 10–11; collective actions, 11, 79–82; *divagaciones* (digressions), 83–84; expansion of, 13–14, 78–79; gender and, 83; generational divisions, 83; globalized repertoires, 3, 10, 82–83; HIV/AIDS crisis, 41, 59, 68, 72–73, 76, 80–82; Lesbian and Gay organizations, 41, 59; local strategies, 10–11, 79–80, 82; neoliberal funding, 82–83; new cohorts of, 79–80; queer cultural life, 1, 103, 111n2; strategic universalism, 83; trans women in, 80, 128n9
LGBTIQ+ identity: Afro-Caribbean religious beliefs, 96–98; class and gender privilege, 47, 53–54, 82–83, 93; creolized queerness, 2–4, 74, 82; global signifiers, 2–7, 9–10, 82–83, 107, 112n32; international media, 56, 59, 124n10, 124n11; media representations, 57–63, 67, 102; police harassment, 60, 81; public roles and, 25, 40; queer subjectivities, 40–43; rural spaces and, 87–92; silence and discretion, 3–6, 8–10, 112n32; streetwalking, 10–11, 15, 79; visibility in media, 57, 100–101, 123n3; whiteness and, 21, 37, 54, 82, 112n32
LGBTIQ+ studies: academic forums, 80; gender in, 8; Latin American, 3–4, 9, 107–8; queer relationalities, 97–98; secreto abierto and, 9; *Vértice*, 80. See also Queer Caribbean studies
Literature and drama: alternative cultural spaces, 61–62; anthologies of gay representations, 4, 57–59, 109–10, 124n10, 124n11; Colección Trujillo, 25; creolized queerness, 2–4, 107–10; cuir Dominican, 104; cultural genealogies, 1–4, 11, 13, 62, 69, 71, 83–84, 88, 125n22; Hispanophone Caribbean, 3–4; homoerotic writing, 28–32; homophobic texts, 4, 57–58, 70, 85; international art events, 62; lesbian writing, 11–12, 70, 84–86, 109–10; LGBTIQ+ representations, 57–59, 68–69, 103–5; marginalized characters in, 63–68; performance art, 70–72; post-insular writers, 44; queer embeddedness in, 105; queer urban nightlife in, 13, 42–43; relationalities, 71–72, 84; rural spaces in, 14, 87–92; same-sex desire in, 4–5, 12–16, 37, 43, 103–4; *travestis/tranformistas* in, 13, 58–59, 63–66. See also Theater

Livingston, Jennie, 103
López, Arturo, 67
López Rodríguez, Nicolás de Jesús, 60
Los Muchachos y Las Muchachas de la Mesa de Atrás (MMMA), 83
Lugo-Ortiz, Agnes I., 33
"Lulú or the Metamorphosis" (Alcántara Almánzar), 58–59
Lyle O'Reitzel Gallery, 61

Macía, Alex, 124n3
Male sex workers: beaches and, 29–31, 84; contradictory sexuality, 5, 46; gay tourism and, 31, 39, 46, 91–94; homosocial relations, 91; masculinity and, 46, 91–92; mobility and, 121n50; queer urban nightlife and, 45–47; relationship dynamics, 93–94; secretive same-sex relations, 91; tacit acceptance of, 91–92. See also Bugarrones
Mamey, 104
Manley, Elizabeth S., 18, 118n5, 119n6
Mar en Calma, 110
"Mariconfianza" (Valdez), 104
Márquez, Laura, 109
Marrero de Munné, Melba, 25–26, 115n45
Marrero Oller, Héctor, 26
Marte, J.M., 109
Marte Chalas, Jenny Marbelle, 109
Martínez Tabares, Vivian, 63–64
Martinique, 9
Masculinity: bugarrones and, 46, 92; colonial discourses, 6, 8, 107; contradictory sexuality, 5, 53, 120n23; critique of, 106–8; female, 33–34, 37, 48–49, 100–101; gender performance, 19; heteronormative, 16–17; interrogation of, 107; male sex workers and, 46, 91–92; non-effeminate, 6, 8, 51, 54, 91; non-heteronormative sexuality, 5, 20; normative performances, 6, 8, 13, 16, 46, 91–92; police force and, 50–54, 123n66; privileges of, 8, 49–50; public spaces and, 48–50, 91; same-sex practices, 6, 8; sex tourism and, 92; *tígueres* and, 49; Trujillo regime and, 16–17
Mast, Raina, 71
Mateo, Andrés L., 28
Mayes, April J., 19, 23
Meccariello, Pascal, 69–70
Mejía, Hipólito, 78

Mena, Miguel D., 25, 28, 31–32, 40, 43–44, 104, 113n2, 113n3
Méndez, Danny, 59, 106
Mercado, Walter, 9
Mercedes, Henry, 1, 67–68, 71, 84
Merette, Checo, 70
Mexico, 9, 75, 85
Mieses Burgos, Franklin, 25
Migration: attempts to reach Puerto Rico, 89, 93–94; Caribbean, 64; Dominican society and, 56, 67, 70; open same-sex desires through, 87; to Santo Domingo, 89, 95; tacit same-sex desire and, 8, 21; to the U.S., 8, 38–39, 41, 64, 66, 87
Mijail, Johan: Afro-Dominican religion, 106–7; Black trans subjects, 106–7; on Cartagena Portalatín, 32; Catinga Ediciones, 104; conversation with Hernández works, 105–6; creolized queerness, 98, 105; critique of racism, 105–6; decolonial project, 107; Dominican literary scene, 104–6; Lecturas Cuir, 104–5, 107; LGBTIQ+ scholarship, 107–8; Morla and, 108; performance art, 104; play on Báez works, 106; rejection of masculinity, 107; South-South genealogy, 107–8; *travesti* positionality, 108
Mijail, Johan. Works: *Chapeo*, 104–6; *Escrituras del otro cuerpo*, 105; *Inflamadas de retórica*, 104–7; *Manifiesto antirracista*, 106; *Metaficciones*, 104; *Pordioseros del Caribe*, 104–5; *Santo Domingo is Burning*, 104, 106
Minalla, Patricia, 70
Modafoca, 69
Molina, Julia, 22
Molloy, Sylvia, 3
Morel, Elisa, 87
Morla, Rafael S., 2, 68–69, 108
Mota, Jennifer, 101
Moya, Antonio de, 5, 17, 113n1
MULA, 101
Muñoz, Jochi, 70
Muñoz, José E., 107
Murray, David A. B., 9
Museo de Arte Moderno, 61
Museo de Casa de Tostado, 61
Museo Memorial de la Resistencia Dominicana (Memorial Museum of Dominican Resistance), 17, 19
Music and musicians: female masculinity in, 100–101; LGBTIQ+ images, 59, 61; listening sideways, 101–2; merengue, 99; performance art, 71, 99; queer dembow, 101; queer embeddedness in, 100, 103; queer nightlife and, 46, 51; queer politics and, 101; Rita Indiana y Los Misterios, 1, 71, 99–101; *tigueraje*, 100

Nacidit-Perdomo, Ylonka, 25, 27
National School of Theatre, 108
Negrón-Muntaner, Frances, 12
Nicaragua, 9
Nixon, Angelique V., 10
Noches de Penthouse, 42
Norman, Lissette, 85, 87
Nuñez, Micheline, 109

Obama, Barack, 82
Ortiz/Soriano, Carlos, 71, 127n45
Otero, Manuel Ramos, 4
Otras visiones exhibit, 69–70
Outfest: Festival Internacional de Cine GLBT, 1

Padilla, Mark, 5, 8, 31, 46, 48–49, 51–52, 74–75, 77, 80–82, 92
Paiewonsky, Denise, 80
Paiewonsky, Raquel, 69
Palacios, Rita M., 47
Pancrazi, Jean-Noël. *Dólares de arena*: Afro-Dominican *bugarrón* relationship, 14, 84, 87–88, 91–94; economic precarity in, 91–92; financially motivated love, 94–95; rural same-sex desires in, 14, 88; visibility of gay writer's relationship, 91–92
Parada 77, 51–52, 123n66
Paradox of Paternalism, The (Manley), 18
Paris is Burning (1990), 103
Partido Revolucionario Dominicano (PRD), 40–41, 78, 119n13
Patín Bigote, 69
Peña, Susana, 9
Peña Batlle, Manuel Arturo, 26
Peña Gómez, José Francisco, 105
Penthouse club, 42, 47, 102
Pepín, Ercilia, 23–24
Peralta, Cesar, 104
Pérez, David (Karmadavis), 70
Perlongher, Néstor, 107
Pineda, Jorge, 1–2, 67, 69

Piñera, Virgilio, 4, 107
Polanco, Grimaldy, 70
Police force: Afro-Dominicans and, 50, 55; anti-gay policies, 51; harassment in public spaces, 60, 81, 89; hierarchy in, 43; hyper-masculinity and, 50–54, 123n66; raids on queer nightclubs, 51
Portorreal Liriano, Fátima, 5
Postales (Báez), 106
Pourette, Dolores, 9
Preciado, Paul B., 108
Presidential Council on AIDS (COPRESIDA), 68, 81, 128n7
Private spaces: colonial discourses, 11; female sex workers, 51; gender and, 14, 22, 31, 86; middle/upper class status, 21–22; same-sex desire in, 12, 14, 21, 36–37, 46–47, 86; white identity and, 21–22; women and, 12, 31–32, 36, 49, 91; women's same-sex desires, 11, 18–19, 22, 31–32, 36–37
Public spaces: explicit same-sex desire, 9, 81, 100–103; gender in, 13–14, 44–45, 48–49, 54–55, 89; gender transgressions, 8, 13, 89; homoerotic encounters in, 31, 51; LGBTIQ+ events, 11, 59, 80–81, 102–3; masculinity and, 48–50, 91; non-heteronormative personas, 20–22; policing of, 60, 81, 89; queer embeddedness in, 29, 40, 91, 100; repression in, 10, 12; same-sex desire in, 5, 9–10, 13–15, 40, 49–50, 60, 80–81, 100; streetwalking, 10–11, 15, 79; tacit understandings, 81, 100; women and, 18, 55. *See also* Queer nightlife
Puello, Ju, 104
Puerto Rico: Dominican migration to, 89, 93–94; non-heteronormative public figures, 9; queer nightlife and, 42; same-sex desire in literature, 4; secreto abierto and, 9
Pumarol, Homero, 44, 106
Punto de Cruz (Taylor), 72

Queer Caribbean studies: decolonizing, 3, 7; globalized LGBTIQ+ frameworks, 2, 10, 82; LGBTIQ+ activism, 10; on secreto abierto of same-sex desire, 9–10; sex-gender discourse, 8
Queer Caribbean Visualities symposium, 2
Queerness: artists and performers, 100–101; chronologies, 5–15; Dominican, 15, 61, 112n40; genealogies of, 1–5, 15; global signifiers, 2, 102. *See also* Creolized queerness

Queer nightlife: Balaguer regime, 13, 39–40, 42–43, 54; *bugarrones* and prostitution, 13, 45–46; as cultural alternative, 42; Draguéalo parties, 102–3; non-heteronormative encounters and, 43–44; police raids on, 51; PRD years, 40; public spaces and, 40, 42; queer subjectivities, 40–43; racial and social class in, 47–48, 54; Santo Domingo, 39–40, 43; semi-privacy of, 13, 46–47; sex work and, 45–47; *travestis/tranformistas*, 13, 40–42, 52
Queer Nightlife (Adeyemi, Khubchandani and Rivera-Severa), 54
Quinn, Rachel Afi, 61, 82–83, 112n40
Quintapata, 69
Quiroga, José A., 9

Race: colonial discourses, 7–8, 107; inequalities and, 12–13, 47, 53, 64, 71, 75; LGBTIQ+ representations, 67, 73; police force and, 50; queer nightlife and, 48; sexuality and, 28, 55, 67; sex workers and, 46–48, 92–93; social class and, 47–48, 53–54; tacit understandings, 22. *See also* Whiteness
Race and the Education of Desire (Stoler), 7
Ramírez, Belkis, 69
Ramírez, Jary, 124n3
Ramos, Juanita, 11, 85
Ravelo, Jissel, 85
Recio, Raúl, 70
Religion: Afro-Caribbean, 95–99; Afro-Dominican, 96, 106–7; Catholicism, 19, 59–60, 69, 96; gender and sexual variance, 96–98; Santería, 96–97; Vodoun, 14, 88–90, 95–96, 98
REMEZCLA, 101
Repertorio Español, 62–63
RevASA (Red de Voluntarios de ASA), 80–81, 83
Reyes Banks, Liberka, 109–10
Reyes Bonilla, Dulce, 85–86
Reyes-Santos, Alaí, 97
Ricart-Guerrero, Nelson, 61, 103
Rita Indiana y Los Misterios, 1, 71, 99–101
Rivera, Bethania, 67
Rivera, Claudio, 67
Rivera-Velázquez, Celiany, 79–80, 83, 103, 108–9
Rodríguez, Carlos, 102–3
Rodríguez, Evangelina, 19
Rojas, Mario, 68

Rojas, Rachel, 101
Rueda, Manuel, 25–26, 43

Salomé U (Vicioso), 67
Same-sex desires: beachscapes and, 29–31; colonial discourses, 6–8, 102, 113n1; Dominican artists, 12; in Dominican literature, 4–5, 12–16, 37, 43, 103–4; el secreto abierto, 9–10, 12, 22; epistemic frameworks, 15; gendered differences, 15, 22, 31, 33, 37, 40, 48, 55, 86, 89, 95, 105; Indigenous, 5–6; invisibility of women's, 22–23, 34, 37; media representations, 13, 57, 59, 123n3, 124n5; multiplicity of ways, 10, 15; privacy and, 12, 21–22, 86; public spaces and, 5, 9–10, 13–15, 40, 49–50, 60, 80–81, 100; race and social class in, 12, 21, 37, 45–48, 50, 53–54; rural settings, 14, 87–92; silence and discretion, 5–6, 37; trauma and, 53, 123n66; white identity and, 12, 21, 37. *See also* Tacit same-sex desires
Same-sex tourism: backlash against, 81; gay males, 31, 39, 46, 88, 91–94; lesbian, 95; masculinity and, 46, 92; nightlife and, 39; relationship dynamics, 93–95; secretive relations, 91. *See also* Sex workers; Tourism
Sánchez, Luis Rafael, 4
Sánchez Marte, Leonardo E., 76, 80
Sanchíz, Francisco, 124n3
Sand Dollars (*Dólares de arena*) (2014), 14, 84, 94–95
Santana, Nives, 67
Santería, 96–97
Santo Domingo: gay social actions, 82; infrastructure and modernity in, 68; Institute for Young Women, 23–24; literary and intellectual circles, 24; public LGBTIQ+ events, 11; queer cultural life in, 1, 84; queer nightlife in, 13, 39–40, 43, 54; racial and social class in, 54
Santo Domingo OutFest/Festival de Cine GLBT, 41
Santos, Vicente, 1, 71
Saunatopía (Morla), 69, 108
Schneiderman, Eric T., 80
Scott, David, 2
Secreto abierto: Caribbean same-sex desire and, 9–10, 12, 22; gender and, 22–23; mother-daughter relationships, 27; respect and discretion, 9; visibility and, 22–23
Serrano Poncela, Segundo, 27

Sexile=Sexilio (Lam), 39, 103
Sexuality: colonial discourses, 6–8, 107, 113n1; gendered transgressions, 6, 8, 88, 100; Indigenous, 5–6, 113n1; open secret/secreto abierto, 9; regulation of women's, 22, 86–87, 91, 100; sexual repression discourse, 6–7
Sex workers: in Dominican society, 42–43, 46, 51; female, 51, 54, 95; gay tourism and, 31, 46, 91–92; long-term relations, 84, 91, 93–94; queer nightlife and, 45–47; relationship dynamics, 93–94; same-sex, 13, 81. *See also* Male sex workers
Small Axe Project, 2
Smith, Paul Julian, 3
Sólo quedan las palabras (Ricart-Guerrero), 103
Soy Leife, El pájaro malo (Ricart-Guerrero), 103
Spartacus International Gay Guide, 39, 119n6
Spencer, Antonio Fernández, 29
Spencer, Isabel, 1–2, 11, 68, 71, 84
Starocean, Karol (Damien), 103–4
Stevens, Camilla, 64, 71
Stoler, Ann Laura, 7–8
Streetwalking, 10–11, 15, 79
Strongman, Roberto, 88, 96
Suriname, 9

Tacit same-sex desires: artists and performers, 60; Contín Aybar and, 28; discretion and respectability, 21–22, 36; Dominican media, 20–21; gay-identified men, 8, 20, 86; gender and, 22–23; HIV/AIDS crisis, 72–73, 77; male sex workers and, 91–92; masculine identification and, 8; private spaces and, 21–22; queer Dominican literature, 15; queer networks and, 28; religious communities, 89; shared understanding, 12, 14–15, 21; threat of the explicit, 34–36
Tacit Subjects (Decena), 5, 8, 28, 86
Tallaj, Angelina, 57–58
Tavárez Labrador, Rafael, 20. *See also* Escribano, Paco (Paquita)
Taylor, Francis, 70–72, 84
Teatro Nacional, 71
Teatro Simarrón, 67
Tejeda, Eddy, 80
Theater: countercultural critiques, 69–71; gender and, 67–68; HIV/AIDS crisis in, 13, 72–77; impact of Waddys Jáquez, 62–63, 125n21, 125n22; innovation in, 67–68; LGBTIQ+ representa-

tions, 13, 63–66, 68–69, 73–74; marginalized characters in, 63–68; performance art, 70–72; queer cultural life, 1–3, 13; questioning of gender/sexuality norms, 60–61; trans workshop, 2, 68. *See also* Literature and drama
Thiefing Sugar (Tinsley), 31
Tigers of A Different Stripe (Hutchinson), 100
Tinsley, Omise'eke Natasha, 2, 4, 31, 88, 96–97
Tokischa, 101, 108
Torres, Luis Alfredo, 43
Tourism: Caribbean and, 118n5; Dominican literature, 14; Dominican Republic, 39, 56, 78, 89, 95, 119n6; sexual exploitation, 60, 68. *See also* Same-sex tourism
Trans'it (2015), 102
Transnational Black Feminist Retreat, 97
Trans Siempre Amigas (TRANSSA), 80
Travestis/tranformistas: bardaje tradition, 6; in Dominican literature, 58–59; in Dominican theater, 13, 63–66; in drag shows, 66; homophobic discourse, 58–59, 66; humanization of, 66; queer nightlife and, 13, 40–42, 52; theater workshops, 2, 68; trans women, 80, 128n9; visibility in media, 66, 123n3
Trinidad/Tobago, 10, 31
Tropics of Desire (Quiroga), 9
Trujillo, María Martínez de, 25, 115n45
Trujillo, Rafael L., 4, 16–17, 23, 38
Trujillo dictatorship: heteronormativity and, 12, 16, 18, 21–22, 26, 28, 37; homophobic discourse, 16–19, 36; masculinity and, 16–17; massacre of Haitians and descendants, 89; persecution of homosexuals, 17–18, 21; same-sex desire in, 4, 12, 16, 20, 33, 37; tacit understandings during, 21–23, 36; transfer of properties to the state, 38; writer critique of, 24–25

United States Agency for International Development (USAID), 119n17
Ureña de Henríquez, Salomé, 23

Valdez, Elena, 42, 47, 101, 120n23
Valdez, Juan, 104
Vargas, Chabela, 9
Varones (Morla), 2, 68–69
Vauzelle, Christian, 61, 103
Ventura, Deivis, 102
Vértice, 80
Vicioso, Chiqui, 67
Vizcaíno, Nancy, 70
Vodoun, 14, 88–90, 95–96, 98
Volonteri, Mónica, 62–63, 66, 68

Walcott, Rinaldo, 2
Wekker, Gloria, 9
Whisky Sour (Vicioso), 67
Whiteness: LGBTIQ+ identity, 21, 37, 54, 82, 112n32; social class and, 23, 35, 37, 54
Women: access to spaces of homoerotic encounter, 31–32; creolized queer love, 84, 93–96; demonization of lesbianism, 19, 87; domestic/private space constraints, 12, 31–32, 36, 49, 91; erotic ambivalence, 33; family surveillance of behavior, 19, 22, 27, 32, 36–37, 86; female cohabitation, 18–19, 34, 37, 85, 109, 113n13; female masculinity, 33–34, 37, 48–49, 100–101; gender norms, 18, 32, 48, 90; gender performance, 19; invisibility of same-sex desires, 22–23, 34, 37; labeled as "puta," 48, 87, 101; mother-daughter relationships, 85–87, 109; as political threat, 18; public secular education, 23–24; public spaces and, 18, 55; regulation of sexuality, 19, 22, 86–87, 91, 100; same-sex desires, 14, 18–19, 22–23, 85–87, 90; socialization of, 22; tourism industry, 60, 89, 118n5; transgender, 80, 128n9. *See also* Femininity; Lesbians

Yaras, 109

Zabala, Mari, 85–86

MAJA HORN is professor in the Department of Spanish and Latin American Cultures at Barnard College. She is the author of *Masculinity after Trujillo: The Politics of Gender in Dominican Literature*.

www.ingramcontent.com/pod-product-compliance
Lightning Source LLC
Chambersburg PA
CBHW020417230426
43663CB00007BA/1201